RUSSIA AND THE
GOLDEN HORDE

The
Mongol Impact
on Medieval
Russian History

RUSSIA AND THE *GOLDEN HORDE*

CHARLES J. HALPERIN

Indiana University Press • Bloomington

In loving memory of my father,
Louis Halperin

First Midland Book Edition 1987

Copyright © 1985 by Charles J. Halperin

Manufactured in the United States of America

Library of Congress Cataloging in Publication Data

Halperin, Charles J.
　Russia and the Golden Horde.

　　Bibliography: p.
　　Includes index.
　　1. Soviet Union—History—1237–1480. 2. Golden
Horde. I. Title.
DK90.H28　1985　　947'.03　　84-48254
　　c1. ISBN 0-253-35033-6
　　pa. ISBN 0-253-20445-3

　　　3 4 5 6 7 91 90 89 88 87

CONTENTS

Preface		vii
Acknowledgments		x
I	The Medieval Ethno-Religious Frontier	1
II	Kievan *Rus'* and the Steppe	10
III	The Mongol Empire and the Golden Horde	21
IV	The Mongol Administration of Russia	33
V	The Mongol Role in Russian Politics	44
VI	The Russian "Theory" of Mongol Rule	61
VII	Economic and Demographic Consequences	75
VIII	The Mongols and the Muscovite Autocracy	87
IX	The Mongols and Russian Society	104
X	Cultural Life	120
XI	Conclusion	126
Notes		131
Bibliography		158
Index		175

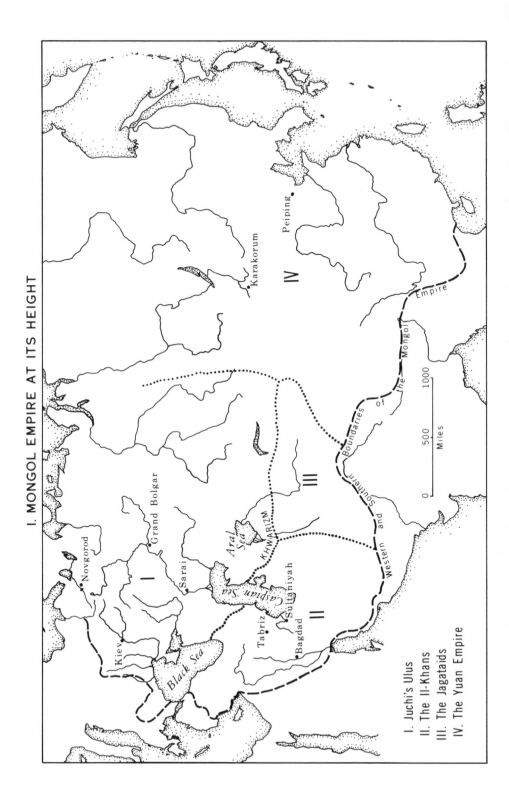

I. MONGOL EMPIRE AT ITS HEIGHT

I. Juchi's Ulus
II. The Il-Khans
III. The Jagataids
IV. The Yuan Empire

Boundaries of the Mongol Empire

Western and Southern

Peiping

Karakorum

Grand Bolgar

Novgorod

Sarai

KHWARIZM

Aral Sea

Caspian Sea

Sultaniyah

Tabriz

Bagdad

Kiev

Black Sea

500   1000
Miles
0

PREFACE

Among historians of Russia, neglect of the period of Mongol domination has been the rule rather than the exception. As Michael Cherniavsky aptly observed, "There seems to have prevailed a vague desire to get rid of, to bypass, the whole question as quickly as possible."[1] Most specialists in medieval Russian history have described the Mongol influence as negligible or entirely deleterious and then moved on rapidly to other topics of investigation.[2] Russia's historical experience since the "Tatar Yoke" has itself contributed to this traditional prejudice among Russian writers. During the imperial period, when Russia was constantly at war with such Asiatics as the Ottoman Turks, the Central Asian Muslims, and the Japanese, the Russian populace tended to regard Muslims, nomads, and Asians with contempt and suspicion. Westernization, initiated by Peter the Great, introduced European feelings of superiority into eighteenth-century Russian historiography and racist and colonialist ideologies into nineteenth-century Russian historical writings. Imperial Russian policy toward minorities at the turn of the twentieth century engendered rabid chauvinism. The scholarly discipline of Inner Asian studies bloomed only at the end of the nineteenth century in Russia, too late to influence the treatment of Russo-Tatar relations in the classic multivolume histories of Russia.[3] Even the early Russian oriental studies reflect all the prejudices of their times against nomads and Muslims.[4]

Soviet scholarship since the Russian Revolution has made great strides in the study of medieval Russia and the Mongol Empire. At the same time, it has perpetuated some of the prejudices of Imperial Russian historiography and interpolated some newer dogmas.[5] Among Russian emigré scholars, the Eurasian movement of the 1920s tried to reinterpret Russia's relationship with the steppe but foundered in metaphysical partisanship. Eurasianism did inspire George Vernadsky, the recognized

American specialist on Russo-Tatar relations, but his contributions to the subject contain their own idiosyncratic flaws.[6] Western scholarship, with its own set of biases, has too often echoed, at various levels of sophistication, the famous but apocryphal epigram, "Scratch a Russian and find a Tatar."[7] Thus nationalistic prejudices, cultural condescension, and scholarly ignorance have contributed to the continued neglect of the impact of the Golden Horde on Russian history.

In recent years the situation has begun to change. A number of Western and Soviet historians, archaeologists, and philologists have shed much needed light on the period of Mongol rule. Thus far, however, no one has attempted to integrate their findings or to present a new overall interpretation of the role of the Mongols in Russian history. In this monograph I will approach this task using the paradigm of the medieval ethno-religious frontier as a comparative framework.

NOTES

1. Michael Cherniavsky, "Khan or Basileus: An Aspect of Russian Medieval Political Theory," *Journal of the History of Ideas* 20 (1959), p. 459.

2. For surveys of Russian historiography on this topic consult B. D. Grekov and A.Iu. Iakubovskii, *Zolotaia orda i ee padenie* (Moscow-Leningrad, 1950), pp. 247–261; V. V. Kargalov, *Vneshnepoliticheskie faktory razvitiia feodal'noi Rusi. Feodal'naia Rus' i kochevniki* (Moscow, 1967), pp. 219–255; N. S. Borisov, "Otechestvennaia istoriografiia o vliianii tataro-mongol'skogo nashestviia na russkuiu kul'turu," *Problemy istorii SSSR* V (Moscow, 1976), pp. 129–146; and Michel Roublev, "The Scourge of God," unpublished manuscript, Chapter I, "Introduction."

3. V. V. Bartol'd, "Obzor deiatel'nosti fakul'teta vostochnykh iazykov" and "Istoriia izucheniia Vostoka v Evrope i Rossii," reprinted in V. V. Bartol'd, *Raboty po istorii vostokovedeniia* (=*Sochineniia,* tom IX; Moscow, 1977), pp. 21–196 and 197–482 respectively.

4. I. N. Berezin, "Ocherk vnutrennogo ustroistva ulus Dzhuchieva," *Trudy Vostochnago otdeleniia Russkago arkheologicheskago obshchestva* 8 (1864), pp. 387–394; V. V. Grigor'ev, "Ob otnosheniiakh mezhdu kochevymi narodami i osedlymi gosudarstvami," *Zhurnal Ministerstva Narodnago Prosveshcheniia,* ch. 178, 1875, otdel nauk (III), pp. 1–27.

5. Charles J. Halperin, "Soviet Historiography on Russia and the Mongols," *Russian Review* 41:3 (July 1982), pp. 306–322.

6. Charles J. Halperin, "George Vernadsky, Eurasianism, the Mongols and Russia," *Slavic Review* 41:3 (Fall 1982), pp. 477–493; Charles J. Halperin, "Russia and the Steppe: George Vernadsky and Eurasianism," *Forschungen zur osteuropaischen Geschichte* 36 (1984), forthcoming.

7. *Macmillan Book of Proverbs, Maxims and Famous Sayings,* ed. Burton Stevenson (New York, 1948), p. 2019; Bergan Evans, *Dictionary of Quotations* (New York, 1968), p. 602. I could not find the epigram in Bartlett. It seems clear that the original version of the epigram was French—"Grattez le russe et vous trouverez le tartare!"—and that it arose in the second half of the nineteenth century. It is most plausibly attributed to Napoleon. See Victor Hugo, *Le Rhin* (Paris, 1900), v. 3, p. 186.

ACKNOWLEDGMENTS

I have benefitted greatly in the preparation of this monograph from the research and knowledge of two scholars. Larry W. Moses contributed a great deal to my understanding of Inner Asian history, the Mongol Empire, and the Golden Horde. Michel Roublev made available to me a typescript of his essay, *"The Scourge of God,"* in which he analyzes the impact of Mongol raids upon the medieval Russian economy and the Mongol role in the rise of Moscow. While Roublev's methods, aims, and premises often differ strikingly from my own, I have found several of his conclusions persuasive. Neither Larry W. Moses nor Michel Roublev is responsible for the use I have made of his research.

Financial assistance from the International Research and Exchanges Board during 1980–1981, when my participation in the scholarly exchange with the Soviet Union was precluded, permitted the writing of the basic draft of this book. Additional financial assistance during Fall 1981 enabled me to continue my research in the Soviet Union on the Senior Scholar/Ministry Exchange. I am also grateful to the Russian Institute of Columbia University for making me a Senior Fellow during Spring 1982 and providing both financial assistance and an office.

I should also like to express my sincerest appreciation to Walter Michener for editorial assistance.

RUSSIA AND THE
GOLDEN HORDE

II. EASTERN EUROPE, RUSSIA AND THE GOLDEN HORDE

Grand Duchy of Vladimir
Grand Duchy of Lithuania

White Sea

URAL MTNS.

Baltic Sea

Novgorod

Riga

Volkhov

Tver'

Vladimir

Kazan

W.

Dvina

Moscow

Nizhnii
Novgorod

Grand Bolgar

Vilna

Kasimov

Riazan'

Warsaw
POLAND
Cracow

Volga

Kiev

Dnieper

Dniester

Sarai

0   100   200   300
Miles

Astrakhan

Caspian Sea

Black Sea

I

The Medieval
Ethno-Religious Frontier

DURING THE MIDDLE AGES TWO UNIVERSALISTIC CREEDS, CHRISTIANITY AND ISLAM, struggled for control of Europe, the Mediterranean world, and the Middle East. Christians and Muslims believed devoutly that all peoples would eventually convert to their own faith, the only true one, and that all false religions would be swept from the earth. In the meantime, theologians of both religions condemned infidels to eternal damnation. Religious doctrine proscribed all (nonviolent) contact, even the breaking of bread, as an abomination. Inevitably, the religious conflict was accompanied by mutual bad feelings, ranging from contempt and suspicion to outright hatred.

Enmity between the two faiths was based, of course, on more than theological differences. Though both Christians and Muslims spent much time fighting their coreligionists, sometimes over matters of doctrine, they also made war on one another. The forces of Islam swept out of the Arabian desert in the seventh century to conquer the Middle East, North Africa, and parts of Spain and the Balkans and soon threatened all of Europe. Christian Europe retaliated, with varying success, and through the fifteenth century sought to stem and reverse the Muslim tide. In these wars the sack of towns, the massacre of populations, and all the in-

1

humanities of medieval warfare exacerbated the acrimony between the two cultures and reinforced their prejudices.

Even hostilities, however, require a certain degree of intimacy. The efficient prosecution of the wars depended on accurate knowledge of the enemy's political organization, social habits, and economic resources, not to mention his military strategies and the nature of his lands and defenses. Ironically, the fighting necessitated occasional peaceful contacts, if only for negotiating surrenders, exchanging prisoners, and arranging truces. Such delicate interactions called for at least a modicum of understanding of each other's cultures to avoid potentially dangerous *faux pas*. For the same purposes interpreters and bilingual emissaries had to be found, or if necessary, trained. While Christians felt assured that in the long run all Muslims would be brought into the Christian ecumene, and Muslims were confident that someday all Christians would bow to Allah, the fact remained that in the short run both inhabited the same earth, often in close propinquity. Unable to exterminate one another, the two sides were forced to develop some sort of *modus vivendi.*

On the frontiers between Christendom and the world of Islam it was inevitable that a wide variety of suspiciously friendly contacts would arise. It was often expedient for each side, when warring with one group of infidels, to make alliances with another; politics has always made strange bedfellows. Convenience and economic need often dictated that Muslims and Christians trade with one another, and traveling merchants from both sides penetrated into the lands of the unbelievers. In the interest of profit, visitors and hosts alike learned to make concessions to each other's faiths, diets, and customs. The obvious benefits of cooperation demanded social and cultural accommodation that was difficult to reconcile with religious doctrine and religious prejudices.

Cordial personal relationships unavoidably arose between individual Christians and Muslims. Rulers and warriors grew to respect the political acumen, military prowess, and integrity of their adversaries. Merchants were impressed with the business sense or honesty of their counterparts of the other faith. Christian clergy and Muslim theologians studied the languages and scriptures of their opponents the better to refute their doctrines and win over their adherents. Research of this kind could lead to grudging admiration for the other side's philological skills or analytical abilities. In theory, of course, it was possible to recognize in an infidel good qualities that did not change his essential wickedness. (Thus a Christian could consider a Muslim a good man, but only compared to other Muslims.) However, in practice the personal bonds created by intercourse between the two faiths obscured the pristine simplicity of religious bigotry.

The ebb and flow of Christian-Muslim warfare led to the creation of conquest societies in which the two faiths lived side by side. Islam from its inception had had to deal with significant religious minorities, including Christians, in the Middle East. Some Christian states in the outlying areas of Europe—the Iberian peninsula, the Balkans, Eastern Europe—faced the same problem in reverse. The territories of the Umayyad Arab Empire and the early Ottoman Empire included large Christian populations, and at times the Byzantine Empire won back lands that had in the interim acquired sizable Muslim populations. Usually conquerors were greatly outnumbered by their subjects, as the French crusaders were in Palestine. When King James's Spanish Catholics took Valencia in the thirteenth century, the kingdom was eighty-five percent Moorish.

Massacre or expulsion of the entire taxpaying populace of a conquest state would have deprived its rulers of the economic wherewithal to continue to wage the holy war. Yet these multireligious societies faced practical problems of cooperation far beyond those of two cultures making selective contacts across a common border. As a result, though the avowed purpose of Christian conquest was the spread of Christianity, and the aim of the *Jihad* the spread of Islam, the rulers of conquest societies were often forced to tolerate or even adopt parts of the culture of their subjects. To lessen the strain of foreign domination, it was expedient to retain local political divisions, bureaucracies, and taxing systems. Conquest invariably depleted population, and many states turned to the infidels to recoup these demographic losses. King James, in the thirteenth century, invited Muslims to settle in Valencia, and Sultan Mehmed II ordered Orthodox Christians to relocate in Constantinople after he had made it the capital of the Ottoman Empire in 1453. Social intercourse between Muslims and Christians rose precipitously in precisely those conquest states created to eliminate the need for, or even the possibility of, such contact. In addition the ruling elite had some tendency to imitate the customs of the indigenous population. Catholics in Valencia took to the communal baths; the French in Jerusalem adopted the local diet; Umayyad rulers lived in Byzantine palaces decorated with very un-Muslim representational art. To be sure, religion and politics set very sharp limits on social assimilation. Political supremacy depended on maintaining social divisions, and religious prejudices precluded much cultural osmosis. Nevertheless, the very existence of conquest societies where Christians and Muslims dwelt together confounded the logical basis of religious warfare.

Muslim and Christian clergy attempted to some degree to adjust their theologies to the realities of life on the ethno-religious frontier. Both agreed that involuntary conversion lacked conviction, and that forcible proselytization violated religious ethics. (In practice the line dividing persuasion and coercion frequently became blurred, and religious enthusiasm often overrode such scruples.) Muslims were obliged to wage *Jihad*, the holy war, only when success was guaranteed. Therefore truces with Christian states, if not eternal peace treaties, could be justified. The theologians of both cultures conceded the unavoidable if unpalatable necessity of permitting the infidel to continue to exist both within and without one's borders. Christian theorists argued that a Muslim state might have natural legitimacy if it did not oppress Christians, did not inhibit missionary activities, did not impede pilgrimages, and did not occupy non-negotiable Christian zones such as Palestine and perhaps any territory once part of the Roman Empire. According to Islamic doctrine, Peoples of the Book, such as Christians, could live among Muslims if they refrained from insulting the Muslim faith, did not ring church bells, did not interfere with conversion to Islam, paid special taxes, and accepted inferior legal and political status. Of course, no self-respecting Muslim or Christian community under foreign rule could live up to the excessive and unrealistic demands of these convoluted theories consistently or for long. Similarly, they were of little practical value to the rulers of conquest states in dealing with their infidel subjects. Nonetheless, theologians had tried to accommodate the de facto coexistence in the frontier world.

Not even the flimsiest theological rationale could be found to justify borrowing institutions from unbelievers. Yet it occurred in every frontier conquest state in medieval times. The Arab and Ottoman conquerors may simply have lacked alternatives. Neither had previous experience with advanced political institutions. But the Catholic Spaniards in Valencia, for example, had their own Arago-Catalonian institutions but simply chose at first not to impose them on the preponderantly Islamic population. The sheer numbers of their potentially hostile subjects dictated that existing political structures be left in place, and they were. To do so was shrewd and pragmatic but this strategy could not possibly be reconciled with the religious foundations of the Christian cause. Muslim states, too, confronted, or rather avoided confronting, this same problem.

In some areas the conquerors were able to maintain distance from the subjugated culture by using as intermediaries interstitial ethnic groups that spoke both languages. In Spain, for example, Jews who spoke both Arabic and Spanish were used as officials, clerks, translators, and interpreters. In Crusader Jerusalem Eastern Christians (Semites such as Nestorians, of heretical or schismatic Christian sects) played an analogous role. Such groups helped minimize direct contact between the dominant elite and the bulk of the population. Thus they softened the disparity between the proclaimed goal of spreading the faith and the glaring fact that many Muslim states were Muslim, and Christian states Christian, in only the most technical of senses. The paradoxes posed by the very nature of the frontier states could be only slightly mitigated by such buffer systems, which after all merely substituted contacts with one unbelieving people for those with another. Wherever Muslim and Christian populations overlapped they could not remain unaware of the contradiction that campaigns undertaken in the name of conversion or extermination had led instead to cohabitation. The emptiness of theological attempts to rationalize this distasteful state of affairs was self-evident. Nor did the conquest societies of the frontier have the leisure and economic resources to subsidize such pursuits. Instead, to deal with the discrepancies between their prejudices and aims on the one hand and their experiences and accomplishments on the other, Muslims and Christians all along the frontier resorted to a different method—the ideology of silence.

The mixed Christian and Islamic societies of medieval times in effect resolved—by common consent or mass conspiracy or social convention—not to draw conclusions from the evidence around them. The realities of daily life simply were not allowed to intrude into the realms of religious ideology or to disturb religious prejudices. The sacred tenets that defined unbelievers as deadly foes were never questioned; nor were they allowed to interfere with peaceful social, political, and economic relations between the faiths. Alien institutions were borrowed or adopted but not acknowledged. Only the old names betray the origins of the Moorish tax structure used in Valencia or the Byzantine bureaucracies in the Umayyad and early Ottoman Empires. Sixteenth-century Ottoman histories pass over in silence the widespread use of Christian soldiers, farmers, artisans, and bureaucrats in the early Ottoman Empire.

Thirteenth-century Church documents from Valencia record in glowing terms the creation of a Christian infrastructure. New orders of nuns and friars were established and monasteries, religious hospitals, and churches built. The archives discreetly omit to mention that only fifteen percent of the people worshipped the Christian god. The churches were paid for by people who never entered them.

In a Christian state, the less said about alliances with one group of Muslims against another, about the use of Muslim mercenaries, trade with Muslim merchants, importation of Muslim settlers, consultation of Muslim doctors, the better. In Islamic states, of course, friendly contacts with Christians caused comparable embarrassment. If one could not speak ill of the enemy, it was better not to speak of him at all. For both faiths, explicit acceptance of any aspect of the other's civilization was potentially very dangerous. Any suggestion that the other faith might have political or religious legitimacy undermined the exclusivist claims of one's own religion and hence the very foundation of one's own political and social order. Christians and Muslims alike went on with business as usual, kept quiet about it as much as possible, and waited for circumstances to improve.

Eventually they did. When the Abbasids had absorbed enough Persian bureaucratic expertise, they dispensed with the Byzantine apparatus used by the Umayyads. The later Ottoman Turks came to feel sufficiently confident of their bureaucratic skills and orthodox religious credentials to do away with Christian officials and institutions. When the Spaniards had accumulated enough resources, they expelled or converted the Moors. (There were so many Christians in the Middle East and the Balkans that no Arab, Persian, or Turkic empire could seriously hope to exterminate them, though rare extremists were willing to try.) No ideological adjustments needed to or could possibly accompany these efforts to bring reality into line with religious doctrine. To acknowledge that the gap had existed would be unseemly. Thus the true nature of the medieval ethno-religious frontier remained historically without intellectual articulation.

The delicate balance of hostility and peaceful cooperation characteristic of the frontier simply outlived its usefulness. Yet in its time it constituted a major historical phenomenon. The pervasive reluctance to draw unwanted conclusions from self-evident facts made it work. This could perhaps be dismissed as regrettable evidence of human hypocrisy. However, in certain times and places the ideology of silence made possible pluralistic societies far more tolerant than many modern states.[1]

In the Kievan period that preceded the Mongol conquest, from the ninth to the thirteenth centuries, relations between Russians and the Turkic peoples of the steppe resembled those of the ethno-religious frontier in all essential respects (though Russia's conversion to Christianity came only at the end of the tenth century). Islam was only one of a variety of faiths practiced by the nomads, but Russian ethnic and religious prejudice did not discriminate among unbelievers. Although Russian sources from the Kievan period excoriate the nomads in no uncertain terms, relations followed the pattern just described. The East Slavs and their Turkic neighbors traded with each other, borrowed institutions, and even intermarried.

With the Mongol conquest began that period of Russian history known as the "Tatar Yoke." The Mongol successor state to the vast empire of Chingis Khan, the Golden Horde, ruled over Russia from 1240 to 1480. Mongol conquest and exploitation provided the thoroughly antagonistic basis for relations between the two cultures. Contemporary Russian sources spare no effort in portraying and lamenting Mongol pillage, destruction, and oppression. Yet with prolonged contact, the Russians inevitably became intimately acquainted with Mongol administration, politics, society, and language. Commercial and social interaction arose, joint military campaigns were undertaken against East Europe and Persia, and institutional borrowing and intermarriage occurred.

The Mongols who arrived on the Pontic and Caspian steppe in the thirteenth century practiced various forms of shamanism, as did most of the indigenous Turkic population into which they became assimilated. The newly agglomerated Turko-Tatars converted to Islam during the second half of the century, and Islam, at the turn of the fourteenth century, became the state religion of the Golden Horde. With this the Russo-Tatar conquest society entered the mainstream of medieval Christian-Muslim frontier life.

At the same time, because the Tatars were nomads and also had contacts with civilizations to the east, the results of the coexistence of Muslims and Christians in Russia were profoundly different than in Spain, the Balkans, and the Middle East. The Mongols' pastoral way of life kept them on the steppe; they did not move into the Russian forest zone. From their eastern and southern neighbors in Central Asia, Persia, and Egypt, the Mongols assimilated Islamic cultural and political structures rather than Russian ones. Whereas the Catholics in Valencia, the Crusaders in

Palestine, and the various Arabic and Turkic peoples who seized former
Roman and Byzantine lands had all adopted the institutions of their new
subjects, the Tatars did not. They remained uninfluenced by Russian life.
It was the Russians, rather, who came to imitate the ways of their Mongol
rulers. Thus the direction of the primary flow of influence in most conquest societies was reversed.

The Russian experience under Mongol rule was also uniquely set
apart from that of the Persians or the Chinese, conquered in the thirteenth
century and ruled by the Mongols until the end of the fourteenth. Persian
and Chinese intellectuals had the philosophical means to explain and
legitimize nomadic conquest; their Russian counterparts did not. In
China any change of dynasty, whether it involved alien invaders or not,
could be explained by the fickle Mandate of Heaven. In Persia the cycli-
cal theory of empires reassured the Muslim populace that the time of the
Mongols would pass. (In any case, the conversion to Islam of the Ilkhanid
Mongol dynasty greatly relieved the religious dilemma in Persia.) The
situation in Russia was different. The Russian "bookmen" (writers, redac-
tors, scribes, copyists) of the Kievan past were accustomed to explaining
Russian victories and defeats in skirmishes with nomads as signs of God's
pleasure or displeasure with his people. They had never been called
upon, however, to rationalize absolute conquest. Instead of confronting
the ideologically awkward fact of utter defeat, the bookmen finessed the
fact of Mongol conquest by presenting Russo-Tatar relations as merely a
continuation of Kievan relations with the steppe with no change of
suzereignty involved. Thus the Russian bookmen raised the ideology of
silence to a higher level and threw a veil over the intellectual implications
of Mongol hegemony.

Russia as part of the Golden Horde, therefore, shared many features
with the rest of the medieval ethno-religious frontier, including the ideology of silence. At the same time, the Russian experience paralleled to a
degree that of the rest of the territories spanning the length of Asia where
the Mongols held sway until at least the end of the fourteenth century. As
among the major sedentary civilizations the Mongols conquered elsewhere, the consequences for Russia of Mongol domination were complex.[2] On the one hand, the Mongols destroyed much of the Russian
economy and severely depleted the population. They imposed foreign
administration and onerous taxes and interfered in Russian politics and
princely succession. On the other hand, the Mongols fostered international commerce, from which Russia profited. Under Mongol protection

the Russian Orthodox Church grew enormously in material resources. The Tatars defended against East European enemies such as Poland and Lithuania, and provided many military, fiscal, and bureaucratic models used by the later Muscovite state.

Clearly the Mongol impact on Russia cannot be defined in simple terms. This book will explore the complexities of the Golden Horde's effect on Russia from the thirteenth to the fifteenth centuries, when Russia lay on the common border of two worlds—European Christendom and the Mongol realms.

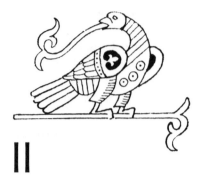

II

Kievan *Rus'* and the Steppe

HISTORIANS USUALLY CONSIDER THE KIEVAN PERIOD OF RUSSIAN HISTORY, from the migration of the East Slavs into the modern-day Ukraine in the sixth through eighth centuries until the Mongol conquest in the mid thirteenth century, as a golden age of national glory. The heart of the Kievan state was the Dnepr' valley along the river route that ran from Novgorod in the north, gateway to the Baltic, down south past Kiev to the Black Sea and Constantinople. Kiev, as the seat of the grand prince, became the capital from the ninth century on, and following the baptism of grand prince Vladimir in 988, Kiev became also the seat of the metropolitan of the Russian Orthodox Church. Separatist tendencies in peripheral regions like Novgorod, Vladimir-Suzdalia, and Galicia-Volhynia were actually a symptom of Kievan prosperity as these regions forged new economic networks apart from the trade along the Dnepr'. The vibrant and devoutly Christian Kievan culture was rich in church architecture and religious literature, and in the eleventh and twelfth centuries the Russian elite felt themselves very much a part of the Christian ecumene. With its active international commerce, flourishing cities, "democratic" institutions, and cultural achievements, Kievan *Rus'* has been idealized by historians.[1] This vision has tended to darken historical

10

judgments of the subsequent Mongol period. A demythologized appreciation of Kievan history provides a surer foundation for estimating the significance of the Mongols in Russian history.

The East Slavs, throughout the Kievan period, had to deal with steppe-dwelling neighbors to the south and east in the Pontic and Caspian steppe and along the Volga river artery. Although warfare between the people of Kievan *Rus'* and these nomads was commonplace, the amount of fighting should not be exaggerated.[2] A number of different pastoral peoples occupied the steppe during Kievan times, and their relations with the Russians varied with conflicting and joint interests. Russian sources, laced with religious invective, dwell on the episodes of hostility but ignore much of the evidence of mutually beneficial cooperation. The impression given is that all such efforts ended in failure and recrimination. While it will not do to omit the hostile side of the Russians' relations with their neighbors on the steppe, interactions were a great deal more complex than contemporary sources allow. A survey of Kievan dealings with a succession of steppe peoples—the semi-nomadic Khazar empire, the sedentary and urban Volga Bolgars, the nomadic Pechenegs, the border vassal Chernye Klobuky, and the pastoral Polovtsy—will provide a context for examining the later Russian response to the Tatar Yoke.

The first nomads the East Slavs had significant contact with, from the eighth to the tenth centuries, were the Khazars, a people probably of Turkic origin, whose ruling elite had converted to Judaism. The Khazars themselves were pastoralists, but their empire, from its capital Itil' on the Volga, controlled international trade and played a prominent role in international affairs, particularly in opposing the spread of Islam north of the Caucasus. It is difficult to infer much about their relations with the Slavs from the scant legendary material recorded centuries later in the Russian Primary Chronicle.[3] According to the Chronicle, the Slavs were forced to pay tribute to the Khazars until the coming of the Scandinavian Varangians, the supposed founders of the Kievan state, in the ninth century. In the tenth century the Kievan prince Sviatoslav conquered the Khazars and liquidated their empire.

Not enough is known of social, economic, and political conditions among the East Slavs in the eighth and ninth centuries to accept the assertion that East Slavic farmers paid tribute to Khazar officials. Certainly it would be a weak basis for any conclusions about Kievan-Khazar contacts. There is, however, an instance of Russian borrowing that is suggestive. The Khazar ruler bore the title *kagan,* emperor. This is the supreme

Inner Asian title, borne only by sacred clans possessing a divine mandate. The Khazars may have derived it from the Türk Empire; *kagan* appears in eighth-century Türk inscriptions on the Orkhon river in Mongolia. Three sources apply this title to the ruler of Kiev: the *Annales Bertiani sub anno* 839; the sermon "On Law and Grace" delivered by Metropolitan Ilarion in Kiev in the eleventh century; and "The Tale of the Host of Igor' " *(Slovo o polku Igoreve)*, an epic about the Russian campaign against the Polovtsy in 1186.[4] This may be the only case of the title's use by a non-nomadic people. That a steppe title was used in Kiev suggests considerable cultural interaction, and the significance of this trace of Khazar influence has long been recognized.[5] For a Christian prelate to laud his ruler with a shamanist title is highly anomalous.[6] That it was set down in writing so rarely indicates that this religious incongruity was apparent to the bookmen of the time.

The Khazar Empire had included the great urban commercial emporium of the Volga Bolgars on the upper Volga. After the defeat of the Khazars by the Russians, the Volga Bolgars became an independent state and survived as an autonomous entity until the coming of the Mongols in the thirteenth century. The Volga Bolgars were Muslims (according to the fictitious tale of the "testing of religions" in the Russian Primary Chronicle, one of their missionaries tried in the late tenth century to convert St. Vladimir). Their relations with the Russians consisted primarily of trade, though the chronicles have little to say about this. The American historian Thomas Noonan has proposed that the northeastern Russian principality of Vladimir-Suzdalia established a trading co-dominion with the Volga Bolgars to monopolize the western termini of the caravan routes that brought silk and spices from Asia to Eastern Europe. No marriages between princely families of Kievan *Rus'* and the Volga Bolgars are recorded, probably because of the religious barrier. Although there is little evidence of overt hostilities, in the late twelfth century the Russian Grand Prince Andrei Bogoliubskii ostensibly launched a "crusade" against Grand Bolgar, the capital of the Volga Bolgars. This attack was probably atypical. Religious antagonism was evidently held in check, at least most of the time, by mutually beneficial trade. Because of the silence of the sources, Russian familiarity with the Volga Bolgar state and its language, customs, and political organization remains a matter of speculation.[7]

The first thoroughly pastoral Turkic tribal confederacy the Russians had to deal with were the Pechenegs (Patzinaks), who migrated to the Pontic steppe in the tenth century and dominated it until the second half of the eleventh century. Although contacts between the two peoples were almost exclusively military, there are indications that the Russians knew this enemy well. The Kievan chronicle *sub anno* 968 contains the legend of a Pecheneg siege of the city. To warn the grand prince, a resourceful Kievan youth escapes through the encircling Pecheneg camp by waving a bridle as he runs through the camp, calling out for his missing horse.[8] It is apparent from the way the chronicler presents the story that he doesn't expect his audience, the Kievan urban elite, to be surprised that a boy should be able to speak the Pecheneg dialect, pass for a Pecheneg, and contrive a Pecheneg bridle. The story celebrates the boy's cleverness; his familiarity with Pecheneg ways is taken for granted. This vignette is an early example of the tradition of using an intimate knowledge of nomads as a weapon against them.

The Pechenegs had already ceased to be a major threat by the time Kievan *Rus'* converted to Christianity in 988, and most references to them in the chronicle are to the period before this, earlier in the tenth century. In these annals the Pechenegs are not called pagans, nor are any religious epithets used at all. The pre-Christian East Slavs perceived the Pechenegs as different from themselves, as nomads, but not as infidels.[9] Hostility between pagan East Slavs and pagan Pechenegs did not find religious expression.

In the eleventh century the Pechenegs and several other lesser tribes, such as the Berendei and Torki, were swept out of the Pontic steppe by the people who would be Russia's most powerful nomadic neighbors, the Polovtsy. Driven from their pastures, the refugees formed a single non-ethnic confederacy usually called the Chernye Klobuky (Black Caps). As sworn enemies of the Polovtsky, the Chernye Klobuky readily entered the service of the Kievan princes. Their military skills were invaluable. The Chernye Klobuky were the match of the Polovtsy in steppe warfare as mounted archers and were precious sources of intelligence, as well as serving as border guards[10] and scouts. Their influence was not confined to military matters, for their military capabilities soon gave them considerable political weight. A garrison was quartered in the capital itself, and the bulk of the Chernye Klobuky was stationed near enough to Kiev to intervene in succession disputes and civil wars. The Vladimir-Suzdalian princes who took over Kiev soon learned that they had to sever their alliances with the Polovtsy to stay on good terms with the Chernye Klobuky.

Soviet scholars have been too ready to detect the influence of the more "developed" Kievan culture on the nomadic Chernye Klobuky. Allegedly this led to the adoption of Orthodox Christianity, "feudal" relations, agriculture, and the sedentary life. However, most of the Chernye Klobuky must have remained nomadic, if only to preserve their steppe military skills, which atrophied rapidly when the nomadic way of life was abandoned. (Perhaps nomads fresh from the steppe were rotated regularly into the Kievan garrison.) Certainly the Chernye Klobuky became integrated into Kievan society and polity to a considerable degree. In a chronicle entry from 1151 they express their willingness to die for the "Russian Land" (russkaia zemlia). This concept expressed the highest loyalties of the Kievan Rus' elite. The Kievan chronicles would not lightly have projected such an expression of Russian political ideology onto the Chernye Klobuky.[11]

The Russian emigre historian D. A. Rasovskii acutely observes that no one ever asked if Kievans were influenced by the culture of the Chernye Klobuky, since it was assumed that nomads had no culture. He raises the question of the "Asiatic cast" of Kievan politics, in which competing princes employed rival contingents of Turkic nomads, and in which steppe ornaments, dress, and modes of fashion prevailed.[12] While Rasovskii exaggerates the archaeological evidence, his approach to the question remains promising.

The most formidable confederation of Turkic nomads the Kievans confronted was the Polovtsy (in Turkic, Kipchaks; in Latin and Greek, Cumans or Kumans), who preempted the Pontic and Caspian steppe in the eleventh century and held it until the Mongol onslaught. Polovtsian sway extended from Siberia and Central Asia across the Urals and the Volga to the Balkans. They played a major role in the histories of the Kievans, the Volga Bolgar state, the Crimea, Hungary, Bulgaria, Khwarizm in Central Asia, and, indirectly, Byzantium. The Polovtsy surpassed in stability and dwarfed in magnitude all other Turkic nomad groups on the pre-Mongol western Eurasian steppe.[13]

Warfare between the Polovtsy and Kievan Rus' was common, but often what the records present as Polovtsian raiding was in fact Russian civil war. In the twelfth century Russia became decentralized. While the city of Kiev retained its symbolic importance as the capital and the residence of the metropolitan, the peripheral principalities, especially Galicia-Volhynia to the southwest, the city-state of Novgorod to the north, and Vladimir-Suzdalia to the northeast, arose as major powers. Civil war, never dormant among the East Slavs, became more frequent. In the course of this internecine strife, rival princes turned for allies to all of Russia's neighbors, including Scandinavians, Poles, Hungarians, and Polovtsy. Chroniclers in victimized regions called down the wrath of God on princes whose collusion brought on infidel raids, while the scribes of more successful princes remained discreetly silent on the subject of such outside help. On the whole, though, chroniclers tended to characterize these wars as foreign invasions and smooth over the awkward fact of civil war.

Like Russia's other neighbors, the Polovtsy used the Russian turmoil to further their own ends. While the Russian princes were busy bloodying one another, they launched more and deeper raids into East Slavic territory. Yet despite the continual raiding and counter-raiding, some frontier always held, and none of the forests of the East Slavs was ever lost to the nomads. The battle between the East Slavs and the Polovtsy was militarily a stalemate.[14] The nomads proved themselves perfectly capable of storming and looting even strongly fortified Kiev, but not of holding the lands they overran. The Russian forests and cities could be garrisoned only by abandoning the nomadic way of life that gave the Polovtsy their military edge over the sedentary Russians. Even if the nomads had been willing or able to make this change, they simply lacked the political and administrative abilities to sustain imperial ambitions. For just these reasons, no people of the Pontic and Caspian steppe, except perhaps for the Khazars, ever attempted to bring the cities and farms of the Russian forest region into a steppe empire. The Polovtsy apparently had no aspirations to do so. However, the Pontic steppe was too poor to support the usually self-sufficient pastoralists. Economic need then, as well as intermittent alliances with various Russian princes, brought the Polovtsy repeatedly into Russian lands as raiders, but they always returned to the steppe when they were through with their raids.

The Russian princes for their part embarked on raids of their own. When they were united they could strike deep into the steppe, destroying the Polovtsy's winter quarters, running off their herds, and enslaving the women and children. These raids were safest and most effective when the men were off on some other business. Some of the most devastating Russian raids were timed, perhaps with Byzantine connivance, to coincide with Polovtsian campaigns in the Balkans, where they were aiding the Bulgarians against the Byzantine Empire. The Russians were no more inclined than the nomads to occupy the lands they ravaged. They lacked the skills to hold their own on the steppe and could neither provision garrisons so distant from their own fields nor survive on the products of pastoralism. The best they could do was try to impede Polovtsian raids by extending further south lines of earthen walls and forts, as St. Vladimir had done when threatened by the Pechenegs.[15]

In the continual warfare between the Polovtsy and Kievan *Rus'*, the nomads, with their superior mobility, had the decided advantage. Even their "homes," after all, could freely be moved about. Nonetheless, this was not a war that could in any sense be won. Battles, of course, were won and lost, but lands never were, and there was always sure to be another battle in the near future. From the eleventh until the early thirteenth centuries, warfare with the Polovtsy was a simple fact of Russian life. While this prolonged contact did not fundamentally alter Kievan social structure, it did exert a subtle influence on Kievan social history. Through their continuous presence and the resulting Russian familiarity with their geography, language, and culture, the Polovtsy became, in effect, a part of the social fabric of Kievan *Rus'*.

This can be seen in the "Instruction" *(Pouchenie)* to his son of prince Vladimir Monomakh, who, in the late eleventh and early twelfth centuries, was the ablest and most vigorous military commander in the war with the Polovtsy. In this blend of autobiography and fatherly advice, Monomakh lists the Polovtsian princes he has defeated, captured, or killed: "The two brothers Bagubarsova, Asinia and Sakzia, Boniak, Aepa, Sharukan, Osenia, Koksus', Burevich', Azgului, Urusobu, Kchiia, Ar-'lanapu, Kitanotpu, Kumana, Kurtka, Cheregrepu, Sur'baria," and others.[16] Monomakh expected his son and other readers of the "Instruction" to recognize these as men of political importance or military prowess. For Monomakh the enemy was clearly neither undifferentiated nor dehumanized. His familiarity with individual Polovtsy and ability to transcribe their names accurately is typical. The chronicles list scores of Polovtsy by name, and the bookmen would occasionally translate their Turkic names.[17]

The author of the *Slovo o polku Igoreve*, the epic about a Russian-Polovtsian battle of 1186, possessed a superlative knowledge of steppe flora and fauna, geography, and ethos. It is disingenuous of him to refer to the Polovtsian steppe as the "unknown land"; his epic, more than any other text, proves that to the Russians the "Polovtsian Land" *(polovetskaia zemlia)*[18] was precisely the opposite—*terra cognita*. (Though the Russian chronicles usually identify the various clans and tribes of the Polovtsy as "our" [allied] or "wild" [hostile] Polovtsy,[19] they use specific names often enough that it has been possible to map the "Polovtsian Land.") The Kievans needed an enormous amount of knowledge about the steppe and its people, whether they were fighting groups of Polovtsy or one another.[20] To create alliances with nomads, the Kievans had first of all to know what the current alliances and hostilities were among the clans of Polovtsy. Then they had to be able to find their prospective allies, which required knowledge of their summer and winter pastures. In negotiations there were diplomatic courtesies to be observed and elaborate ancestries to be praised. The Kievans had to be sure that the gifts they brought symbolized alliance rather than vassalage or slavery, which might have been fatal. The new allies had to have a clear understanding of each other's military capabilities to coordinate effective strategies. In short, military survival for the Kievans depended on exhaustive knowledge of steppe geography and the nomads' annual migrations, customs, tabus, genealogies, and language. This knowledge constituted in itself a Polovtsian contribution to Kievan culture.

The Polovtsy are usually accused of interdicting the trade route along the Dnepr' river from Kievan *Rus'* to Byzantium. Along this route the products of the Russian forests and captives taken in Kievan slave-raiding expeditions were sent south to purchase Byzantine luxury goods. It is likely that the decline of trade on the Dnepr' caravan route had more to do with the growing Italian monopoly of trade in the Byzantine Empire than with the Polovtsy. The nomads wanted, through "customs" and extortion, to exploit this trade rather than extinguish it. Since this meant smaller profits for Russian princes, the chronicles interpret this interference as wanton and malicious destruction. In fact, trade along the Volga river, which benefited Novgorod the Great and Vladimir-Suzdalia as well as the Volga Bolgars, flourished at the height of Polovtsian power. Down both the Volga and the Dnepr' the nomads traded directly with the East Slavs, exchanging salt, fish, and livestock for manufactured goods. The products of Russian artisans (and some of the artisans themselves) made their way to the winter grounds of the Polovtsy, the Russo-Alan[21] "cities."[22] The balance of trade cannot be determined. On the whole the Polovtsy's influence on the Kievan economy was probably negative, but class distinctions decided who suffered and who benefited. The peasants were most likely to be killed or enslaved during Polovtsian raids into the Russian forests, while the aristocracy, merchants, and some artisans continued to trade profitably with the nomads.

There is no evidence that the Kievans borrowed any political institutions from the Polovtsy, who had never had occasion to develop any administrative apparatus. However, though Kievan princely succession remains a subject of controversy, within the Riurikid clan there was clearly a preference for collateral succession, i.e., brother to brother rather than father to son. It is perhaps significant that the only other known examples of this practice are among nomadic Inner Asian peoples.[23]

Marriages were sometimes arranged between the families of Russian princes and friendly Polovtsy. The religious barrier was not a problem when Russian princes took shamanist wives from the steppe, since the Polovtsian princesses converted to Russian Orthodoxy. (Russian women did not marry Polovtsy, however, as this would have meant moving to the steppe and possibly being only one of several wives of a nomad prince.) In Kievan *Rus'* such marriages were sufficiently common in some family lines that in the late twelfth century some Russian princes were seven-eighths Turkic by blood.[24] They could hardly have been unaware of their heritage.

The extent of linguistic borrowing from Turkic languages in the language of Kievan *Rus'* has unfortunately never been established. Clearly the Russians and the Polovtsy were able to communicate, but for the most part the evidence for bilingualism is indirect. The nomad princesses who married Kievan princes must have learned Russian in order to pray and converse, and they may well have brought with them servants who did the same. The various Turkic nomads who entered the retinues *(druzhiny)* of Kievan princes could have been bilingual, and the same is true of the many Kievan princes, nobles, and merchants who dealt regularly with the Polovtsy or Chernye Klobuky. There are no records of Russians speaking the Polovtsian language, but this is perhaps not surprising, since it might have seemed improper. The Kievan sources do not, to my knowledge, mention the use of interpreters. They may have been unnecessary or so common as not to elicit comment. Informants and translators are necessarily implied by the presence of Polovtsian tales in Kievan writings.[25]

Most claims that the nomads influenced Kievan culture are difficult to substantiate.[26] Their literature, however, presumably oral and folkloric, is recorded in the Russian chronicles. The chronicler records, for example, that the Pecheneg prince Kuria turned the skull of grand prince Sviatoslav into a drinking goblet.[27] Other stories show more subtlety. The legend of Otrok and the Wormwood is a complete narrative of beauty and pathos.[28] In it the Polovtsian prince Otrok is driven from his native steppe by Vladimir Monomakh. Later, after Monomakh has died, an envoy brings some feather grass from the steppe for Otrok to smell. The aroma so overwhelms him with homesickness that he returns. (Inner Asian specialists have recently begun to realize that clans of pastoral nomads did not just wander in search of pastures but had traditional summer and winter pastures with inherited rights of usufruct. Their sense of attachment to the land was as strong as any farmer's.) The story is included in the chronicle because the chronicler and his audience empathize with Otrok's love of his homeland and are moved by it.

The same cross-cultural understanding is apparent in the Kievan *Slovo o polku Igoreve,* though some scholars consider it a later forgery.[29] Igor' Sviatoslavovich, prince of Novgorod-Seversk, launches a campaign in 1186 against the Polovtsian princes Gza and Konchak, hoping to dip his helmet symbolically in the Don river after his victory. Igor' is captured but treated with great honor. He is allowed to send for a priest to tend to his spiritual needs; he is given freedom of the camp; his son is betrothed to Konchak's daughter. The Polovtsian chieftains even take him hunting, a great honor among Inner Asian pastoral societies. This rapport between military aristocracies could transcend religious and cultural barriers from one end of the Mediterranean to the other and was apparent in other chivalric epics—"El Cid," "La Chanson de Roland," and "Digenis Akritas."

In their relations with the steppe peoples, Russians of the Kievan period faced problems very similar to those that vexed Christians and Muslims in the Mediterranean world. Their interactions with the nomads were fundamentally ambivalent. For every steppe alliance, there was a steppe war; for every peaceful business transaction, a raid on a caravan; for every act of friendly cooperation, one of violent hostility. The presence of hostile unbelievers on the steppe was not something the Kievans could do anything about. At the same time the mutual familiarity and periodic cooperation that naturally evolved were at odds with their most deeply held principles and threatened the Russian Orthodox basis of Kievan society. In the tradition of the medieval ethno-religious frontier, Russian intellectuals resolved this dilemma by turning to the ideology of silence. The essential ambivalence of Russian dealings with the infidels scarcely appears in the records of the time. The Kievan bookmen treated the nomads with unequivocal hostility and carefully recorded raids and atrocities while ignoring equally significant peaceful cooperation. When

Monomakh fought against the nomads, his bookmen lauded him as a defender of Christianity. When Monomakh made alliances with groups of Polovtsy and fought with them, as he did on innumerable occasions, his bookmen, or Monomakh himself, recorded the fact without comment or omitted it altogether. The religious ideology of the Kievans required that they be the implacable foes of the pagans and Muslims of the steppe. As this was not always practical in real life, they made it so in their writings.

The Mongols first appeared in the south Russian steppe in 1223. The Russians had not seen this people before, but they thought they knew the type. "No one knew who they were, or where they came from," wrote the Kievan chronicler, "or what their language is, or what tribe they belonged to, or what their religion is. Some say they are Tatars, and others call them Taurmeny, and others, Pechenegs."[30] The Russians believed, after centuries of contact with steppe peoples, that they knew what to expect. They were mistaken. The destructive power of the Mongol war machine eclipsed anything the Russians had seen before.[31] Other steppe nomads had contented themselves with raids and forays. This time Kievan *Rus'* found itself rapidly subjugated and annexed into the huge Mongol Empire. For the first time in their history the Kievan principalities felt the weight of foreign domination. This was the one aspect of the Tatar presence for which the Russians' long experience with steppe peoples had left them totally unprepared.

It is not surprising that the Russian bookmen, who were already practitioners of the ideology of silence, responded as they did. In describing the Mongol conquest, they preserved the stance of earlier times. When the resisting Russians lost a battle, they were being punished for their sins; when they won, the might of the Christian God and the truth of their faith were confirmed.[32] The chronicles recorded the events of Mongol rule using the now obsolete vocabulary of the earlier period of raids and counter-raids. Warfare between Kievan *Rus'* and other nomads had consisted largely of discrete military encounters without overarching political consequences.[33] By presenting Russo-Tatar relations in the same terms, the bookmen sought to deny that the Mongols had changed the rules of the game. Russian intellectuals wrote of the Mongols as if they were merely the successors to the Polovtsy and so avoided directly addressing the change in Russia's political status. In a refinement of the ideology of silence, Russian authors and chroniclers from the thirteenth to the fifteenth centuries denied that Russia had been conquered.

III

The Mongol Empire and the Golden Horde

MONGOL RULE OVER RUSSIA IS TRADITIONALLY CONSIDERED TO HAVE LASTED FROM 1240 to 1480, a century longer than in China or Persia, where the Mongols had maintained their supremacy for nearly a century and a half. The longevity of the Mongol Empire and its successor states, including the Golden Horde, owed much to their flexible and creative administration and to the legacy of Chingis Khan's charismatic leadership and political acumen. Though he died before the Russian conquest, the figure of the World-Conqueror looms large in any consideration of the Mongol impact in history.

Evaluations of Chingis and his accomplishments tend toward the extremes. For some historians he is the noble savage, the illiterate sky-worshipper whose inspired leadership, flawless judgments of human character, and military genius catapulted the obscure Mongols to the height of world power. For others he is a monumental gangster whose bloodthirsty cruelty and indifference to human life mobilized the barbarian Mongols for a worldwide rampage of death and destruction. Both images derive from uncritical reading of the medieval sources. The demigod emerges from the pages of the so-called *Secret History of the Mongols*. Though the origin and often the meaning of this text are obscure, it has the virtue of expressing the Mongol point of view.[1] Critics of Chingis have relied on chronicles written in the sedentary civilizations overrun by the Mongols, in particular China, Persia, and Russia. These sources attribute the excesses of Mongol conquest to innate depravity. Obviously neither of these views can be taken at face value. Empire-building is an invariably destructive process, unwelcome to the conquered. Tacitus immortalized the darker side of Roman expansion when he noted that the Romans made a wilderness and called it peace. Chingis Khan's military and political genius and charismatic leadership cannot be questioned; neither can the number of lives lost during his pursuit of glory. The same is true of Alexander the Great, Julius Caesar, and Napoleon. Chingis was no more cruel, and no less, than empire-builders before and since. Moral judgments are of little help in understanding his importance, and none is advanced here.

Chingis Khan's great abilities were not alone responsible for his success, which depended on the conditions of the Inner Asian steppe and the culture of the nomads who dwelt there.[2] The central unit of nomadic society was the clan, which served all economic, social, political, and military functions. Women and children looked after the herds, which freed the men for warfare. Males were trained from boyhood as mounted archers. They fought as a unit under the command of the clan elder, who also determined the political allegiance of the clan as a whole. Steppe wars could arise over grazing rights, politics, or personal feuds, but the nomads fought no more often than medieval European knights. When one clan defeated another, the victors assimilated the losers into their own clan as a military unit, perhaps with a new officer. The defeated clan assumed the name of their conquerors. Since the hierarchies created by this process required social validation, legendary backgrounds were fabricated. It would be discovered that both clans were descended from a pair of brothers, the victors from the elder. In more one-sided cases it might be decided that the losers were the heirs of a vassal or slave of the ancestor of the more powerful clan. The ranks swelled with each success, and victory bred victory.

Military successes also fostered political ambition and fed reputations of charismatic personality. As a rising warlord became the immediate vassal of increasingly important rulers, his essential political skill was knowing when to betray his current overlord to further his own aims. Inner Asian politics at the highest level inevitably overspilled the steppe, and any increasingly powerful nomad leader in Mongolia attracted the worried attention of China. In resisting Chinese manipulation, the best defense was offense. Thus a petty border lord, with some military and political skill and a healthy helping of luck, could rapidly become a potential conqueror of China. Many Inner Asian princes followed this path, among them Chingis Khan.

Chingis had a divine mission and a higher purpose than glory and booty: Tengri, the Inner Asian Great Blue Sky, had granted him the right to rule all who lived in felt tents.[3] From the Türk Empire Chingis took the imperial title *khan (kagan)*, which became part of his name. It was Chingis' military insight, in part, which allowed him to surpass the achievements of previous steppe warlords. He realized that to defeat China and other sedentary societies, the superiority in the field of his mounted archers would not be enough. To storm cities he needed experts in siege warfare. He drafted these from among the Muslims and the Chinese and built an army capable of besieging any city in the world. The Mongols did not improve on the military technology they acquired; they simply increased the sheer numbers of siege weapons hurled at an enemy city. With this advantage and the tactics and iron discipline of all nomad armies, Chingis fashioned an almost unbeatable war machine, capable of coordinated operations on an immense scale.

His "Mongols" were actually a tribal confederation of various Uralo-Altaic peoples, many of them Turkic, led by Chingis and his Mongol tribe. The armies were held together by the nomadic clan-tribal system, and as they advanced their ranks swelled with the peoples they conquered. Though Chingis' original Divine Mandate applied only to nomads, his armies did not stop when they reached the ends of the steppe. The Mongols kept riding until they were stopped, as they eventually were by the Mamelukes of Egypt and by the Japanese, or until they chose to withdraw, as they did in Europe. Chingis Khan died in 1227, before the Mongol Empire reached its greatest size. Without the social structure of the steppe clans and the superiority it gave his mounted archers, Chingis could have achieved nothing. Yet the conditions and way of life that made his rise possible existed for several millennia, and no one else, not Attila or Tamerlane, ever exploited them as successfully.

Though Chingisid ideology had its roots in the steppe and had not originally extended beyond it, the Divine Mandate soon had to be modified to a concept of universal empire. This interpretation followed rather than motivated Mongol conquests outside the steppe.[4] There is no need to seek the influence of "civilized" theories of world empire. To the

Chinese, "world" supremacy referred to the Middle Kingdom, and Christian universalism, which allegedly reached Chingis through the Nestorian tribes in the confederation, was singularly inappropriate. Chingis worshipped Tengri; his concept of empire came from the Türk Empire; and his mandate was born in the steppe when he did not yet aspire to dominion over all men. It was success, not Chinese or Christian theory, that transformed a limited steppe conception of "world" rule into a geographically universal ambition. Chingis remained true to Tengri and in his will divided not the lands of his empire but the nomad armies that had conquered them, so many clans and tribes to each of his heirs.

Chingis Khan's empire did not fragment after his death as had those of Alexander and Charlemagne. His personal legacy was an important building block of Mongol strength and unity. Only his descendants, the Golden Kin, could rule within the Mongol Empire and its successor states.[5] Chingis' life story became the basis of seventeenth-century Mongol historiography,[6] and his relics and standards became objects of veneration.[7] When the Mongols converted to Buddhism in the sixteenth and seventeenth centuries, Chingis became a Buddhist saint. The significance and power of his name and memory in the successor states of the Mongol Empire is reflected in the Yasa, the fictive legal code created after his death but attributed to the great conqueror.[8]

Chingis never abandoned that sophisticated blend of shamanism, polytheism, and totemism endemic to the steppe. His successors considered the clergy of all religions sorcerers, and, though they adopted exclusivist religions, retained his tolerance for other faiths.[9] For this they were, ironically, much praised. Christians, Muslims, Taoists, Buddhists, and Confucianists all perceived Mongol tolerance as special sympathy for their own creeds. Clerics and chroniclers of each faith recorded the Mongol era in largely religious terms and from the vantage points of their own religions. Thus, depending on the source, Chingis quotes from the Koran, favors Nestorian Christianity, or holds Taoist beliefs. These sources, concerned mainly with religion, fail seriously to address the administrative structure of the Mongol Empire and thus create the impression that it had none.[10] This skews the picture of Mongol rule, and the religious consequences of the Mongol conquest have been allowed to crowd out other aspects in some scholarly literature.

Mongol administration was in fact complex and eclectic. The large sedentary populations in the new empire presented political and administrative problems never envisaged in the steppe, and the Mongols responded with the resources at hand. In Mongolia they had already developed what were essentially feudal concepts.[11] Vassals received fiefs of herds and clans, with accompanying rights to pastures. The feudal hierarchy was imbedded in Mongol political organization. In building their empire, the Mongols retained features of their customary law, borrowed bureaucratic structures from various sources, and formulated new laws to cover new situations. The strength of the Mongol Empire, as Larry W. Moses has suggested, lay in its ability to integrate feudal, clan-tribal, and bureaucratic and imperial social structures and political institutions.[12] A single Mongol might be simultaneously a feudal vassal, a clan aristocrat, and a bureaucratic official. The clan-tribal nomadic base was perpetuated even as the aristocratic elite assumed new military, political, and bureaucratic responsibilities. The fusion of identities and meshing of systems and forms gave cohesion to the empire, and the passage of time proved its viability.

The Mongols conquered nearly all of Asia and achieved what all Inner Asian steppe empires had dreamed of, control of the continental caravan routes from China to Persia. The enormous destructive cost of the Pax Mongolica cannot be denied, but the Mongol Empire made significant contributions to the political institutions, economic development, and cultural diversity of many lands. No history of the Mongol Empire, no matter how erudite, which dwells only on Mongol destruction can be satisfactory.[13]

The Golden Horde was the inheritance of Chingis' son and grandson, Juchi and Batu. Though its boundaries varied and cannot be delineated with precision, basically they included the upper Volga, the territory of the former Volga Bolgar state, Siberia to the Urals, the northern Caucasus, Bulgaria (for a time), the Crimea, and Khwarizm in Central Asia.[14] The core of the Golden Horde and the key to its identity and its success was the Pontic and Caspian steppe. In the mid thirteenth century, following the conquest of Russia, the Golden Horde was still part of the great Mongol Empire. The census of the Horde and Russia was directed from the far-off imperial capital Karakorum in Mongolia, and the Horde's rulers still held fiefs in China and Persia. Troops from the Golden Horde took part in the campaigns of the Mongol Empire. However, before the turn of the century allegiance to the mother state had become largely symbolic and ceremonial. (This fiction was worth maintaining up until the liquidation in 1368 of the Mongol Yüan dynasty in China, the repository of Mongol tradition.) Though the Chingisid heritage remained important, the Horde became fully autonomous. Its rulers assumed the title khan, coined their own currency, and vied with the other Mongol successor states for power and influence.

The Golden Horde's ideological foundations and initial institutional apparatus were those of the Mongol Empire. It used the Mongol census, decimal organization of the army, postal system *(yam)*, and steppe taxes. During its long history, however, the Golden Horde evolved in response to the exigencies of its position in the Pontic and Caspian steppe and in the world. With the adoption of Islam in the fourteenth century came the most sophisticated bureaucratic apparatus in the Islamic world, the Persian *diwan* system.[15] A central council of four *bekliaribeks* replaced the Mongol family council of the *quriltai*; a vizier was put in charge of the treasury; and the entire Muslim religious establishment of qadis, muftis, and the like arose in Sarai, the Horde's capital on the lower Volga. Islamic diplomatic forms were combined with Mongol chancellery practices dating back to Chingis Khan.[16] From the immunity charters the khans issued to the Russian Orthodox Church can be inferred the extent and complexity of the taxation system.[17] Thus in both internal and external affairs the Golden Horde possessed a fully functional paper bureaucracy, one which had a decisive effect on each of its successor states. (Unfortunately, Tamerlane destroyed the Horde's archives when he sacked Sarai in the 1390s.)

Such an administration could not operate on horseback. Using labor and artisans conscripted from peripheral areas like Russia and the Volga Bolgar and Khwarizmian territories, the Horde founded new cities like Sarai in its heartland, the lower Volga. While most of the rank-and-file Mongols remained on the steppe as nomads, preserving their military effectiveness, a permanent urbanized bureaucracy took shape in Sarai. The traveler ibn Batuta who visited Sarai in the second quarter of the fourteenth century described it as a normal Muslim city, with running water brought by aqueducts, mosques, meddresses, caravansaries, foreign merchants' quarters, and aristocratic and imperial palaces.[18] From written and archaeological evidence the complexity of the Golden Horde's social structure is obvious.[19] The khan might still roam symbolically up and down the Volga, accompanied by much of the military camp *(orda)*, but the Golden Horde was at its height a delicately balanced symbiosis of nomadic clans and sedentary bureaucratic elements. In this it resembled the great Mongol Empire.

During the nearly two and a half centuries that the Mongols ruled the Pontic and Caspian steppe, this system proved its resiliency. Both emir Mamai, after his defeat by Dmitrii Donskoi at the battle of Kulikovo Field in 1380, and Tokhtamysh, after his disastrous loss to Tamerlane on the Terek river in 1391, were able to recover and raise new troops. The Horde's grip on Russia was never loosened, despite its own court rivalries and dynastic intrigues. In the imperial palaces of Rome and Constantinople life expectancy was often short, but the Roman and Byzantine Empires had resources whose effectiveness was not destroyed by disturbances at the highest levels. The same was true of the Golden Horde.

The scope and sophistication of the Golden Horde's diplomacy show that they were not, as the great Imperial Russian historian S. M. Soloviev dismissed them, a bunch of petty bandits. International diplomacy on a large scale required a coherent and reasonably efficient governmental apparatus. The major thrust of the Golden Horde's foreign policy was directed south toward the rich pastures and profitable trade routes of Azerbaidjan, held by the Mongol Ilkhanids of Persia. In pursuit of this prize, the Golden Horde made common cause with the Mamelukes of Egypt, coercing the Byzantines into relaxing their friendship with the Ilkhanids enough to permit communication from the Black Sea to the Mediterranean through the Straits of Constantinople.[20] These diplomatic efforts were both extensive and expensive. Fifty major embassies to Egypt are recorded, each requiring gold and silver gifts and horses, camels, and falcons for the Mameluke sultan. The Mongols observed all the niceties of Islamic diplomacy. Correspondence had to be on paper of the correct size, written in the proper scripts with the right pens and inks and special gold letters, and expressed in elaborate formulas that only poets and scholars could fully master. The Mamelukes reciprocated, employing a Mongolist[21] in their chancellery and paying scrupulous attention to Mongol custom and Chingisid genealogy in their letters to the khan at Sarai. The alliance between the Mamelukes and the Golden Horde survived interrupted contact and failed dynastic marriages and was maintained even after the Ilkhanids renounced their sympathy for Nestorian Christianity and adopted Islam. The Horde's struggle with the Ilkhanids for Azerbaidjan endured as long as the Ilkhanid state itself.

The Golden Horde's foreign policy also actively embraced all of Eastern Europe, the Middle East, and Central Asia. Armenian and Georgian princes, Italians from the Genoese colonies in the Crimea and on the

Black Sea, Khwarizmians and Egyptians, Papal envoys and missionaries all came to Sarai, as did ambassadors from the Mongol houses of Persia, Central Asia, China, and Mongolia. It is hard to see how Mongol rule could have had an isolating effect on Russia during the thirteenth and fourteenth centuries. Though Russia's role in the Mongols' foreign policy was small, consisting largely of contributing manpower and taxes to the Azerbaidjan campaigns, it was vital to Russian self-interests to stay abreast of the Horde's foreign affairs. Certainly the Russian princes who frequently traveled to Sarai witnessed the parade of foreign dignitaries visiting the lower Volga. The Golden Horde's significant European contacts would also have tended to expose Russia to the international community. After the overthrow of the Yüan, the Golden Horde lost touch with China and Mongolia and by the turn of the fifteenth century had become more a provincial East European power than a major Middle Eastern one.

The economy of this internationally active state was based on pastoralism and commerce. (The products of farmers and artisans did not create economic surpluses; they were for domestic consumption, necessary but not lucrative.) While most Mongols lived off their herds, the cream of the economy was international trade fostered by the security the Mongols enforced along the caravan routes. The richest of these were the trade routes from the Orient bringing silk and spices to the Mediterranean and Europe. These passed through Sarai and the other Mongol cities of the lower Volga. The Horde also redirected the fur trade through Ustiug and Sarai to the Caspian, excluding some Russian or Bolgar intermediaries.[22] The Mongols did not engage directly in trade but taxed the foreign merchants who took advantage of the Pax Mongolica, mostly Armenians, Italians,[23] Jews, and Central Asian Muslims. The Horde promoted trade with Poland-Lithuania, the Hanseatic League (via Novgorod), Egypt and Byzantium, the Genoese from Kaffa in the Crimea, Persia, and Central Asia. They minted their own silver coins, indicating a favorable balance of trade; indeed, during civil wars each khan established his own mint.

The Golden Horde's political history can be reconstructed from hostile Russian and Persian sources and friendly Mameluke ones.[24] The first internal division had occurred before the turn of the fourteenth century. Nogai, whose Chingisid legitimacy is questioned, built a power base in the Crimea and the Balkans and contested with the khans of the lower Volga for control of the Golden Horde. The underlying causes of this civil war were clan and tribal rivalries and competition for trade routes. After this perhaps premature separatist attempt was suppressed, the Horde rose in the early fourteenth century to what is generally considered its greatest period, during the reign of Khan Uzbek. Under Uzbek Islam became the state religion of the Golden Horde. Later in the century, civil war and instability reasserted themselves, and near anarchy reigned for twenty years. Khan Tokhtamysh expelled the de facto power of the Horde, emir Mamai, and at last restored some semblance of order. Tokhtamysh's success proved ephemeral. The Horde's urban base had been devastated by the Black Death, and the great Central Asian ruler Tamerlane administered the *coup de grace* in the 1390s, crushing Tokhtamysh in a titanic struggle. Tamerlane sacked Old and New Sarai and rerouted the caravans of the Asian silk and spice trade to the south of the Caspian so that they bypassed the Horde's emporia along the Volga. This staggering loss was more than the economy could bear. The cumulative weakening of the urban centers and the clashing interests of nomadic and sedentary Mongols shattered the symbiosis of city and steppe, and regional separatist impulses were released. Each of the future khanates pursued its own economic ties. Emir Edigei made a final effort to pull the Golden Horde together but failed, and in the middle of the fifteenth century the Horde fragmented definitively.

When the great Mongol Empire had split, it produced, in addition to the Juchids of the Golden Horde, the Yüan dynasty of China, the Chagataids of Central Asia, and the Ilkhanids of Persia. Two hundred years later, after the other successor states had disappeared, the Golden Horde still had enough life to spawn successor states of its own. These were the khanates of Kazan' on the middle Volga, Astrakhan' on the lower Volga, Gireid Crimea, Shibanid Siberia, the Muscovite client state of Kasimov, the nomadic Nogai hordes, and the Great Horde, the remnant of the Golden Horde's nomadic core, still roaming the open spaces in the midst of the peripheral successor states. (The Great Horde was no longer part of the richer commercial world. To avoid losses through customs or extortion, the Golden Horde's urbanized successor states joined forces with Muscovy to liquidate the Great Horde in 1502.)

The legacy of Chingis Khan still remained a potent force. All of these states were ruled, at least in name, by his descendants. As Larry W. Moses has observed, there was no precedent in the Mongol Empire for non-Chingisid rulers like Mamai and Edigei (leaving aside the disputed case of Nogai). Even the mighty Tamerlane, of aristocratic Mongol birth but not a

Chingisid, respected the forms of dynastic legitimacy. Though he did sponsor a spurious genealogy linking him to Chingis, he did not presume to call himself khan. Instead he married into the imperial family and used puppet khans. Non-Chingisid rulers in the Golden Horde's successor states followed this example.

It has been presumed that the Mongols refrained from occupying Russia because they were incapable of administering an urban and agricultural society, because they were daunted by the ferocity of Russian resistance, or some combination of the two. Yet Persia and China fought off the Mongols at least as strongly as Russia and had vastly greater populations to administer. The institutions which permitted prolonged occupation of China, Persia, and Central Asia would hardly have been inadequate to govern Russia. The fact is that Russia remained unoccupied because it had little to offer the Mongols. It was neither part of the steppe nor located on profitable trade routes. Commerce in and through Russia may have been important for the Russians but was minor compared to the trade along the caravan routes east and south of Sarai. Mongol taxes may have been a great burden on the Russian economy, but for the Mongols this revenue was insignificant beside the wealth that flowed from Khwarizm, Bolgar, the Crimea, and Azerbaidjan. Russia was simply peripheral to the Golden Horde's interests.[25] The Mongols replaced the rulers of other sedentary areas like Khwarizm and Bolgar with Mongol officials but left Russia, like Armenia-Georgia, in the hands of native princes. The profits would not have offset the expenses of direct administration. The Mongols wanted to extract maximum benefit at minimum cost; any interpretation of their actions that does not proceed from this assumption is probably misguided.

Russia's position in the Golden Horde is an anomaly, in part because it was never part of the Mongol *ulus*. This term, which meant, essentially, political inheritance, had originally applied to all of Chingis Khan's empire and then to the parts of it, like the Golden Horde, left to his heirs. The Golden Horde, the *ulus* of Juchi and his son Batu, was considered to have four parts—Sarai, the Crimea, Khwarizm, and Desht-i-Kipchak (the Polovtsian steppe).[26] Russia was not included, nor did it fall into the category of areas like Bolgar, which also lay outside the *ulus* proper but merited a direct Mongol presence. No known term from Mongol political theory describes Russia's status, and its theoretical and ideological place within the Mongol hegemony remains indeterminate.[27]

The Mongols who ruled Russia had several profound advantages over the Mongol dynasties in China and Persia. Before reaching Russia, the Mongols had already assimilated many probably Turkic tribes such as the Naiman, Kerait, and Tatars. The indigenous peoples of the Pontic and Caspian steppe, like the Turkic-speaking Polovtsy, were by and large shamanist nomads, culturally and ethnically similar to the new conquerors. The Mongols eliminated the socio-political infrastructure of the Volga Bolgars, the Polovtsy, and the Chernye Klobuky, deporting most of the latter from the western steppe to the Volga. Then the Golden Horde swallowed the enormous Polovtsian population and the other nomads of the steppe and gradually became a Turkic-speaking state. The indigenous nomads lost their original identities and later emerged from the Mongol period in new ethnic groups with Mongol names; Polovtsy, Volga Bolgars, and Chernye Klobuky vanished to be replaced by Tatars, Uzbeks, and Nogais.[28] In China and Persia the Mongol dynasties ruled populations whose culture and religions were very different from their own (though the Ilkhanids eventually adopted Islam). Thus non-assimilation was a problem because of the cultural and religious hostility of their subjects, and assimilation was dangerous because it deprived the Mongols of their traditional sources of strength. The Golden Horde remained largely on the steppe and faced neither of these problems. The absorption of the Turkic-speaking population strengthened the Mongol hold on the steppe and lent the Golden Horde ethnic and cultural unity.[29]

Russia's religion and culture were at least as hostile to the Mongols as those of China and Persia, but Mongol rule lasted longer in Russia because it was indirect.[30] The Pontic and Caspian steppe made this possible. In China, where direct rule was a necessity, the Mongol cavalry was severely hampered by a lack of adequate pasture. The Ilkhanids were better off but had to enforce their rule of southern Persia and other areas with an army based in the pastures of northern Persia and Azerbaidjan. The Golden Horde, on the other hand, had at its center the vast pastures of the Pontic and Caspian steppe, sufficient to support indefinitely a full Mongol army. Russia was too close to the steppe for its own good. Even the most remote Russian city was within easy striking distance. Thus the Mongols were able to control Russia for as long as conditions on the steppe were favorable. Russian liberation came only after the irrevocable disappearance of Mongol political harmony.

The Mongols initially ruled Russia through resident Mongol officials called *baskaki*. Later this system was abandoned, and Russia was ruled from Sarai by means of envoys called *posoly* who communicated the wishes of the Mongol overlords to the Russian princes. The Mongols continued to give commands in the Russian forests for a hundred years after China and Persia had overthrown Mongol dynasties.

Russian historians have blamed both the conquest and Russia's continued inability to free itself on the disunity of the Russian principalities, presuming that a united Russia could have cast off the Tatar Yoke. Hence the glory and importance attached to Dmitrii Donskoi's victory in 1380. In truth, no amount of solidarity would have enabled the Russian princes to withstand the Mongol juggernaut of 1237–1240. Nor, at any time during the thirteenth and fourteenth centuries, could they have overcome the Golden Horde, with its powerful balance of a nomadic army and an urbanized bureaucracy, fueled by the profits of international commerce. Russia was secondary to the Horde's interests. As a consequence, the Golden Horde's foreign relations and internal conflicts did more to determine its Russian policy than did Russian politicking or resistance. Though the growing power of the Muscovite state (and its sheltering of the founders of the Kasimov khanate) did have an impact, Russia had little to do with the eventual collapse of the Golden Horde. Tamerlane did more than Dmitrii Donskoi to weaken the Horde, ravaging those cities not already decimated by the Black Death and cutting the Horde off from the Asian caravan routes.

The Mongols ruled Russia from the steppe, but this did not, as many have claimed, lessen their influence on medieval Russia's political, economic, social, and cultural life. Indeed, by prolonging Mongol hegemony, this arrangement may have contributed to its lasting effects. Any examination of the Mongol impact clearly must begin with Russo-Tatar relations during the centuries of the Tatar Yoke.

IV

The Mongol Administration
of Russia

THE FRANCISCAN MISSIONARY CARPINI, WHO, ON THE POPE'S BEHALF, PASSED through Russia on his way to Karakorum shortly after the conquest, described the first Mongol administrators. These were the *baskaki* (a word of Turkic origin, which the Mongols doubtless acquired from the peoples they overran and assimilated).[1] According to Carpini's report, the *baskaki* oversaw the collection of tribute, conscripted troops, and maintained order, that is, suppressed opposition to Mongol rule.[2] (There were tax-farmers who were not *baskaki*, notably the Muslim tax-farmers expelled from a series of northeastern Russian cities in 1262.)[3] The *baskaki* were stationed in the Russian forest zone, but as circumstances changed the Horde adapted its administrative methods and recalled the *baskaki* to the steppe. Their duties were taken over by envoys who brought directives from Sarai, where the bureaucracy now included specialists who followed developments in specific regions of Russia. The change did not constitute a loosening of the Mongols' grip. Though they left the political infrastructures of the Russian principalities intact, the Mongols exercised authority very effectively in Russia during most of the thirteenth through fifteenth centuries.[4]

To analyze the Mongols' administration of Russia requires meticulous examination both of the extant sources individually and of the larger picture they present. Many of the references to Mongol officials occur in unreliable texts from later periods, showing obvious signs of interpolation. At the same time, the close study of details in the sources must not obscure the broader framework of the Horde's development, which makes the administrative change explicable. Both of these dangers are apparent as we try to establish the impact of the *baskak* system on Russia. This requires determining when the system began and ended, where the *baskaki* were stationed, and how they conducted themselves.

Clearly the Mongols implemented the *baskak* system not long after they conquered Russia, for Carpini describes the system in 1245. The Hypatian chronicle *sub anno* 1254–1255 is the first of a number of Russian sources to mention Mongol administrators, recording that the *boyar* (noble) Milei was named *baskak* of the village (?) of Bakota.[5] In 1267 a *yarlik* (patent) given to the Russian Orthodox Church's metropolitan lists *baskaki* among the officials who should honor the church's fiscal immunities.[6] Two years later, according to the Novgorod First Chronicle, the "great Vladimir *baskak* Argaman" helped grand prince Yaroslav impose his will on a recalcitrant Novgorod and then frightened off the German knights threatening the city.[7] The sixteenth-century Nikon chronicle holds that this Argaman returned to Novgorod in 1273.[8]

The same Nikon chronicler, who was particularly fond of generalizations, is probably responsible for the claim in a redaction of the *vita* of Mikhail of Chernigov that Mongol governors *(namestniki i vlasteli)* were appointed in all Russian cities after the 1237–1240 campaign.[9] The sentence is an interpolation not in the original text, and the use of the Russian terms emphasizes the anachronism. Unfortunately, none of the scattered early references substantiate the assertion, or even that the *baskak* system was implemented throughout Russia at the same time. The Nikon chronicle also asserts that Batu installed a *voevoda* (military governor) in Kiev following the sack of the city in 1240,[10] but the *voevoda* is not named, and this is probably another textual corruption. A later copy of a 1257 Riazan' charter[11] mentions an Ivan Shain appointed *namestnik* of Chernigov, but again the use of the Russian term is suspect. In estimating the distribution of *baskaki*, historians have often depended on later sources of dubious value. That *baskaki* were distributed throughout the Russian forest zone is perhaps suggested by the reference in the 1267 *yarlik*, which applied in all the Russian principalities. No contemporary sources corroborate this.

Collecting tribute and conscripting troops, two of the *baskak*'s primary functions, involved quotas based on population. This suggests a correlation between the taking of a census *(chislo)* and the installation of a *baskak* in a given region. The original redaction of the *vita* of Mikhail of Chernigov records a census in the Kievan region in the 1240s.[12] It may have been used by the *baskaki* Carpini saw. There was no census in Vladimir-Suzdalia until 1257 or in Novgorod until 1259.[13] It is possible that these cities did not have *baskaki* until after the censuses. Unfortunately the connection between the census, the payment of tribute, and the presence of *baskaki* remains more logical than demonstrable. We know that Novgorod had a census and that it paid tribute, but there is no evidence of a *baskak* in the city. Similarly there is no evidence of a census in Galicia-Volhynia, yet it definitely paid tribute, and there is a reference to at least one *baskak* in the area, Milei.

The Soviet scholar A.N. Nasonov tried to address the problem of the distribution of *baskaki* using toponymic evidence. He argued that place names with the root *baskak-* indicated that Russian troops with Tatar officers under the command of a *baskak* had once been stationed there. This fits with the story of the *baskak* Akhmad and with the record of a peculiar incident in Kiev in 1331, both described later. Nasonov attributed the concentration of such names in the Rostov region to an intensified military presence following the *veche* uprisings of 1262. Such place names are widely distributed in Russia, and if Nasonov's theory is correct, the *baskaki* were much more common in the Russian forests than the references in the sources suggest.[14]

Nasonov's conclusion has been disputed by another Soviet scholar, V.V. Kargalov. He argues that Mongol punitive expeditions were known to originate in the steppe during the period of *baskak* administration, and that therefore *baskaks* did not have powerful forces at hand. The sources contain no mention of standing Russo-Tatar armies in the Russian forest zone. In Kargalov's opinion, the village names reflect *baskaki* land holdings.[15] Kargalov's point has a good deal to be said for it, though it is not widely accepted among Soviet historians. It is unlikely that high Mongol officials would have been stationed in minor Russian villages. It is more probable that they were assigned to the major political centers and accompanied by small retinues of troops.

A cryptic incident in Kiev raises more questions than it answers. In 1331 Vasilii, the archbishop of Novgorod, and his entourage were set upon by a Prince Fedor of Kiev, an anonymous *baskak,* and fifty men who extorted a ransom *(okup)*.[16] Nothing is known of Prince Fedor, the nameless *baskak,* or whether Kiev at the time owed obedience to the Golden Horde or to Lithuania. Nor can it be proven that these were Russo-Tatar troops belonging to a *baskak* army.[17]

The sixteenth-century *vita* of Pafnutii of Borovsk contains another problematic reference to a *baskak.* Allegedly the saint's grandfather was a *baskak* who raped a Christian girl but saved his life and soul by converting to Christianity and marrying his victim. When or if any of this happened is open to serious question.[18]

The only extended narrative about a *baskak* is in the Laurentian chronicle, the major source for the history of northeastern *Rus'* in the thirteenth century. Oddly it makes no mention of that Argaman described in the Novgorodian chronicle as wielding such might in Vladimir, the northeastern capital. Instead, in its account of the 1280s, the chronicle includes the tale of Akhmad, who held the *baskach'stvo* (a delightful Russianized nominative) in the southern city of Kursk in Chernigov province.[19] *Baskak* Akhmad farmed the tribute *(dan')* in Kursk and founded two tax-free enclaves *(slobody)* for artisans. The political situation in Kursk was unstable, as two local Russian princes took different sides in the dispute within the Golden Horde between Nogai in the Crimea and Telebuga on the Volga. The princes believed that by playing the two Tatar factions against each other, they could avoid reprisals for disobeying Akhmad. Akhmad was unable to impose his will with the Russian troops and Tatar officers at his disposal and eventually summoned a punitive expedition from the steppe. Local nobles were massacred and one of the princes executed. Akhmad, in the end, fled to the steppe. His tenure, as described in the Laurentian chronicle, was exploitative and brutal.

For a number of reasons, Akhmad's career cannot be assumed to be typical of the *baskak* system in all of Russia or even in the southern region.[20] There are no other accounts of the same type to compare it to. That the story appears in the chronicle of a distant city poses further problems, and the tale's origins and when and where it was first written down are unknown.[21] Thus we cannot conclude that *baskaki* regularly founded *slobody* or farmed tribute or even that they controlled military units. The unusually turbulent state of affairs in Kursk also makes extrapolating from Akhmad's career risky.

Akhmad certainly did not further the interests of the Chernigov princelings, and other evidence of the relations between the *baskaki* and Russian princes is scarce, obscure, and contradictory. The first *baskak* mentioned in Russian sources, Milei of Bakota, earned the disapproval of Grand Prince Daniil of Galicia-Volhynia, though just what Milei did is difficult to determine.[22] In the next decade, however, *baskak* Argaman placed the power of the Tatar state behind Grand Prince Yaroslav in his troubles with Novgorod. Whether the *baskaki* generally supported the princes is impossible to say. Probably only princes loyal to the Tatars could count on the backing of the *baskaki*.

Since the *baskaki* definitely were powerful men, it is probable that they were members of the Tatar aristocracy. The names which have been preserved, however, suggest a variety of backgrounds. Argaman sounds Armenian; Milei, Slavic (he was said to be a *boyar*); Akhmad is a Muslim name used by various peoples; and Telebuga, the *baskak* of Rostov, whose death is recorded *sub anno* 1308,[23] probably has a Turco-Tatar name. This heterogeneity is intriguing, but we cannot infer ethnicity from names with any assurance.

The arbitrariness of the references to *baskaks* in the chronicles is striking. Why should a tale about Akhmad, the *baskak* of a political backwater, be recorded rather than one about the obviously influential "great Vladimir *baskak* Argaman?" The chronicles say nothing of the deaths of Akhmad or Argaman but record the passing of Telebuga of Rostov, about whom absolutely nothing else is known. The notice of Telebuga's death appears in annals assumed to come from Rostov, at the time the center for chronicles written for princes. Chronicles that were being written elsewhere, however, make no mention of their own *bas-kaki*. What little data we have seems accidental.

The Mongols discontinued the *baskak* system in the fourteenth century. The evidence of when and how it was abandoned is as scanty as the evidence concerning its implementation. One mention of *baskaki* in the fourteenth century can be discounted. The Nikon chronicle interpolates an allusion to *baskaki* as participants in a Russo-Tatar expedition against Smolensk in 1339, when the city was already under Lithuanian control.[24] The latest reliable allusions to *baskaki* come from the second half of the century. Several documents and charters from the 1350s to 1382 refer to *baskaki* installed in the Riazan' border region[25] by *Tsaritsa* Taidula (i.e., *Khansha* Taidula, the wife or widow of a khan). On the other hand, in contemporary literary works about the battle of Kulikovo Field in 1380, emir Mamai expresses his intent to restore the *baskak* system. This implies that *baskaki* were no longer in use at the time.[26] (Given Mamai's evil reputation, the passage also suggests that the *baskak* system was hated.)

⸱Possibly the Mongol administrators were removed from different parts of Russia at different times (just as they may have been installed at different times). The *baskaki* of the Riazan' border region may have been the last to leave Russia.

Most historians argue that the Golden Horde installed and then removed the *baskaki* in response to specific events of the Russian resistance. According to this theory, the Mongols stationed officials in Russia after the Russians ejected Muslim tax-farmers in 1262. The Tver' uprising of 1327 then compelled the Tatars to recall the *baskaki* and allow the Russian princes to collect the tribute. This view begs a number of questions. It ignores the possibility of regional variation in Mongol policy. It disregards the fact that *baskaki* were not just in charge of tribute collection but were also supervisors and intelligence-gatherers.[27] Moreover, the earliest trustworthy evidence that princes were collecting tribute for the Mongols dates from the third quarter of the fourteenth century. This leaves a gap of at least twenty-five years between the 1327 uprising and any proof of the Tatars' putative response. Indeed, the Horde, then at the zenith of its power under Khan Uzbek, savagely repressed the Tver' uprising, and the argument that they did away with an entire administrative system in deference to Russian opposition is unconvincing.

The "Russian" theory of the rise and fall of the *baskak* system places far too much emphasis on the Russian influence on Mongol policy and far too little—indeed, essentially none—on the interests of the policy makers and the Golden Horde's internal dynamics. Given the Mongols' demonstrable bureaucratic flexibility, we can assume that they used *baskaki* when these were the most efficient means of overseeing Russia and extracting tribute and conscripts and removed them when this ceased to be the case. Russian resistance would have been a factor, but only one among many.

A "Mongol" theory of the evolution of the *baskak* system provides an alternative perspective in terms of the Golden Horde's internal history. Maintaining and supervising a network of resident Mongol officials in Russia must have required central control from Sarai and sophisticated record-keeping. Thus this phase of administration could not have preceded the Golden Horde's development of an urban bureaucracy to complement its nomadic army. Further, this bureaucracy had many concerns more urgent than Russia, and would not have turned its attention to the East Slavs unless it were thriving. The period of *baskak* administration, then, probably corresponded to the heyday of the Horde's bureaucratic urban base and ended when the Black Death, civil war, and Tamerlane's assaults weakened the Mongol cities.

The new political environment on the steppe in the fourteenth century naturally caused a restructuring of the Mongol administration of Russia. Responsibility for overseeing the Russian principalities seems to have passed from the *baskaki* to absentee administrators called *darugi*.[28] This Mongol term, also used in Yüan China, was synonymous in the thirteenth century with the Persian *shikhna* and the Turkic *baskak* (in Inner Asia, Anatolia, and the future territories of the Golden Horde, *baskak* was used by nomadic states with sedentary subjects before the coming of the Mongols). In the fourteenth century the term *daruga* replaced *baskak* in use both among the Mongols and their various subjects and clearly had ceased to mean the same thing. This shift apparently accompanied a change to a remote (and less expensive) form of administration, for the *darugi* of the fifteenth century clearly resided in the Mongol cities on the Volga. Each was apparently assigned to a specific Russian principality. If the *baskaki* can be likened to British colonial viceroys, the *darugi* resembled State Department desk officers. *Darugi* advised the khan on Russian affairs but lacked operational responsibility.[29]

Although the late-fifteenth-century Simeon chronicle *sub anno* 1272 refers to one Temir, *doroga* of Riazan',[30] other contemporary chronicles make no mention of him, and this is probably an interpolation. Indeed there is no other evidence that *dorogi* had authority over Russia until the fifteenth century. The *doroga* of Moscow, Min Bulat, was active in the Horde's debates in 1432 and 1438 over Muscovite dynastic succession, and there are references to *ulusnye dorogi* (*dorogi* of the *ulus?*) and the *darag'* prince Usein of Sarai.[31] The Golden Horde may have used *darugi* elsewhere earlier than in Russia. In 1376 a combined military force from Moscow and Nizhnii Novgorod briefly seized Grand Bolgar. The *doroga* and *tamozhnia* (customs collector) they imposed until the Tatars took the city back probably were filling existing offices.[32] The Russians may well have been familiar with the *darugi* system before it was applied to Russia.

When the Mongols removed the *baskaki* from the Russian principalities and replaced them with *darugi* operating from Sarai, they were not relaxing their control of the East Slavs. During the *baskak* period it was the nearby presence on the steppe of the formidable nomad army that ensured that Mongol wishes were obeyed, and that presence had not changed. The only difference was that the Golden Horde now made its wishes known by sending envoys from Sarai to the Russian princes. These envoys were called *posoly,* a literal Russian translation of the Mongol *elichi/ilichi.* The chronicles show no abrupt switch from *baskaki* to *posoly;* however, a primitive statistical analysis of the references indicates that *posoly* were used with increasing frequency as *darugi* took over the duties of the *baskaki.* There are a handful of thirteenth-century references: in 1257 unnamed envoys came to Novgorod;[33] in 1262 an envoy named Kutlubuga appeared in Vladimir-Suzdalia;[34] and in 1277 four envoys from Nogai—Tegichag, Kutlubuga, Eshimata, and Man'sheia—arrived in Galicia-Volhynia.[35] It was in the fourteenth century, however, when the Golden Horde presumably was in the process of dismantling the *baskak* system,[36] that the greatest number of visits from envoys was recorded.[37] References to *posoly* became fewer as the Horde's influence declined, particularly after the middle of the fifteenth century, when fragmentation drastically reduced the Tatars' ability to interfere in Russian affairs.[38]

The *posoly* were important officials, very likely Mongol aristocrats, and they traveled on the imperial post *(yam),* probably bearing some insignia of office (perhaps the *paiza,* a seal of gold, silver, copper, or other material). The Russian chronicles identify them by name, sometimes adding the adjectives *silen* (strong) or *liut* (evil).[39] The chronicles rarely mention that they are accompanied by retinues, the most famous exception being Shevkan in Tver' in 1327, but it is unlikely that envoys rode without escorts. I know of no records of envoys using interpreters, but they probably did not speak Russian. Certainly the princes were visited by *posoly* often enough to keep Turkic-speakers on hand. Princes loyal to the Tatars could expect at least as many visits as hostile princes (Ivan Kalita, a prince of Moscow in the early fourteenth century, is a prime example).[40] The Mongol envoys requisitioned taxes and troops as the *baskaki* had done and brought the Russian princes messages and announcements of Mongol decisions or summoned them to Sarai. The envoys were the major link between the principalities and the Golden Horde during most of the Mongol period of Russian history.

The shift from reliance on *baskaki* to the use of *darugi* and *posoly* was designed to decrease the costs of administering Russia. Officials living in the steppe rather than in the forests could be supported cheaply by the pastoral economy, and were also available for other, perhaps more lucrative tasks. Through the absentee system, the Golden Horde was able to keep its grip on Russia even after the crises of the late fourteenth century.

The efficient administration of Russia required that the Mongols divide it into districts, which were superimposed over Russia's existing political divisions without either replacing them or subverting them. The basic unit they used was the *tumen,* rendered in the Russian sources as *tm'a,* which meant ten thousand. In the steppe this meant ten thousand adult males, which, among nomads, was the same as ten thousand troops. Among sedentary populations things were less simple; ten thousand households could not possibly produce that many troops without destroying the local economy. We know that in China and Persia some *tumens* fielded far fewer than ten thousand troops, in one case only one thousand. Furthermore, the term took on different meanings in the different Mongol successor states. Thus, whether a *t'ma* comprised ten thousand troops, adult males, taxpaying households, or some other units is not known.

The Russian sources are not of great help in addressing this problem, as references to *t'my* are intermittent and unreliable. The Rogozh chronicle records that in 1360 Khan Nevruz settled a dispute over the throne of the grand princedom of Vladimir by awarding the throne and its fifteen *t'my* to Andrei Konstantinovich rather than to the minor Dmitrii Ivanovich (later Donskoi).[41] The *Khronograf* of 1512 records that before the grand prince of Lithuania Vitovt lost the battle on the river Vorskla in 1399, he promised his puppet-client Tokhtamysh the grand principality of Moscow and its seventeen *t'my* as well as Great Novgorod and Pskov, but not Tver' or Riazan'.[42] On the basis of these two entries, Michel Roublev and other historians have concluded that the grand principality of Moscow-Vladimir, excluding Novgorod, Pskov, Tver', and Riazan', contained fifteen or seventeen *t'my.* A 1445 treaty between princes of Suzdalia and Galich (in Vladimir-Suzdalia, not Galicia-Volhynia) alludes to the five *t'my* of Nizhnii Novgorod, apparently also administered separately from those of the grand principality of Vladimir.[43]

Both the Rogozh chronicle and the *Khronograf* are from the fifteenth century, each roughly a century later than the events it describes. Earlier and presumably more accurate accounts of the events of 1360 and 1399 in chronicles of northeastern Russia do not mention *t'my.* The Rogozh chronicle is of mid-fifteenth-century origin, but survives only in sixteenth-century manuscripts which had passed through Muscovite hands.[44] The *Khronograf* is particularly suspect. Scholars have traditionally attributed it to Pakhomii the Serb, an emigre writer of the mid fifteenth century. More recently it has been proven that the *Khronograf* was written in the late fifteenth century in Russia.[45] Its only original Russian material, a fantastic and completely inaccurate account of the death of Batu, does not inspire confidence.[46] Although these two references to the *t'my* of northeastern Russia are interesting, they should not be accepted uncritically. Fifteen is not seventeen. Further, both are interpolations and may testify more to the imaginations of the later bookmen than to their expertise.

Two much more reliable sources, neither of them Russian, come from the south. The first is a 1507 *yarlik* from the Crimean khan Mengli-Girei ceding territories to King Sigismund I of Poland. (The Mongols had in fact long since lost control over the lands involved.) The second is a letter from Sigismund to Khan Said-Girei written in 1540.[47] Together they name fourteen *t'my,* thirteen of them in Slavic territory—some in north-eastern Russia—and the Egol'da *t'ma* created in the Ukrainian steppe in the mid fifteenth century. These are official documents, not literary chronicles. The two lists overlap and their data are consistent.

The Crimean khanate, more than any other, had preserved the traditions and institutions of the Golden Horde, even as part of the Ottoman Empire. Only Chingisids ever sat on the throne at Bakchisarai, and their charters and bureaucratic practices perpetuated those of the Golden Horde and the Mongol Empire. The Crimean khanate is therefore the logical place for the Golden Horde's organizational charts of East Slavic territories to have survived.[48] How these escaped Tamerlane's destruction of the archives is unknown.

The Polish-Crimean evidence is not without problems. Logically a census would be an absolute prerequisite for establishing districts based on the number of adult males, potential recruits, households, or some such measure. Yet the Crimean documents mention *t'my* in areas for which no record of a census exists. (Logically, too, there should be a correlation between *t'my,* the census, and *baskaki.* The *vita* of Mikhail of Chernigov mention a census in the south, and one of the *t'my* in the Crimean document is Kursk, residence of *baskak* Akhmad. Unfortunately, this neat alignment of evidence stands alone against many disparities.) Nonetheless, taken together, the northern and southern sources that refer to *t'my* indicate that the Mongols divided all of Russia, including Great Russian, Ukrainian, and Belorussian lands, into fiscal or military districts. Because it suggests that the Mongols considered all of the East Slavic territories equally subject to their rule, this is a significant conclusion.[49]

The Russian bookmen of the Mongol period must have known how they were governed, but no thirteenth-century Russian chronicler ever mentions the *t'my*. Obviously they were familiar with the word, for they used *t'ma* to mean ten thousand[50] and derived from it the nominative *temnik*, an officer of ten thousand troops.[51] Perhaps the word's association with alien domination, when used in its administrative sense, made it distasteful, though the bookmen freely record the comings and goings of the *posoly*. Possibly bureaucratic terms simply had no place in the literary prose of the chronicles. In any case, during the Tatar Yoke, the Russian bookmen scarcely used the word at all. Most curious is that in the late fifteenth and sixteenth centuries, when Mongol power had declined, the chroniclers began to use the word with evident familiarity.

Where the boundaries of the Russian *t'my* lay and how they were determined remain unclear. Yet the evidence at least allows us to confirm that the Golden Horde divided all of Russia into districts for censuses and for levying troops and tribute. Similarly, despite the incompleteness of the evidence, an overall picture of the Golden Horde's administration of Russia does emerge. While we cannot say with certainty when the *baskak* system was begun, how widely it was used, or when it was discontinued, we at least know that Mongol rule began with a direct administrative presence, supported by the massive Mongol power on the steppe. This same power allowed the Mongols to rule with fewer and fewer men, as they transferred responsibility for Russian affairs from the *baskaki* to the remote *darugi*. The details of this transfer and the enhanced use of envoys that accompanied it are unclear, but it is apparent that Mongol power in the Russian forest zone remained as great as ever. Russia was within easy reach of the long arm of the khan for most of the two and a half centuries of Mongol rule.

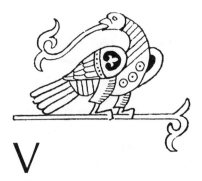

V

The Mongol Role in
Russian Politics

THE MONGOL EXPANSIONIST CAMPAIGNS OF THE THIRTEENTH CENTURY
decisively altered the political fates of many lands, including those, like
Russia and Eastern Europe, that the Mongols chose to leave with some
degree of autonomy. Though these areas retained their political institutions and indigenous ruling classes, the Mongol presence on the steppe
was a powerful factor in their politics. Mongol manipulation was a matter
of course, and forcible coercion not uncommon. In Eastern Europe, the
Golden Horde's influence declined in the fourteenth and fifteenth centuries, though it never ceased, but in Russia the Tatars' interference in
regional politics continued almost unabated until the complete collapse
of Mongol power west of the Urals.

Despite the importance of the Mongol factor, Russian politics continued to evolve internally, and as a result, the Golden Horde had perforce to react to developments not of its own choosing. The Horde's
tactics changed in response to new conditions in the Russian principalities, but its long-range goals remained essentially the same. Since the
Golden Horde's archives did not survive Tamerlane's sack of Sarai, historians must infer these goals from the Mongols' behavior during their
lengthy overlordship. In doing this they run the risk either of underes-
timating the Mongols' political sophistication by reducing their motives

to simple extortion or of crediting the Horde with excessively subtle intentions. As our knowledge of Tatar activities is based largely on the Russian chronicles, the danger of distortion is especially great. Keeping in mind how things looked from Sarai and the internal dynamics of the Horde's socio-political structure is the best way to analyze the Golden Horde's policies.

The impact of these policies on Russian politics has too often been reduced to a search for heroes or cowards. Patriotic Russian historians have understandably sought to identify the princes and polities that most steadfastly withstood the Tatars, and they have been inclined to emphasize the importance of Russian resistance. This tendency has been more than offset by the many Western historians who have been prone to highlight the incidents of collaboration and to minimize the extent of opposition to Mongol rule. Russia, in fact, resisted the Tatars as fiercely as Eastern Europe or the Middle East. Further, as we have seen, her prolonged subjugation was the result of circumstances beyond Russia's borders rather than of her waning opposition to alien domination. As far as collaboration is concerned, the Mongols found accomplices wherever they went. This was as true in China and Persia as in Armenia-Georgia and Russia. If politics is the art of the possible, then politicians can always be criticized for opportunism. Discussions of the political dealings of the Russians with the Mongols would benefit from less partisanship and more perspective.

To idealize or malign the moral character of medieval Russia's political elite is less productive than analyzing when principalities chose to cooperate with the Tatars and when they chose not to. The complex relations between the Russian princes and the Mongol khans do not make this easy. The impact of Tatar actions varied over the years, and a principality bitterly opposed to the Mongols in one decade might be allied with them in the next. Since both Russia and the Golden Horde underwent considerable internal changes, adjustments by both sides could hardly be avoided. The fluid mosaic that emerges is unamenable to any simplistic formulation, but is a more accurate reflection of Russian history. While a comprehensive analysis of Russo-Tatar political relations would fill several volumes, a selective survey, without succumbing to superficiality, should convey the variety and complexity of the Tatar role in Russian politics.

In 1223 a Mongol scouting expedition, actually a reconnaissance in force, smashed through an alliance of Polovtsy and Alans north of the

Caucasus and invaded the Pontic steppe. Their appearance was a surprise to the Russians, who had never seen these people before. With some misgivings, a group of Kievan princes agreed to an alliance with the Polovtsian refugees. To forestall this, the Mongols sent envoys to the Russians, protesting that they were only making war on their "slaves and herders," the Polovtsy, and had no quarrel with the princes of Kievan *Rus'*. They went so far as to promise that after they had defeated the Polovtsy, they would let the Russians have the booty. The Mongols had just used this same divide-and-conquer strategy to disrupt the Polovtsian alliance with the Alans. They had appealed to the Polovtsy as fellow nomads and urged them to abandon the Alans. The Polovtsy agreed to this, only to find that after the Mongols had annihilated the Alans at their leisure, they turned on their brother nomads. The Polovtsian survivors probably brought news of this duplicity to the Russians, who suspected that the Mongol offer was a ruse. They violated the steppe custom of diplomatic immunity by executing the Mongol ambassadors and, with this insult to Mongol honor, guaranteed war.

It is remotely possible that the Mongol embassy was sincere. Chingis Khan was still alive at this time, and the Mongol Empire was still primarily concerned with the conquest of the steppe. While it is true that the Alans were not nomads or steppe-dwellers, they had occupied an area of much greater strategic importance to the steppe than Russia. Be that as it may, the Kievan princes had committed themselves. An army of Russians and Polovtsy met the Mongols in battle at the river Kalka and was disastrously defeated.

The pious Russian chronicler concluded his record of this debacle with the heartfelt wish that the Mongols would go back where they came from and never visit *Rus'* again. The Slavs, obviously, had yet to learn of the Mongols' grand strategy for conquest.[1] That first raid was just a prelude to the full-scale invasion to come. The Mongols did, in fact, disappear for fifteen years, but the causes and significance of this hiatus escaped Russian attention. Though the Russians were quite familiar with the western Kipchaks/Polovtsy, they had no information about events further to the east. Thus they were unaware that the Mongols had not gone back where they came from but were busy subduing the eastern Kipchaks and opening the steppe passage westward.[2] What the Russians did not know did hurt them, for they were caught unprepared when, in the late 1230s, the Mongol hordes reappeared.

In swift campaigns in the winter of 1237–1238 and in 1239–1240 the Mongols, under Chingis' grandson Batu, devastated northern and southern *Rus'* before sweeping Galicia-Volhynia to the south-west en route to Eastern Europe and the Balkans. The advance through Eastern Europe halted only when news of the death of the Great Khan, Ugedei, overtook the nomad armies. To attend the *quriltai,* the council to elect his successor, the Mongol leaders turned back.[3]

That an accident of history, namely the timely demise of Ugedei, saved Europe from further destruction has struck many historians as un-persuasive and superficial. The argument has been made, especially by Soviet historians, that the opposition of the Russians and other Eastern Europeans had so weakened the Mongol armies that they used the death of Ugedei as an excuse to withdraw from a campaign that they no longer had the resources to win. Though some of the East Slavic resistance was certainly heroic, it was not Russian blood that saved European civiliza-tion. Mongol strength had not been greatly depleted by the Russian cam-paigns, and Batu's hordes overran European armies of knights and infantry whenever they encountered them. Though they had not brought sufficient siege weapons to take every city, the Mongols were never de-feated in open battle. Because of their greater mobility armies from the steppe, even if outnumbered, could generally defeat the armies of seden-tary civilizations; so it was with the Mongol armies in Eastern and Central Europe in the 1240s, for they were more than a match for every army sent against them.

A second theory about the Mongol withdrawal from Europe is based on a sophisticated appreciation of Inner Asian history. Some historians have suggested that the Mongols advanced no further because the Hun-garian plain simply was not extensive enough to support the vast numbers of horses necessary to any nomad army. In this view, long-term domina-tion of Central Europe from a Hungarian base would have been ecologi-cally impossible. Previous nomadic groups like the Huns and the Avars had failed to build permanent power bases in Hungary; the Magyars remained only by abandoning their nomadic way of life. Thus the Mon-gols could not have held Central and Eastern Europe under any circum-stances.[4]

This analysis is serious but not entirely to the point. Whether the Mongols could have retained political control of Europe is moot; the question is why they did not try to. While it is possible that they realized the limitations of the Hungarian plain as a base for an army of nomads, nothing in the history of Mongol expansion suggests that they wasted much time on such calculations. Palestine and Egypt were climatically unsuited to the Mongols, but only defeat at the hands of the Mamelukes kept them out. The Mongols in China, influenced, to be sure, by Chinese geopolitical pretensions, invaded southeastern Asia and even attempted to invade Japan, both areas profoundly unfit for pastoralists from the Inner Asian steppe. The primary impetus of Mongol expansion was the momentum of successive victories rather than a sober appraisal of prospects for the future, and in Europe, Batu and his hordes certainly had the momentum. No European army had yet been able to withstand them, and probably none could have. The Mongols sent messages to European monarchs proclaiming themselves rulers of the continent. It was indeed the death of Ugedei, rather than exhaustion or geography, that forced Batu to postpone his European plans. Subsequent divisions in the Mongol Empire kept the Mongols from ever returning.

The succession crisis in the Mongol Empire that saved Europe from conquest came too late to help Russia. Some historians have seen Russia's defeat as the culmination of Kievan decline, but it is doubtful that Russia could have withstood the full force of the Mongols even at its height in the eleventh century under Yaroslav the Wise. The Mongol military machine, after all, was capable of conquering China, Turkestan, and Persia, all areas with immense populations and gargantuan walled cities. (The Mongols subdued China in sixty years, Russia in three.) Thus the Mongol conquest can hardly be cited as evidence of Kievan decline. A more coordinated Russian resistance might have prolonged the conquest but could not have prevented it.

Following the subjugation of Russia, the Mongols imposed their administrative apparatus, with its *baskaki* and *t'my*, on Russia's existing political structure, which was left intact. Through indifference, rather than impotence, the Tatars allowed the Russian princes to keep their thrones, though each had to make a personal obeisance to the khan. Some, like grand prince Yaroslav and his son Alexander Nevskii, were required to visit the great khan at Karakorum. Though the Mongols were the ultimate arbitrators of succession in the Russian principalities, they strictly respected the dynastic legitimacy of the Riurikid clan[5] and in the thirteenth century even honored Russian collateral succession, from brother to brother (perhaps because it was a practice from the steppe).[6] They let the Russian political infrastructure stand, in all its untidiness. The grand prince of Vladimir, titular overlord of Vladimir-Suzdalian *Rus'*, continued his ambiguous dominance of other principalities in the north-east and his often nominal suzereignty in Novgorod. Changes in the south were more drastic; the devastation had left little worth ruling, and the throne of the grand prince of Kiev fell vacant. Some historians have credited the Mongols with uniting Russia, but the feuding between the principalities and city-states continued throughout the Mongol period. It was only after the demise of the Golden Horde that Muscovy, using some administrative methods learned from the Mongols, succeeded in unifying northeastern Russia.

Russia's acquiescence to Mongol hegemony ought not to be exaggerated. Until at least the middle of the fourteenth century, for a Russian prince to face the Mongols in open battle was suicide; yet in spite of this many princes and nobles in the northeast stood, fought, and died during the Mongol assault of 1237–1240.[7] Under the circumstances, those princes who chose submission can hardly be castigated; timely propitiation usually helped to mitigate the Tatars' destructiveness. One attempt at concerted rebellion was a complete failure. Two southern princes who had originally fled when the Mongols appeared, Mikhail of Chernigov and Daniil of Galicia-Volhynia, joined forces with Andrei Yaroslavovich of Vladimir-Suzdalia in an effort to liberate Russia. The coalition was unable even seriously to challenge the Mongol might, and each of its members paid for their audacity. Daniil had taken an oath of obedience to the pope in the expectation that Catholic crusaders would come to his rescue. Then, though his lands were the furthest removed from the Golden Horde, he personally submitted to the khan and waited for help which never came.[8] Mikhail was summoned to the Horde and executed for rebellion. The Russian sources presented him as a religious martyr.[9] Andrei Yaroslavovich took refuge abroad and was allowed to return only after submitting to his brother Alexander Nevskii, who was loyal to the Golden Horde.

Nevskii, rather than Russia, was the beneficiary of these machinations, and his collaboration with the Tatars has been an embarrassment to patriotic historiographers ever since.[10] Still, his victories over both the Teutonic knights and the Swedes prove his bravery and military skill,[11] and he used his political capital with the Golden Horde to ameliorate the harshness of Mongol rule. Nevskii's willingness to cooperate with the Horde may well have saved Russia from more severe exactions. Nevskii died on the way home from pleading for leniency in response to the expulsion of the Muslim tax-farmers by cities in northeastern *Rus'* in 1262. Perhaps it was his mission which prevented the Tatars from sending an army to punish the uprising.[12]

Nevskii seems to have been directly responsible for bringing the city-state or urban republic of Novgorod into the Mongol fold. Novgorod's stance toward the Golden Horde has been idealized and badly distorted, its reputation for staunch resistance resting on an uncritical interpretation of a single episode, the census under the aegis of Alexander Nevskii. It is true that the city was not sacked during the conquest, but many cities in northeastern Russia escaped this fate, and it cannot be taken as evidence of extraordinary heroics. Indeed, Novgorod's long-term relations with the Golden Horde, though in some ways unique, contain ample examples of the pragmatism and opportunism characteristic of the Russian response to the Golden Horde.

On the eve of the Mongol conquest, Novgorod had already perfected the strategy for maximizing its independence that it would use with modifications throughout the Mongol period. Novgorod was necessarily subservient to outside Russian princes, but by manipulating rivalries among the Riurikids, the city managed to maintain considerable autonomy. If a prince proved overweening, the Novgorodians offered the city to a more responsive one from a rival principality. In this way they resisted the encroaching power of the grand prince of Vladimir in the twelfth and early thirteenth centuries by inviting in princes from Smolensk or the Dnepr' valley.

It did not take long for Novgorod to adapt these techniques to the changed political climate that followed the conquest, but for a time its options were severely limited. Since the Mongols had devastated the south, Novgorod could no longer turn there for help in fending off the grand prince of Vladimir, now doubly dangerous as a Tatar client. Resistance to the grand prince, now Alexander Nevskii, was tantamount to defying the Golden Horde, and Novgorod did not force the issue. The Mongols never reduced Novgorod militarily because they did not need to. The arrival of census-takers from the Golden Horde indicates that the city's submission was already arranged. The census was conducted under Nevskii's protection,[13] and the Novgorodian chronicler greatly exaggerates the popular resistance to it. If there had been serious opposition in Novgorod the Tatars would have sent an army, not civilian head-counters.

Novgorod's ability to maneuver politically remained constricted after Nevskii's death, but the city's political establishment readily turned to the Mongols when it needed help. Dissatisfied with grand prince Yaroslav Yaroslavovich, Nevskii's brother and successor, Novgorod accepted an offer of assistance from a third brother, Vasilii, and sent a delegation to the Horde to request redress of grievances. Yaroslav, however, secured a Tatar punitive force to buttress his demands. Fortunately, the efforts of the Novgorodian delegation and the arbitration of the metropolitan led to a reconciliation of all parties. Yaroslav remained prince of Novgorod, but the city was spared from the Tatar forces. Novgorodian funds no doubt helped influence the Mongols to recall their troops and permit a peaceful resolution of the conflict.[14]

In the next century Novgorod was still seeking to influence Tatar decisions so as to increase its autonomy. In 1353 the city sent envoys to persuade the khan to award the grand principality of Vladimir to Konstantin Vasil'evich of Suzdal' rather than to Ivan II of Moscow. Novgorod extricated itself from a ticklish situation in 1371 by promising to acknowledge Mikhail Aleksandrovich of Tver' as grand prince of Vladimir and hence overlord of Novgorod *if* the Horde awarded him the *yarlik.*[15] Though Novgorod lost its case on both of these occasions, they show that the city was always willing to play politics by the Mongols' rules, which meant paying the tribute and the additional sums necessary to get a sympathetic hearing at Sarai. Novgorod was also happy to accept commercial privileges from the khan, including the customs charter that permitted its merchants free transit across northeastern Russia during the fifteenth century.[16] Obviously, Novgorod was not an enclave of fierce resistance to Tatar rule. Instead, the city incorporated the Mongol factor into its complex strategies to promote its independence by propitiating and manipulating greater powers.

In southern *Rus'* there was no one to contest Mongol power in the thirteenth century. The Dnepr' valley and the city of Kiev were not entirely depopulated, but this area proved less resilient than the northeast. Peasants constituted the bulk of the remaining inhabitants, and most organized political life disappeared.[17] Even the metropolitans abandoned Kiev, moving their de facto residence to Vladimir in 1299 because of "Tatar oppression" *(ot nasiliia tatarskogo).*[18] The independence of Galicia-Volhynia has been badly overdrawn by some historians.[19] The failed rebel Daniil had submitted personally to the khan, albeit in bad faith, and his successors acceded to Mongol demands. Princes and troops from Galicia-Volhynia joined the Tatars in campaigns against Poland, Lithuania, and Hungary.[20]

The Ukraine, however, fell away from the Golden Horde in the fourteenth century. The growing grand principality of Lithuania, having already acquired Belorussia, annexed Galicia and Kiev, and Poland annexed Volhynia. Some historians have argued that the Belorussians and Ukrainians welcomed Lithuanian rule as a relief from Tatar exploitation. The Lithuanians were still pagans, but, unlike the Catholic Poles, did not threaten Orthodox Christianity. Besides ignoring the fact that the Mongols, too, practiced religious toleration, this is an argument from silence. While it is true that the sources do not mention East Slavic opposition to the Lithuanians, other explanations are possible than that there was none. The lack of chronicles from the area is certainly such an explanation. Further, Russian resistance to Lithuanian aggression may not have been effective enough to have been mentioned in chronicles from other parts of Russia. It is unlikely that the East Slavs welcomed being overrun by any foreign power.

Mongol dominion in the Russian territories in the thirteenth century had embraced Galicia-Volhynia, the Kievan south, and perhaps Belorussia. Following the Lithuanian and Polish annexations, these lands came under "western" influence, and in the fourteenth and fifteenth centuries the Golden Horde attempted to intervene in the politics of Belorussia and the Ukraine with increasing irregularity[21] while holding fast to northeastern Russia. Some have seen this as the cause of the split of the East Slavs into distinct Great Russian, Ukrainian, and Belorussian peoples. Doubtless the political division contributed to this ethnic divergence, but the process is too complex for us to isolate the influence of the Tatar Yoke.

The Mongol impact on the politics of northeastern Russia has been better recognized by historians, but not necessarily better understood, than their role in Belorussia and the Ukraine. In the thirteenth century the khans of the Golden Horde followed Russian genealogical principles in awarding the throne of Vladimir, the most powerful in Russia, to rival princes of Vladimir-Suzdalia. Near the end of the century there was a split in the Golden Horde, and the feuding princes of Vladimir-Suzdalia aligned themselves with rival khans. The division in the Horde gave shape and coherence to preexisting hostilities within Russia, as often happens in minor states in the orbit of major powers. At the congress of princes held in Vladimir in 1297 to assess the current political situation, grand prince Andrei Yaroslavovich, prince Feodor of Yaroslavl', and prince Konstantin of Rostov opposed princes Daniil of Moscow and Mikhail of Tver'.[22] Several hierarchs of the Church apparently served as mediators, and a later chronicle mentions the Tatar envoy Ivrui, who may have played a similar role.[23]

The congress of 1297 was noteworthy as the first and last time that Tver' and Moscow found themselves on the same side of a dispute. By the turn of the fourteenth century, the political map of northeastern Russia had been redrawn, and for the rest of the century Russian political history is dominated by the vicious struggle between Moscow and Tver' for supremacy in Vladimir-Suzdalia. In the drive for power, both states had to address Sarai, for the Golden Horde had the uncontested prerogative of determining succession to the symbolic throne of the grand prince of Vladimir. In this new political climate, the Mongols abandoned the now obsolete policy of respecting the traditional Russian lines of succession.

The hostilities among the Russian princes gave the Golden Horde additional leverage, and it used its control of the throne of Vladimir to neutralize Russian power. Thus, since in the early decades of the fourteenth century Tver' was the strongest principality in Vladimir-Suzdalia, the Mongols awarded the throne of Vladimir to Moscow, though that city's pretentions were genealogically unjustified. A rebellious Mikhail of Tver' defeated a combined Russo-Tatar punitive force (the Tatars stayed neutral in the battle) and captured Agafiia, the wife of his rival, Yurii Daniilovich of Moscow. This triumph, however, eventually proved fatal for Mikhail. Agafiia was the baptismal name of Khan Uzbek's sister Konchaka, who had converted to Russian Orthodox Christianity for her marriage to Yurii. Disastrously, Agafiia died in Mikhail's custody, and he was accused of poisoning her. (Her death was surely an accident. The consequences of harming a Chingisid would have been obvious to Mikhail.) At Yurii's instigation, Mikhail was summoned to Sarai and executed.[24] His son Dmitrii avenged his father by murdering Yurii Daniilovich while he was in Sarai. For having done so without the khan's permission, Dmitrii Mikhailovich was also executed.[25]

Another of Mikhail's sons, Aleksandr, was grand prince of Tver' when that city's opposition to the Tatars peaked. In 1327 a spontaneous revolt erupted against a Mongol embassy led by Chol khan (Shchelkan). Chol khan's immoderate behavior in Tver' led to an uprising in which he and most of his retinue died. Thus it seems unlikely that his mission was to provoke the city and compromise Aleksandr, as some have claimed.

When the Tatars wanted to punish a recalcitrant Russian prince, they could always accuse him of embezzling the tribute. Chol khan's mission was probably to raise conscripts and revenue for another campaign against the Ilkhanids for Azerbaidjan. Given the fact that the Mongols had executed Aleksandr's father and brother and that Chol khan's comportment, while typical, was far from circumspect, it is not surprising that the Tatars' demands sparked an urban riot. Aleksandr fled the city in the wake of the revolt, and Ivan Kalita of Moscow led the inevitable Russo-Tatar punitive expedition. The Tatars later made Kalita grand prince of Vladimir, while Aleksandr, after further but unknown activities, was summoned to Sarai, with the expected consequences.[26]

The special relationship between the Golden Horde and Moscow was strengthened in the middle of the fourteenth century, when the Mongols faced a new challenge to their hegemony. Grand prince Olgerd of Lithuania struck deep into the Tatar orbit by bringing both Tver' and Riazan' into his sphere of influence and applying pressure to Novgorod. Olgerd's opposition to the Mongols was not rooted in principle, and he played politics by the same rules as everyone else. Thus, with his eye on Moscow, he sent a delegation to the Golden Horde to negotiate a rapprochement. The Mongols, however, had decided, logically, to use Moscow as a counterweight to the growing power of Lithuania. The Muscovites were therefore successful in their attempts to undermine the Lithuanian embassy, and the Mongols, in a fine display of political delicacy, arrested the Lithuanian envoys and handed them over to Moscow. Olgerd was compelled to ransom his emissaries from his enemies.[27] Thus Moscow benefited from its allegiance and the Golden Horde's support for its obedient vassal state helped to maintain stability in Russia and to protect the Tatars' interests there.[28]

Bloody civil war and domestic unrest in the Golden Horde eventually destroyed the Tatars' alliance with Moscow, during the score of years the Russian chronicles call the "great troubles" (velikaia zamiatnia). Since Russian vassals contributed both to their prestige and to their treasuries, rival khans vied for the allegiance of Russian princes. The lack of a central authority in the Golden Horde presented the Russians with new options, and traditional alliances shifted. The confusion resulted in a number of political anomalies, such as two competing khans each awarding Dmitrii Donskoi the yarlik to the throne of Vladimir.[29] At the same time the breakdown of order made it hazardous for princes and metropolitans to visit Sarai because of the danger of a coup d'etat. Furthermore, free-lance Tatar bandits stepped up their raids on Russian territory, and there was no khan in a position to control them for the Russians to bribe.[30] Yet despite the chaos within the Golden Horde, the importance of the Tatars in Russian affairs did not diminish.

The most powerful Mongol grandee to emerge from this turbulent period was emir Mamai, who ruled through Chingisid puppets from a power base west of the Volga, near the lands earlier held by the rebel Nogai. Mamai's major Russian ally was Tver', whose princes now served Tatar interests as assiduously as the Muscovites had before. Relations between Moscow and Tver' remained acrimonious, with Moscow now pitted against the Mongols as well. Mamai awarded the *yarlik* to the throne of Vladimir to Mikhail of Tver', but this attempt to strengthen his client state misfired. When Mikhail arrived at Vladimir, the citizens refused to open the gates to him, and a massive expedition led by a coalition of princes of northeastern Russia under Muscovite leadership imposed a humiliating treaty on Tver' in 1375, forcing it to accept inferior status as a "younger brother" of Moscow.[31] Mamai sent a force commanded by his general Begich against the Muscovite alliance in 1378, but the rebels defeated them on the river Vozha.[32] Moscow also seized Grand Bolgar and installed a customs collector, in a premature attempt to extend her control down the Volga.

Matters came to a head in 1380, when Dmitrii Ivanovich of Moscow led a largely Muscovite army into the steppe for an enormous battle with Mamai and his armies. The terms of the treaty with Moscow obliged Tver' to help her fellow Russians, but no Tverian troops joined the army marching to meet the Tatars. Mamai, too, failed to receive help from allies. Riazan' was allied with the Tatars, but her troops did not take part in the battle. More significant was the default of the Lithuanian grand prince Jagiello. Jagiello had succeeded where Olgerd had failed and allied himself with the Tatars against Moscow. His troops, however, did not arrive in time to take part in the battle. (Soviet historians believe that Jagiello tarried deliberately because his East Slavic conscripts were unenthusiastic about aiding the Mongols against their compatriots. This is an ingenious interpretation with little evidence to support it.) Dmitrii and Mamai met "beyond the Don river" (i.e., *Zadonshchina,* title of the famous epic), where Dmitrii won one of the most celebrated victories in Russian history, earning his epithet, Donskoi—"of the Don." Belatedly arrived Lithuanian troops and Riazani units contented themselves with looting the baggage train and harassing the victorious but depleted Moscovite columns as they exhaustedly returned to Moscow.

The victory of Kulikovo Field was the first major Russian victory against the Tatars in 140 years of Mongol rule, and Moscow made full use of it to enhance her status and prestige in northeastern *Rus'*.[33] Thus Moscow, which had for so long collaborated with the Golden Horde, emerged as the savior of Russia, while Tver', which had struggled against the Tatars during the same period, became the beaten lackeys of the Mongols. In fact, neither city had superior claims to patriotism. Tver' had simply peaked too soon and tried to resist the Mongols while they were too powerful. Moscow had been more patient and seized a propitious moment when the Mongols were weakened. Like Lithuania, Moscow and Tver' were both opportunistic, and Moscow happened to be more successful.

Despite its drama, however, Moscow's battlefield triumph of 1380 had remarkably little effect on Russia's status within the Golden Horde's hegemony, and the Tatar Yoke was not shattered. (Some have claimed that Donskoi's victory broke the spell of Tatar invincibility, but proof of the existence of such a spell has eluded them.) Indeed, the cost to Moscow of the battle was devastating. The *Skazanie o Mamaevom poboishche,* a lengthy and highly rhetorical account of Donskoi's exploit, records that of the 300,000 men who marched to meet Mamai, 253,000 did not return. These fantastic figures cannot be accepted, but it is clear that Moscow had won a pyrrhic victory. Russian losses were so great that Moscow could not raise another army to take advantage of Mamai's defeat. Mamai, on the other hand, mobilized more troops and prepared for a second campaign against Russia.

Luckily for Moscow, the arrival of Tokhtamysh, pretender to the throne of the Volga khanate and client of the powerful Tamerlane, caused Mamai to abandon his Russian scheme. Unluckily for Moscow, Tokhtamysh had the same plans and carried them out after defeating emir Mamai on the river Kalka. In 1382, with the connivance, in part coerced, of the princes of Tver', Riazan', and Nizhnii Novgorod, Tokhtamysh launched a surprise attack on Moscow. The Tatar army rode from the steppe to the gates of Moscow without meeting resistance. Once there, the princes of Nizhnii Novgorod, Donskoi's brothers-in-law, tricked the citizens into surrendering the city.[34] The Tatars broke their word and immediately razed Moscow for having had the temerity to resist Mongol authority.[35]

Tokhtamysh had efficiently reestablished the Golden Horde's power in the Russian forest zone, and he did not choose to take the throne of Vladimir away from Moscow. He did, however, impose a heavy tribute on all of Vladimir-Suzdalia and took Dmitrii Donskoi's son, Vasilii Dmitrievich, as a hostage. (Vasilii escaped on his second attempt.)

Moscow benefited more from the deteriorating relations between Tokhtamysh, now undisputed khan of the Golden Horde, and his former patron, Tamerlane, than it had from the victory of Kulikovo. The threat from Tamerlane made Tokhtamysh eager to secure his Russian rear and probably motivated him to grant the recently subdued city several concessions. Tokhtamysh sanctioned Donskoi's will, in which he passed the throne of Vladimir to his son, and then in 1393 allowed Vasilii, now grand prince, to take over Nizhnii Novgorod.

When Tamerlane attacked the Golden Horde, Moscow did lose some contingents of troops fighting in Tokhtamysh's service, but it suffered worst from the invasion scare of 1395. The Muscovites were convinced that Tamerlane planned to ravage the city. Tamerlane, in fact, planned nothing of the sort; he was dreaming of Peking, and Russia was of no interest to him. The terrified people of Moscow, however, firmly believed that only the miraculous intercession of the Virgin saved them from destruction at his hands.[36]

Tamerlane expelled Tokhtamysh from the Golden Horde. The deposed khan fled to Lithuania, where he became the client of grand prince Vitovt. That occasional crusader against the Tatar infidels now proclaimed his intention of restoring the Golden Horde's rightful khan, incidentally assuring Lithuanian hegemony over the Pontic steppe. This was not to be. Tamerlane's new agent in the Horde, emir Edigei, led an army which massacred the Lithuanian forces on the river Vorskla in 1399.[37]

During these wars, Moscow for a time was left to its own devices, but Edigei decided to reinstitute the Horde's power and in 1408 laid siege to the city. He summoned troops from Tver' to his aid, but the Tverian prince took the cautious course of sending his troops with orders not to arrive fast enough to be of any use.[38] Edigei did not take Moscow but extracted a ransom from its people before returning to the steppe. His subsequent attempts to hold the Horde together failed, and eventually he, too, was forced to flee. Like Tokhtamysh, he ended up in the service of Vitovt, his former enemy.

In the second quarter of the fifteenth century, the Golden Horde became embroiled in a succession dispute—actually, a civil war—in

Muscovy. When Dmitrii Donskoi composed his will, his son Vasilii had yet to produce a son of his own. Therefore Donskoi named his second son, Yurii, as Vasilii's heir. Subsequently Vasilii did indeed father a son, Vasilii II, whose accession to the throne when Vasilii I died was challenged by his uncle Yurii. Vasilii was still a minor at this time, and his guardians were his grandfather, grand prince Vitovt of Lithuania (Vasilii I had married Vitovt's daughter), and the metropolitan Photius.[39] While these two were alive, Yurii could take no decisive action. Neither Muscovite faction rejected Mongol sovereignty in Russia or questioned the khan's right to determine the successor to the throne. In 1425 Yurii and Vasilii agreed to present the problem to the khan, but this led to nothing. The death of Vasilii II's protectors revived Yurii's efforts, and in 1432 the two men actually traveled to Sarai for a judgment. The Horde's own centrifugal tendencies influenced the proceedings. The Crimean prince Taginia, of the powerful Shirin clan, favored Yurii, but the *doroga* for Moscow, Min Bulat, supported Vasilii II. After much politicking (and probably much bribery), khan Ulu-Mehmed awarded the grand prince's throne to Vasilii II, but confirmed Yurii in his appanage *(udel)* of Galich and granted him Dmitrov as well.[40]

When Vasilii and Ulu-Mehmed met again under different circumstances, things turned out less well for the prince. Another civil war in the Golden Horde had resulted in Ulu-Mehmed's expulsion from Sarai. After some mysterious peripatetics, he defeated and captured Vasilii II near Suzdal'. To gain his own release, Vasilii II had to guarantee a huge ransom and also make some political concessions.[41] Given that Ulu-Mehmed had no political base of his own, it is hard to imagine what he could have done with his distinguished prisoner other than release him. Nonetheless, this incident cost Vasilii II his throne and much grief. His enemy Dmitrii Shemiaka, son of Yurii of Galich, exploited public discontent with the onerous ransom. Without ever having shown anti-Tatar proclivities himself (indeed, he had sought a *modus vivendi* with Ulu-Mehmed), Shemiaka was able to portray Vasilii II's policy toward the Tatars as soft. He organized a coup d'etat. Vasilii was overthrown, blinded, and exiled.

Assistance from Ulu-Mehmed at this point would not have enhanced Vasilii's reputation among his subjects, and the leanings of the new khan at Sarai are not known. However, Tatar assistance came from an unexpected quarter. One of Ulu-Mehmed's sons assassinated his father and founded the Kazan' khanate on the middle Volga. Two of Ulu-Mehmed's other sons fled their patricidal sibling and, as vassals of Vasilii II, founded the khanate of Kasimov. In part because of their help, Vasilii II was able to regain his throne. Kasimov served Moscow as a forward post against Kazan' for the next hundred years.

When Vasilii's son Ivan III ("the Great") succeeded him on the throne of Moscow, the political map of the steppe had changed dramatically and with it the pattern of Moscow's relations with the Tatars. The Golden Horde had ceased to exist, and in its place arose a number of smaller khanates, each with its own relationship to the Russian principalities. Muscovy's relations with the Kazan' khanate were complex, her aggressive intentions tempered by the lure of trade and her own limited military capability. Because Crimea and Moscow had common foes in Poland-Lithuania (united dynastically since 1386) and the Great Horde (the nomadic remnant of the Golden Horde), the Crimean khanate, despite its subordination to the Ottoman Empire, became one of Moscow's allies. Moscow also fostered intimate contacts with the Nogai Hordes, whose mobile nomadic forces could match those of the Great Horde.

In this web of alliances and hostilities, the jockeying for position to control the Volga trade routes climaxed in the famous "Stand on the Ugra river" in 1480. In this legendary incident, a Muscovite army faced the army of Khan Akhmad of the Great Horde, which was massed on the other side of the Ugra. Akhmad was depending on ever-promised but never-delivered Polish-Lithuanian troops, which were being held down in the Ukraine by Moscow's Crimean allies. At precisely the same time, perhaps not without the connivance of Ivan III, resistance to Polish-Lithuanian rule flared up in the Ukraine and Belorussia, effectively preventing Sigismund I from keeping his pact with Akhmad. Meanwhile, the Russians and the Tatars exchanged insults and arrows across the Ugra, which could only be crossed when frozen over. As soon as the river did freeze, however, which would have allowed the armies to engage at last, both sides simultaneously retreated. The Muscovite bookmen hailed this coincidence as a miracle.[42]

Such was the episode in which Russia supposedly won its liberty at last and threw off the Tatar Yoke. It occurred without a pitched battle and with the Russians allied with one group of Tatars against another. Nor was it apparent to anyone at the time that the Great Horde's 1480 offensive against Russia was to be the last. However, the Nogais killed Akhmad the next year, and the Crimeans eliminated the Great Horde altogether in 1502. Though no khan ever again tried to assert Mongol power in the Russian forest zone, ambiguities surrounded this political denouement. The grand princes of Moscow continued to collect tribute for the Tatars;

in his will, Ivan III allocated tribute (admittedly, smaller sums than before) to Kasimov, the Crimea, Astrakhan', and Kazan'.

The ad hoc alliance of Muscovy, Kasimov, Kazan', Astrakhan', the Crimea, and the Nogais collapsed almost immediately after accomplishing its purpose of destroying the Great Horde. Now that the Great Horde was no longer a threat to the trade routes, the coalition dissolved in quarrels over the profits. More warfare, in the post-Mongol period, eventually decided the outcome in favor of Muscovy.

The history of Moscow during the Mongol period makes it apparent that any simple analysis of the Mongol impact on Russian politics must be inadequate. Moscow's constantly changing position is indicative of the pattern of East European politics as a whole during the thirteenth to fifteenth centuries and of the flexibility of all parties. No Russian principality had a monopoly on patriotism or, for that matter, collaboration. Each tried to advance its own interests by whatever means seemed best at the moment, and while there was heroism and treachery, above all there was pragmatism. As usual, the politics of the frontier played havoc with cultural and religious fastidiousness.

As for the Golden Horde's policies toward its Russian territories, these often led to seemingly contradictory results. The Mongols sometimes supported the separatist tendencies of Tver', Riazan', Nizhnii Novgorod, or Moscow. At other times they bolstered political centralization under the grand principality of Vladimir to balance against internal power centers like Novgorod or foreign enemies like Lithuania. It becomes clear that the Horde did not in principle favor either centralized power in Russia or the reverse. Instead, the Tatars adopted whatever tactics seemed best suited under the circumstances to further its abiding goals of extracting tribute and military manpower while fending off neighbors like Poland and Lithuania. In pursuit of these long-term objectives, the Golden Horde used a variety of short-term means.

The Golden Horde's commitment to its Russian interests remained constant. Despite the changes in the administration of Russia, despite the "great troubles," despite the emergence of new power centers in Russia and elsewhere, and despite even Tamerlane's invasion and the Horde's disintegration, the Tatars consistently sought to keep their grip on Russia. Throughout the Mongol period, Russian princes either weighed the Tatars' response to every decision or ignored it at their peril.

VI

The Russian "Theory"
of Mongol Rule

THE MONGOL CONQUEST AND THE YEARS OF OPPRESSION THAT FOLLOWED CREATED awkward problems for Christian Russia's writers and intellectuals. The anomaly of Russia's pragmatic and often cooperative relations with hated religious enemies was of course a familiar difficulty, for the East Slavs had been trading, intermarrying, and allying themselves with steppe enemies for centuries. The Russian bookmen had long since learned to skirt the dangerous logical corollaries of this situation with the ideology of silence, as Christians and Muslims all along the medieval ethno-religious frontier had done in similar circumstances. Now, however, the Russians faced a new and much greater threat to the religious and intellectual basis of their culture: they, the wards and agents of an invincible god, had been rapidly and efficiently subjugated by infidel hordes whose power in the foreseeable future was clearly unassailable. The Russians' solution to this second intellectual problem was an extension of their solution to the first.

Since the roots of the Russian intellectual response to the Mongols lie in the Kievan period, it is necessary to keep in mind how the Russians had chosen to envision their dealings with their earlier neighbors on the steppe. From the time of the East Slavs' conversion to Christianity, their chroniclers had omitted from the records all mention of cooperation with nomads like the Pechenegs or the Polovtsy, of respect for them, and even of knowledge of their ways. Instead they recorded only the military history, the battles and the raids, and presented them as religious rather than political conflicts. Hence in the chronicles the Russian princes are never simply defending their holdings or warring on nomadic political enemies. Rather they appear as defenders of the faith battling to save Christianity from marauding infidels driven by religious animosity. This conceptual framework governed how the Kievan bookmen wrote about, and indeed, thought about, Russian relations with steppe nomads. In ignoring cooperation and idealizing conflict to accord with their religious mandate, the Russians had devised a literary etiquette which safeguarded the Christian ideological foundations of their society. This tradition was already thoroughly assimilated by the time the first Mongol horsemen appeared on the horizon.

Unfortunately, when the Russian bookmen of the thirteenth century were suddenly faced with the stunning fact of a complete Mongol victory, the Kievan legacy proved inadequate. The Kievan models provided for glossing over complex and ambiguous dealings with unbelievers but made no allowance for outright conquest. Absolute and long-term subjugation was unprecedented in Russian history, and the ideological ramifications were shattering.

Of course the Russians were not the only people in the medieval confessional world confronted with the thorny ideological problems of defeat by infidels. Christians everywhere took military losses as evidence of their god's displeasure rather than of his weakness or nonexistence. The god of the Hebrews had often temporarily withdrawn his support from his people when they were disobedient, and when Christians lost battles they inferred that they had failed their god rather than vice-versa. When they mended their ways, Christian victories would necessarily follow. Medieval Christians, apart from the Russians, found that even conquest could be explained within this elementary providential theory without compromising the validity of their religion. The Armenians, to whom foreign conquest was not new, admitted that their subjugation was god's will,[1] and thought it natural that an omnipotent god should use infidels to chastise his wayward followers. Intellectuals in Byzantium, mulling over the coming Ottoman victory, decided that the Turks were actually Christian in their morality, if not better Christians than the Byzantines![2]

Non-Christian peoples, who, like the Russians, had been conquered by the Mongols, already had long-standing theories of their own to help them account for such defeats. The Chinese fell back on the malleable theory of the Mandate of Heaven,[3] and the Persians on their well-articulated theories of the rise and fall of empires.

Thus Russia's response to the Mongol conquest was unique. The Russian bookmen, the caretakers of the religious and intellectual foundations of Russian society, confronted for the first time the volatile fact of complete defeat. Either the Christian god was not omnipotent, which was unthinkable, or else the Mongol conquest was his will. Faced with these two possibilities, the Russian bookmen chose not to choose. Rather than rationalize conquest as other peoples had done, Russian intellectuals implicitly denied that it had occurred. They sidestepped the dangerous implications of Mongol rule by refusing to treat Russo-Tatar relations in terms of sovereignty, that is, by refusing to explicitly acknowledge that *Rus'* had been conquered. Russian writers recorded the events of the Mongol period within the conceptual framework evolved during the Kievan period, using the vocabulary from that earlier era when no actual conquests ever took place. Through an adept and remarkably consistent use of language, in which they eschewed the terminology of conquest and even of liberation, the bookmen avoided coming to grips with the ideological conundrum of their own defeat.

The Russians were, of course, aware that they had been conquered. The chronicles record the events of the conquest and the subsequent manifestations of Mongol rule in graphic detail. Yet they rejected the fact of Tatar rule in the sense that they never acknowledged the causal links between Batu's campaigns and the many evils they later suffered at the hands of the Tatars. Texts from the late fourteenth and fifteenth centuries, generations after the conquest, accuse the Mongols of plotting to rule Russia, as though this had not long been a *fait accompli*. (These designs always come to naught.) Naturally, since Russia had never been conquered, contemporary accounts of the Battle of Kulikovo Field and the Stand on the Ugra River could not hail liberation.

To the extent that the Russian bookmen dealt with the theoretical aspects of Mongol rule at all, the overwhelming tendency was to do so in the most ambiguous terms. The medieval authors mixed Christian providentialism, religious dogma, and "secular" historical analysis, muffling the ideological consequences of Russia's plight under layers of religious rhetoric. Some have attributed this response, or lack of response, to the intellectual poverty of medieval Russia. In this view the Russian bookmen were not so much avoiding the theoretical implications of Tatar rule as incapable of grasping them. While it is true that medieval Russians were not inclined to write ideological treatises, this hardly means that they lacked the acuity to do so. In any case, a culture's ideology finds implicit expression in many ways, among them literature, history, and myth. Russian writings from the Mongol period clearly show a rejection of the fact of conquest.

Much of the discussion that follows is designed to show how this denial is apparent from the vocabulary the Russians used in describing the conquest and the later events of the Mongol period. Dictionaries and lexicons of the Old Russian language are not much use for understanding medieval Russian concepts. The only reliable way to find out what a given term meant when originally used is to analyze its uses over many years before and during the Tatar period. This kind of cumulative *explication des textes* reduces the risks of reading modern assumptions into medieval sources. Russia's intellectual posture is also evident from what the bookmen chose to record and not to record, in particular where the logic of an account seems to demand certain admissions which do not appear. Only a comprehensive analysis of all narrative texts from the Mongol period of Russian history could present all the texture and nuances of the Russian perception of Russo-Tatar relations.[4] Still, the selective analysis that follows should illustrate the disparity between long-standing scholarly assumptions about the sources' content and what they actually say.

When the Mongols appeared out of nowhere in 1223, annihilated a joint force of Russians and Polovtsy, and disappeared, the Russians reacted as most Christian and Muslim peoples did to the Tatars. They identified them with the peoples of Gog and Magog, whose escape from behind the mountains where Alexander the Great had locked them up signaled the apocalypse. Some Europeans invoked instead the legend of Prester John, the fabled Christian monarch of the East whose armies warred on the Muslims.[5] The Prester John legend was known to the Russians and Byzantines, but they were too familiar with Asian nomads to confuse the Mongols with the saviors of Christendom, especially after the disastrous encounter on the Kalka river. In any case, the apocalyptic mood passed as soon as the Mongols rode away, and unlike the Tatars, it did not return.

The Russian narratives of the Mongols' reappearance and the campaigns of 1237–1240 are straightforward: the Mongols arrive and destroy all opposition in Vladimir-Suzdalian *Rus'*. When these accounts record that the Mongols took a city or principality, the verbs they usually use are *vziali* and *plenili*. The first is clearly a generic term, meaning to "take" in the military sense but nothing more. It does not connote that a city that was taken was then held. Consequently this verb is ambiguous, and just what it describes must be determined on a case by case basis. *Pleniti* is far more complex. It is invariably translated "conquered," but Sreznevskii, our only medieval dictionary of Old Russian, actually gives a variety of meanings.[6] The root *plen* means either capture or captive. Thus *plenniki* are prisoners-of-war. A city which had been "captured," like one which had been "taken," could still be either held or abandoned. In the latter case, a better translation of *plenili* would be "plundered."

Russian bookmen of the Kievan period had used the same verbs to describe the depredations of nomads in their own time. By using the same terms their predecessors had used in describing, for example, the sack of Kiev by nomads who then returned to the steppe, writers of the Mongol period implied that the events of their day were of the same order. These verbs continue to appear in the chronicles until the mid sixteenth century in contexts that show that their meanings had not changed since the Kievan era. For example, the chronicles certainly do not mean to imply that the same Russian cities were "conquered" again and again, that the Muscovites "conquered" Tver' in 1375, or that Novgorod's lower classes "conquered" the villages of some *boyare*.[7]

The "Tale of the Destruction of Riazan' by Batu" is an extended literary work which shows that the verbs the Russians used to describe the Mongol conquest contain no hint of a change of sovereignty. In the earliest redaction[8] we find the Tatars "taking" and "plundering" Riazan', Vladimir-Suzdal', and the Russian Land. Afterward Prince Ingvar Ingvarevich restores the churches and city walls, repopulates the city, and brings life back to normal, and "there was great joy among the Christians, those whom God had with his strong hand saved."[9] This closing sentiment would be incompatible with the admission that Riazan' had fallen under a hated alien yoke, and there is no mention of a permanent Mongol presence. Written no earlier than the fourteenth century, the "Tale of the Destruction of Riazan'," after long decades of Mongol rule, does not allude to the real consequences of the Mongol campaigns.

The closest the northeastern texts about the campaigns of 1237–1240 come to admitting that the Tatars had come to stay is in telling how the besieged princes of Vladimir chose martyrdom rather than have to do the "will" of the Tatars. (The nominative is *volia*, but the term appears only in the oblique case as *vole*.) When Vasil'ko Konstantinovich is captured, he too prefers martyrdom to entering Tatar service and doing their "will."[10] Having to obey the Mongols' "will" clearly implies a subordinate relationship, but since the princes avoid this by dying, there is no explanation of what this would have entailed. *Volia* appears elsewhere only in the Galician-Volhynian chronicle of the thirteenth century. This account describes the princes of Galicia-Volhynia summoned to participate in Mongol campaigns against Poland, Lithuania, and Hungary as being either subject or not subject to the "will" of the Tatars. (In the latter situation, the word used is *nevole;* the nominative of this oblique case would be *nevolia*.)[11] The term certainly seems to imply that the Russians were Tatar clients, perhaps even vassals, but the chronicler offers no explanations.

For three or four years after the conquest, chronicles from northeastern Russia do not mention the Mongols at all.[12] Then a series of entries appears which tells how various Russian princes journey to Sarai or Karakorum "for their patrimonies" *(pro svoiu otchinu)*. These princes received *yarliks* granting them the right to retain their principalities.[13] The chronicles, though presumably written for posterity, fail to mention *why* any Russian prince should need permission from the Mongols to remain on his throne. A simple clause—"because the Tatars had conquered *Rus'*"—would have filled the logical gap, but it does not appear.

The *vita* of Mikhail of Chernigov shows a more direct examination of Tatar rule.[14] In this account, after the Mongol campaign *(nakhozhdenie)* of 1240, the Tatars "sat" *(osadisha)* for a certain time *(po koletsekh vremena)* in Russian cities, took a census *(chislo),*[15] and began to collect tribute *(imati dan')*. When Mikhail returns from abroad, Tatar emissaries tell him it is improper for him to live "on the land of the khan" *(zemlia kanova)* if he has not bowed *(pokolniv'shesia)* to Batu. Mikhail takes the hint and travels to Batu but then refuses to perform the shamanist purification rite of passing between two fires. He declares, "I bow to you, oh Tsar, for God has given you the tsardom and the glory of the world . . ." but will not compromise his religion by performing an infidel rite. Mikhail is executed by the Mongols but canonized by the Russian Orthodox Church.

The hagiographer has gone further than other sources in acknowledging Mongol rule and even its legitimacy. Mikhail's speech echoes the apostle Paul's "The powers that be, are of God," as Michael Cherniavsky has pointed out.[16] Still, there are peculiarities. The narrative suggests that the Tatars "sat" in Russian cities (unspecified) only for a while and makes no explicit connection between the Mongol invasion and the fact that Chernigov is now "the land of the khan." Furthermore, the realities of Mongol rule have been relegated to the background of what is presented as a religious rather than a political confrontation. In fact, Batu executed Mikhail because he was a rebel. The khan's tolerance of other faiths and his protection of the Russian Orthodox Church were well known. Nonetheless, in the *vita* Batu and Mikhail become religious rather than political adversaries, their encounter a test of Mikhail's religious conviction, and Mikhail's death a religious martyrdom.

The Pauline doctrine also appears in the *vita* of Alexander Nevskii.[17] This hagiographic account refers to Batu as "a powerful tsar of the eastern land, to whom God has subjected *(pokoril)* many lands, from the east to the west." Batu sends Nevskii the following message: "You know that God has subjected to me many peoples *(iazytsi;* literally, tongues). Do you alone wish not to submit yourself *(pokoritesia)* to my power? Yet if you wish to preserve your land, then come quickly to me and witness my imperial dignity *(chest' tsarstva)*." Nevskii pays the required visit to the khan, who treats him with great honor *(chestno).*[18] Subsequently the khan, angry with Nevskii's brother Andrei, sends his commander *(voevoda,* a Russian term) Nevrui to "war on" *(voevati)* the Suzdalian Land. Much as prince Ingvar had done in Riazan', Nevskii restores the Suzdalian Land in the aftermath of Nevrui's "plundering" *(po pleneni)*. He also helps deflect the Tatars' anger with his gifts and diplomacy.

Nevskii's *vita,* like Mikhail's, is noteworthy both for what it reveals and for what it does not. Batu's power over Russia is not denied, for if it were the story could not be told. Yet Tatar sovereignty is not explicitly acknowledged, and the tale omits to mention that when Nevskii was summoned to the Horde, Russia was *already* one of the lands God had subjected to Batu. Indeed, Nevskii was already bound by the oath of allegiance taken by his father Yaroslav. The story also neglects the fact that Andrei Yaroslavovich's offense was attempted rebellion, and a number of other details that would clarify the real political context of Nevskii's doings, including the *baskak* system, Nevskii's *yarlik,* and the prominent role he played in the Mongol census of Novgorod.

The chronicle of Galicia-Volhynia records grand prince Daniil's formal submission with similar reticence. Daniil, who fled during the cam-

paigns against southern *Rus'*, learns upon his return that the penalty for
not complying with Tatar wishes will be the loss of his patrimony. Accordingly, Daniil travels to the Horde, goes down on his knees before Batu,
accepts the designation slave *(kholop)* of the Tatars, guarantees tribute,
and, like Nevskii, is dismissed with honor.[19] This entry *sub anno* 1250 is
critical of Daniil, while the description in Nevskii's *vita* of Nevskii's visit
to Batu is laudatory. The two accounts are otherwise similar in that they
do not explain why these events occurred or why refusing to submit to the
Mongols would have been political suicide (aside from the obvious threat
of force).

The eloquent sermons of Serapion, bishop of Vladimir, contain the
most poignant evocations of the state of Russia following the Mongol
campaigns. According to Serapion, the Russian cities have been "plundered" *(plenisha)*, "taken" *(vziasha)*, and "destroyed" *(razorisha)*, raids
(rati) and "pagan oppression" *(poganskoe nasilie)* continue, and the
Christians live in "bitter slavery" *(gorkuiu rabotu)*.[20] Serapion's scriptural
cadences are built with the same vocabulary used in the other thirteenth-
century sources and indeed in Kievan sources from before the Mongol
period. He is eager to paint a black portrait of Mongol oppression, but he
is decrying a religious and moral rather than a political oppression. God
is punishing the Christians for their sins, and Serapion's reference to
"slavery" is rhetorical hyperbole rather than a description of political
status. Russia's political subordination *(pokorena)* seems a natural addition to a list of its penances but does not appear.

Thus writers from various parts of *Rus'* avoided the issue of Russia's
change of sovereignty. Chroniclers, hagiographers, and preachers from
Vladimir-Suzdal, Novgorod, and Galicia-Volhynia either did not con-
cede the fact of Mongol rule or, in describing its manifestations, left them
in a logical vacuum. By employing the lexicon left over from the days of
Kievan *Rus'* and by leaving unspoken the causal links between the arrival
of Batu's armies and Mongol rule, the Russian bookmen skirted the intellectual dimension of the Mongol conquest. The ambivalence of the thirteenth-century bookmen echoed through the works of generations of later
Russian writers.

Since the medieval Russian bookmen had denied conquest, they
could not hail liberation. The events of 1237–1240 had been treated as
no more than a great military defeat, so Russia's gradual emergence from
the Tatar period could only be treated in terms of simple military vic-

tories. The fourteenth and fifteenth-century writers who applauded Russian successes were forced to do so within the narrow confines of the thirteenth-century lexicon. Gradually, however, new concepts and a changed perception of the past did penetrate the literary etiquette.

Donskoi's victory over emir Mamai at Kulikovo Field in 1380 is traditionally the most celebrated Russian attempt to break the Tatar yoke, but contemporary literary works do not cast it in this light at all.[21] In the "Short Redaction" of the "Chronicle Tale" of 1380, Mamai's expressed intent is to "plunder" (pleniti) the Russian Land. Instead he is defeated first by Donskoi, then by Tokhtamysh, who notifies the Russian princes that he has "defeated his (own) enemy and theirs," and is now enthroned on the Volga tsarstvo. Donskoi and the other princes send envoys bearing gifts. In the "Expanded Redaction" of the "Chronicle Tale" Mamai, who was not a Chingisid, is accused of lèse-majesté for calling himself khan or tsar'. Here, Donskoi announces that he is willing to pay the same amount of tribute as under Chani-bek. There is not the least indication that Russia's relationship with the Golden Horde has altered.[22]

Recounting the same events, the epic Zadonshchina at least goes so far as to relate the current state of affairs to incidents in the past. As Mamai plots to "take" (vziati) the Russian Land, Donskoi's wife Evdokiia prays that God will not allow a repeat of the disaster on the Kalka, from which Russia still suffers. (This shows some poetic license: the defeat on the Kalka preceded the conquest proper by fifteen years.) It was God's will that Batu had "plundered" (pleniti) Russia, for the Russians had sinned, but now with God's favor Mamai would be defeated. Evdokiia's lament is concerned only with the joy and sorrow of victory and defeat in a great battle, despite the allusion to Russia's long sufferings. Mamai's Tatars will no longer collect tribute, but this is because these particular Tatars will be dead, not because Russia will have won its independence.[23]

The very religious Skazanie o Mamaevom poboishche (Narration of the Battle with Mamai), which completes the Kulikovo cycle, breaks new ground in its depiction of Russo-Tatar relations.[24] In this account, Mamai, besides intending to imitate Batu, who "plundered" the Russian Land and "took" Kiev and other cities, wants to "sit" (sideti) his Tatars in the cities and "rule" (vladeti) from them. He also calls Donskoi his servitor (sluzhebnik) and refers to Donskoi's patrimony as part of the ulus or Mongol inheritance. The Skazanie thus expresses for the first time the very idea of Mongols actually ruling Russia, though it appears only as an ambition. Of course, the stance that Russia's freedom is merely threatened, rather than long since lost, is belied by the reference to Russia as part of the *ulus,* the legacy of the Mongol Empire, but this is ignored. The *Skazanie* goes farther than any previous Russian work toward hinting at Russia's real status, but drowns any connection between Mamai's "ambitions" and Batu's accomplishments in its crusading religiosity. It emphasizes Donskoi's piety without reference to political motives or the idea of Russian liberation.

A final record of Donskoi's victory at Kulikovo appears in the Russian chronicles *sub anno* 1389, the year of his death, in a text usually called Donskoi's *vita.*[25] Here, Mamai, inspired by the Devil and evil advisors, is said to have wanted to install *baskaki* in Russia and impose Islam on the Russians. Both accusations are unreliable and tendentious, and of course the text does not explain why there had ever been *baskaki* in Russia or why they had been removed. Donskoi's piety wins him the battle, and the motives for the encounter and the consequences of his victory are not considered.

The face-off between Ivan the Great and Khan Akhmad of the Great Horde in the famous "Stand on the Ugra River" in 1480 is usually treated as the definitive event in the Russian liberation. This view grossly oversimplifies the case, for Moscow had probably ceased paying tribute to the Great Horde sometime in the 1470s, yet continued formal relations until the Great Horde was destroyed twenty years after the Ugra incident. Furthermore, Muscovy continued to pay tribute, of a sort, to various other Tatar khanates. It was not until three quarters of a century later that Muscovite ideologues began to ascribe to this confrontation the significance it currently holds in Russian historical writings.

There is no indication in the fundamental chronicle account of the Ugra river incident that on that day Russia was liberated or that it needed to be.[26] In this simple narrative, *Tsar'* Akhmad intends to "plunder" *(pleniti),* as Batu had done, all Orthodox Christians. He fails, however, and is later killed. Thus God "saved" *(izbavi)* the Christians. A separate lament extols the bravery of the Russians in contrast to the cowardice of the South Slavs, comparing Muscovite defiance to the Tatars in 1480 (a generous interpretation of Moscow's cautious military strategy) to the South Slavs' acceptance of Ottoman oppression. This raises the intriguing possibility of a parallel between the Balkans under the Ottomans and Russia under the Tatars, but naturally the text does not go that far.[27]

The most famous and often quoted source on the Stand on the Ugra is the "Epistle to the Ugra" *(Poslanie na Ugru)* of Vassian, bishop of Rostov and confidant of Ivan III.[28] Vassian notes that the Tatars' campaign *(nakhozhdenie)* has greatly frightened the people of Moscow and assures Ivan that he can be released in the eyes of the Church from any oath made to Akhmad, since it was extracted by coercion. Vassian insists that Ivan is the Orthodox *tsar'* and that Akhmad is merely a "brigand and savage and fighter-of-God." Though Batu plundered *(popleni)*, enslaved *(porabotati)* the land, and "took the title *tsar'*," he is not one, "nor . . . of an imperial clan" *(ne . . . ot tsarska roda)*. The epistle closes with the thought that God has simply been punishing the Russians for their sins much as he had previously punished the Israelites by reducing them to slavery *(rabota)* to Pharoah and other foreigners *(inoplemenniki)*.

Vassian thus presents for the first time a coordinated analysis of the beginnings of Mongol rule in Russia: Batu plundered Russia and then assumed the imperial title. However, Vassian's epistle is an assault on the legitimacy of that title. Since the Russians used the same word, *tsar'*, to translate both *khan* and *basileus* (the Byzantine emperor), they implicitly accorded the former the same sort of legitimacy as the latter.[29] Vassian must untangle the two before he can assert that Mongol rule has never been legitimate. In Cherniavsky's analysis:

> The archbishop is trying here to destroy the image of the khan-tsar by raising the image of the tsar-basileus; only one tsar is possible, the Orthodox Christian one, and the other is an imposter. Yet in order to fight this imposter it is necessary, Vassian felt, to raise the Grand Prince to the role of tsar himself. What Vassian was trying to do was to solve the ideological problem. Ivan III's reluctance to face the khan in battle was caused by political and military fears, not by his awe before his sovereign. Yet, politically and militarily, the Tatars remained a serious danger for Russia not only during the fifteenth but also during the sixteenth century. Vassian's problem, the ideological problem, was not just to defeat the Tatars in battle—it was to destroy the image of the khan as tsar.[30]

He did this by elevating the grand prince of Moscow to the status of basileus-tsar and denigrating the khan as a mere usurper. Vassian rejects the Pauline doctrine invoked in the *vitae* of Mikhail of Chernigov and Alexander Nevskii and, on the grounds that only a Christian can be a *tsar'*, denies Chingisid legitimacy.[31] In this respect Vassian's epistle is unique in medieval Russian intellectual history. It is also interesting in that it takes for the first time a historical perspective on the origins of Mongol domination and lays the foundation for several subsequent attempts to attach a special ideological significance to the Stand on the Ugra.

The first of these, which seems to date from the 1550s, is an epistle addressed to Ivan IV and variously attributed to metropolitan Makarii or the priest Silvestr, Ivan's father-confessor. This document hails four great events in world history: the deeds of the Hebrew judge Ezekial, the defenses of Constantinople under emperors Constantine and Leo, and the Russian defense against Akhmad in 1480. Though Akhmad wanted to plunder *(pleni)* the Russian Land and become its ruler *(vlastets)*, he, his empire *(tsarstvo)*, and his clan *(rod)* perished, his places *(mesta)* became empty, and his regime *(dershava)* and glory disappeared.[32]

This text presents Akhmad's desire to become sovereign of the Russian Land as though his imperial ancestors had not held that position since 1240. It also conflates the Stand on the Ugra with the demise of the Great Horde in the first decade of the next century. From this perspective, the events of 1480 assume the status of pivotal moments in the history of man.

Elements from both Vassian's Epistle and the Epistle to Ivan IV are used in a novel and arresting way in the *Kazanskaia istoriia* (Kazan' History), in which the reinvention of Russian liberation is made complete. According to this complex, heterogeneous, and ambitious narrative,[33] Batu "plundered," "enslaved," and began collecting tribute in *Rus'* when he founded the Golden Horde *(Zlataia orda*, the first attested use of this term). Without regard to genealogical legitimacy *(ne po koleny, ni po rodu)*, he awarded power to whomever he chose. This evil power *(vlast'*, rule or authority) endured from Batu's time until Ivan III ceased paying tribute to Akhmad ("purchasing" the Russian throne, *vlasti russkiia kupiti)*. When Akhmad sends envoys demanding the tribute and that Ivan reverence Akhmad's portrait *(parsenu)*, Ivan tramples the picture, unable to tolerate further Tatar oppression *(nasilie)*. As a result, Akhmad intends to plunder *(pleniti)* the Russian Land and destroy Moscow as his grandfather Tokhtamysh had done. He fails because while facing Ivan's troops on the Ugra, he learns that the Gorodets (Kasimov) *tsari* have attacked Sarai. This is the final desolation *(zapustenie)* of the Golden Horde, and Akhmad abandons the field. "And thus ended the Horde tsars, and by such divine intervention the *tsarstvo* and great power of the Golden Horde perished *(pogibe)*. And then in our Russian Land we were freed *(svobodi)* from the burden *(yarmo)* of submission *(pokorenie)* to the Muslim *(busurmanskogo)* and began to recover, as if from winter to clean spring."

The Kazan History was probably written in the 1560s, and its author plays somewhat fast and loose with history.[34] For one thing Batu did respect Russian succession principles. For another, Akhmad and his envoys were Muslims—no portrait of him would have been allowed. At any rate, this account is of interest as the culmination of the rethinking of the Tatar yoke and Russian liberation that first appeared in Vassian's Epistle. Though its author does not follow Vassian in attacking Chingisid legitimacy, he too explicitly acknowledges that a long period of Mongol domination began after Batu's campaigns. Then, from the Epistle to Ivan IV, he adopts the telescoping view that equates the Stand on the Ugra, the demise of the Great Horde, and the release of Russian Christians from the burden *(yarmo)* of slavery.[35] Despite the numerous flaws in the historical foundations of the Kazan History, its account of the beginning and end of the Tatar period became canonical in Russian historical writing.

The Kazan History superimposes on Vassian's biblical metaphors a political and historical conception of Mongol suzereignty such as would never have been expressed during the Mongol period. It was not until the flurry of ideological articulation that characterized the reign of Ivan IV, three quarters of a century after the events of 1480, that the Stand on the Ugra achieved its status as the moment of Russian liberation. This lag was the natural consequence of the need of the Russian writers, freed at last from the Mongols, to free themselves from their own tradition of literary and intellectual restraints.

Russia's intellectual reaction to Mongol rule, as reflected in contemporary writings, was both complex and ambiguous. Writers usually showed no reluctance to discuss the Tatars but tended to restrict themselves to graphic descriptions of Mongol atrocities, presented as incidents in a continuous religious war. To the extent that the Russian bookmen dealt with the Mongol presence in political terms, they fell back upon the vocabulary of the Kievan period, forcing the conceptual framework of that earlier era to do service in a world it no longer suited. By using equivocal words in preference to well-known precise ones, by not drawing causal connections, and by presenting the manifestations of Mongol rule without explanation, the medieval Russian bookmen avoided the intellectual implications of the Mongol conquest.

The Russian response stands alone. Religious ideologues in other conquered medieval societies, Christian, Muslim, and pagan, all directly addressed the questions raised by their own defeat. All used existing theories, or elaborations of existing theories, to come to terms with their own defeat without weakening the religious substructure of their civilizations. Russia's past and its peculiar status within the Golden Horde may explain why the Russians did not choose to admit conquest and interpret it as an extreme case of God's displeasure, as other Christians had done. Russia was clearly not part of the *ulus,* and the Tatars had allowed the Russian princes to retain their thrones. Few Mongols actually dwelt in the Russian forest zone. As a consequence, conditions were much more favorable for Russia's unique elaboration of the ideology of silence than they would have been if the Mongols had garrisoned the cities or replaced the princes with Mongol governors. Also, Russia already had a long history of dealings with steppe peoples. The Mongols, after all, were pastoral nomads like the Polovtsy and their predecessors, lived on the same steppes, and in a number of ways interacted similarly with the Russians. Russia's ambiguous position in the Golden Horde, the lack of a continual Tatar presence, and the heritage of Kievan relations with steppe nomads combined to make the Russian response of leaving the relationship between Russia and the Mongols unexplored and unarticulated. Absentee rule made it possible, and the Kievan tradition made it easy.

The medieval writers' reticence about the true nature of Russo-Tatar relations is a sign of neither ignorance nor timidity. Instead, it is itself a form of resistance to oppression. It has, however, had the regrettable result of misleading historians. The bookmen give the impression that the Mongols had no greater impact on Russian history and society than earlier steppe peoples, and historians have accepted this as true. Yet because of the ideology of silence, the Kievan posture did not reflect the reality even of the Kievan period, much less of the radically altered circumstances following the Mongol conquest.

VII

Economic and Demographic Consequences

THE IMMEDIATE IMPACT OF THE MONGOL INVASIONS WAS CATASTROPHIC BEYOND anything the Russians had previously experienced. The Mongols had combined the siege weaponry of the Chinese and the Muslims and used it on an unprecedented scale, assaulting cities with thousands of catapults and battering rams day and night. When cities fell the Mongols would sometimes raze them and massacre the inhabitants, for though they were neither the first nor the last to do so, they were waging a war of terror. Merciless destruction spread panic before the Mongol armies, a powerful weapon, and also assured against armed centers of resistance in the Mongols' strategic rear. Medieval warfare was seldom gallant, and the Mongols were the greatest practitioners of the art.

The corpses pierced with Mongol arrowheads that archaeologists have found amid burned-out rubble vividly evoke the nature of the Mongol conquest. However, archaeology has also been particularly useful in assessing its economic and demographic aftermath.[1] Before the Mongols came, late Kievan *Rus'* had been reasonably prosperous. Its cities carried on extensive international commerce with both East and West while sustaining a variety of artisanal activities, and its farms produced enough to support the urban populations.[2] The Mongol campaigns of 1237–1240 shattered this economy. Many cities lay in ruins, their populations largely slaughtered. From among the survivors and from the cities less harshly dealt with, laborers and skilled artisans were deported to the steppe to raise the new Mongol cities along the lower Volga or else sold into slavery. The permanent decline of a number of artisanal skills reflects the Tatars' most ruinous effects on urban life. Several skills disappeared entirely, including the art of cloisonné enameling for the luxury market. In the countryside crops were burned and livestock run off. The Russian forests probably hid many villages from the Mongol cavalry, but any settlements in the path of the advancing armies were destroyed. Population declined throughout Russia, most precipitously in the plundered cities (the great population shifts the Mongols caused were a later phenomenon).[3] Even if Russia had not been abruptly cut off from foreign markets, the decline in agricultural and artisanal production would have left little surplus for trade. Though the Russians had probably stopped minting coins before the Mongols arrived, it was a century after the conquest before economic conditions were favorable enough to begin again.

The successful conclusion of Batu's subjugation of Russia did not spell the end of Mongol destructiveness, for in addition to the rigorous economic exploitation that now began, Mongol military forays into Russia remained fairly frequent. These incursions, which the Russian chronicles record as "raids," were usually undertaken in support of favored Russian princes or were punitive expeditions against rebellious or recalcitrant principalities. Mongol discipline was often severe. Some historians have suggested that the Dnepr' region in the Ukraine, which was particularly hard hit, may have been entirely depopulated. Though this is an exaggeration, it was a century after the conquest before political activity revived in the heart of the Ukraine. Galicia and Volhynia were not immune to such attacks either, and suffered much harm during the second half of the thirteenth century. In the rich agricultural and urban region of Vladimir-Suzdalian *Rus'*, the Mongols used periodic depredations to neutralize the power of principalities whose waxing strength seemed to pose a threat. Besides the damage done by the various Mongol war parties specifically sent to keep Russia tractable, there was a certain amount of incidental destruction. Slave-raiding forays along the borders were not uncommon, and Mongol contingents returning from joint Russo-Tatar campaigns against Poland, Lithuania, or Hungary thought it meet to loot their allies' villages as they passed by. The Mongols' capacity for violence was kept fresh in the Russian mind.

The cost to Russia of the Mongol conquest was not, of course, confined to the loss of lives and property. The tribute the Mongols demanded *(vykhod,* later *dan')* was the greatest drain on the Russian economy, but there were many others, a variety of direct and indirect levies. The *yarliki,* or patents, guaranteeing the Russian Orthodox Church immunity from taxation, list most of these, including the postal tax *(yam),* the customs tax *(tamga),* and tolls *(myt').* The Russians also had to bear many of the costs of the Mongol administration. Thus they had to provide subsistence for the *baskaki,* in kind or in grants of land, and feed and house the Mongol envoys *(posoly)* and their retinues as they rode to and from the Golden Horde. This could prove a considerable economic burden, and villages along the routes most traveled by Mongol envoys were granted tax exemptions to help them bear it. Nonetheless, expropriations by Horde functionaries forced the abandonment of many villages. For the Russian princes, the incidental expenses of Tatar overlordship could also be great. It was expensive to travel to and from Sarai (in certain cases, Mongolia), to support themselves and their retainers while there, and to offer Mongol grandees and bureaucrats the bribes necessary to make the visits fruitful. The Mongols also extracted ransoms for cities, such as that paid for Moscow in 1408, and for hostages, such as Ulu-Mehmed demanded for Vasilii II. Irregular taxes, essentially extortion, round out the list of means the Tatars used to ensure the constant flow of wealth from Russia to the steppe.[4]

Attempts to calculate the amount of the tribute, as an aid to assessing the drain on the Russian economy, have produced mixed results.[5] There are no records at all for Galicia-Volhynia, the southern Ukraine, Novgorod, Riazan', Tver', Smolensk, all of Belorussia, or Nizhnii Novgorod (except for when this city was briefly held by the Muscovites in the 1390s). Indeed there are no records of any kind from before 1389 and hence no way of determining the tribute before then. In that year, however, Muscovite princes began to note specific amounts of tribute in their wills and treaties. These figures provide a reliable means of at least estimating Russia's annual payments to the Tatars. The lowest possible estimates for the grand principality of Moscow, without the hypothetical sums for the other regions, indicate that the Russians paid the Mongols between five and seven thousand silver rubles a year. For the Golden

Horde, which had other holdings considerably more lucrative, this was not a vast sum, but for the ravaged Russian economy it must have been an enormous burden.

Such, then, were the immediate and most apparent economic and demographic consequences of the Mongol conquest. Batu's campaigns had destroyed a number of Russian cities and greatly depopulated many regions. The severe depression that followed was exacerbated by further raids and continual economic demands, especially the constant flow of tribute from Russia to the steppe. Even in cities which had not been razed, like Novgorod, the building of churches, traditionally the first sign of economic surplus, came to a halt. This gloomy picture must be qualified, however. The damage from the conquest and the rigors of Tatar exploitation were distributed unequally socially, geographically, and through time.

The Russian peasantry felt the Tatars' economic oppression much more acutely than the Russian aristocracy, and indeed the Russian princes profited from the exploitation of their people. The grand princes were in charge of collecting tribute for the Mongols, and this proved so profitable that the throne was more than worth the large bribes the khan required before awarding it. Historians have almost invariably assumed that the grand princes grew rich through embezzling the tribute. This was dangerous, however, since the Tatars treated it as a capital offense. Roublev has demonstrated that at least the Muscovite grand princes enriched themselves in a safer and more sophisticated way. Rather than pilfering from petty cash, the princes manipulated the allocation of the tax burden. They exempted the crown lands from paying tribute altogether and made up the difference by demanding more from their peripheral appanages. The profits from this must have been massive compared to the puny rewards of embezzlement, and the Mongols, as long as they got their due, were indifferent.[6]

In the steppe, Mongol taxes, like those of most pastoral nomadic peoples, if not progressive, were at least proportional to wealth. It was the Russian elite who made the tribute regressive, forcing the poor to pay the most. When, as the Mongol period was ending, the expected tribute fell to a fraction of what it had been, Moscow's princes continued to collect the old amount and pocketed the difference.

Russian princes and nobles also profited by participating in Tatar campaigns against Russia's neighbors and earning a share of the loot. The rewards depended, of course, on how many lives, weapons, horses, and supplies they expended and on how much damage their Tatar allies did to the Russian countryside on the way. The princes of Galicia-Volhynia may have received some recompense for their aid in campaigns against Poland, Hungary, and Lithuania, but many of these were unsuccessful, and any returns may not have compensated for the villages lost to the Tatars in transit. On the other hand, the princes of northeastern Russia who tendered their services to the Golden Horde were definitely properly rewarded. The Rostov princes who took part in the sack of the Ias city of Dediakov in the Caucasus in 1277 won wealth and prisoners, and the Azerbaidjan campaigns too may have proved remunerative.[7] On the whole, Russia's princes at least broke even on these ventures and usually turned a profit.

The economic effects of the Mongol conquest and rule varied in different regions of Russia just as they did among the social classes. Many cities were devastated, but many others, including Novgorod, Pskov, Smolensk, Polotsk, Vitebsk, and probably Rostov and Uglich, suffered little or no damage and were never sacked.[8] Furthermore, after 1240 Mongol destruction was not indiscriminate but carefully designed to impede the development of certain principalities and foster that of others.[9] Different cities benefited from this policy at different times. During the first half of the fourteenth century, for example, since Moscow had allied itself with the Golden Horde, the Tatars directed their raids against Moscow's enemies, Tver' and Riazan'. (Indeed, the capital city of Riazan', after repeated destruction, had to be relocated.) Then, in the second half of that century and in the next, the Tatars perceived Moscow as a threat, and it was that city's turn to be the target of Mongol attacks.[10]

The Mongol raids influenced the balance of power among the Russian principalities largely by affecting the size of their populations. Medieval cities were never either demographically or economically self-sufficient and depended on a flow of food-stuffs and population from the countryside just to feed the urban dwellers and keep their numbers up. Thus no city could sustain itself, much less grow, without a viable agricultural infrastructure at work in the surrounding lands. Furthermore, since increased population meant more food producers, more taxpayers, more recruits, and more administrators, the Russian princes' power was measured in manpower. The Mongols wrought demographic changes which determined the decline and ascendance of the Russian principalities.

Mongol attacks on the regions of Vladimir and Suzdalia in the second half of the thirteenth century produced population shifts to the north, to Ustiug, Beloozero, and Viatka; to the west, to Rostov and Yaroslavl'; and to the southwest, to Tver' and Moscow. In the first half of the fourteenth century, however, Moscow alone benefited from this kind of forced immigration, protected by her alliance with the Golden Horde while the Mongols launched supportive raids against Moscow's enemies. The Tatar attacks weakened the rival Russian cities while augmenting Moscow's growing strength in the most material way by funneling population in her direction. Thus the other Russian cities, though far from debilitated, lost ground just as Moscow tightened its grip on northeastern Russia. Moscow's prosperity owed less to the immediate political and military advantages of her alliance with the Horde than to the economic and demographic results of a Mongol policy designed to systematically impoverish centers of anti-Tatar opposition, notably Tver'. When the Golden Horde's "Great Troubles" began in the 1360s, Moscow was in a position to strengthen itself even further while the Tatars saw to more pressing needs. By the time the Horde recuperated, Moscow was too powerful to be dislodged from her preeminence in Vladimir-Suzdalia. With Moscow now become the greater threat to Mongol power, the Golden Horde lent its support to an eager Tver', but it was too late.[11]

Although devastation, extermination, and extortion were the most dramatic effects of the Mongol presence on the Russian economy, they were not the only ones. The Golden Horde, for reasons of self-interest, played a major role in providing the means for Russia's recovery. Like all Inner Asian nomadic empires before them, the Mongols were solicitous of trade. Nomadic empires had always expanded along the continental Eurasian caravan routes, protecting the merchants who actually conducted the trade and extracting profits through customs taxes. Though they altered existing patterns of commerce to increase their own profits, the Mongols followed in this tradition. The results for Russia, while mixed, were on the whole beneficial.[12]

The Mongols shifted the Urals fur trade route, which had run east and west through Novgorod, to run north and south, channeling furs through Ustiug and Moscow to Sarai. Moscow and Ustiug naturally profited considerably from the flow of furs and silver along this new route.[13] Novgorod lost the income from this trade, but because the Mongols also protected the Baltic and Volga river trade routes, the city flourished in the thirteenth and fourteenth centuries rather than declining. Not only did the Mongols not cut off Novgorod from her western trading partners in the German Hanseatic League, but they gave tax exemptions to Hanseatic merchants entering Russia through Novgorod and passing through Suzdalia (perhaps on their way to Sarai).[14] Novgorod was the entrepot for nearly all Baltic trade entering and leaving Russia, and this Mongol policy probably increased trade and hence income. Historians have been most concerned with Novgorod's commercial ties with the West, but the city was also intimately involved in trade with the Orient, as archaeological finds of silks, glazed pottery from the Muslim East, and Damascus swords attest.[15] Through Novgorod passed oriental goods on their way to the Baltic and European goods on their way to the Golden Horde. Because of the Mongols' commercial policies, Novgorod, like Moscow and Ustiug, prospered.

Historians have always taken it for granted that the oriental trade was in luxury goods and that the items bought and sold ended up, along with the profits of commerce, in the hands of the Russian upper classes—the princes, nobles, and merchants. Archaeologists, however, are beginning to broaden the entire picture of Russia's oriental trade. First, oriental goods entered Russia not only from the Horde and Volga Bolgar but also from the Crimea and even Moldavia. Second, the effects of this trade seem to have penetrated Russian society to a much greater extent than was thought. Oriental goods such as silk, glass, beads, cowrie shells, and boxwood combs have been dug up at village sites throughout the Russian countryside. These are everyday, rather than luxury, items and would have had to have been imported in bulk for trade in them to be profitable. These finds in many Russian villages suggest that the Russian peasant during the Mongol period did in fact have some ties with the international markets.[16]

In addition to the trade that flowed through Russia and the steppe, there was also trade among the peoples within the Golden Horde's hegemony. The Russians traded with such sedentary population centers as Volga Bolgaria, Genoese Kaffa, and, later, Kazan', but their most conspicuous dealings were with the Tatar nomads. The chronicles record an expedition in 1474 from the Great Horde to Moscow comprising thirty-two hundred merchants and others accompanied by an embassy of six hundred. Moscow bought forty thousand horses for its cavalry.[17] Though this is the only such transaction recorded, perhaps because of its magnitude, it cannot have been unique. The Russians bought horses, livestock, and hides in exchange for silver or manufactured goods, in particular textiles. Russian trade with both the sedentary peoples and the nomads of the steppe thus continued to follow the patterns established in the Kievan period.

Naturally the Mongol dynasties of Yüan China and Ilkhanid Persia also sought to foster trade, and the differences in these other successor states to the Mongol Empire illuminate Russia's situation within the Golden Horde. In both China and Persia the Mongols had taken up residence among their new subjects, garrisoning cities and gradually blending to a degree with the indigenous societies. As a result, their economic interests coincided with those of the native peoples, and the Mongols, after the destruction of the initial conquest, promoted diversified economic development.[18] The Yüan emperors built canals to improve transportation and communication.[19] In China agricultural and artisanal production, hard hit in Russia, continued unabated. The same was true in Persia, partly because Persian artisanal traditions were well-established, but also because the Ilkhanids were patrons of the arts. Persian viniculture, which had languished as a result of Islamic taboos, thrived under the Mongols, who were great drinkers, even after their conversion.[20] The Persian silk industry also benefited from the Mongol conquest because of the contacts that opened with China. Cities along the caravan routes, in Persia, Armenia-Georgia, Central Asia, and China, prospered as part of the tax-free customs zones protected by the Pax Mongolica. Government service also offered opportunities for ambitious officials. Chinese and others in China and Persians and even Jews in Persia rose to great prominence in Mongol service, while building, legally or otherwise, great fortunes. A vizier for the Ilkhanids, Rashid ad Din, created a personal empire that makes Ivan Kalita's principality seem minute by comparison.

In Russia, things were profoundly different. The Golden Horde was as interested in the profits of trade as the other Mongol states, and of course preferred a financially viable base of taxpayers, but Russia's position was not analogous to that of China or Persia. The Mongols did not live among the Russians or in any way become integrated into Russian society. The Golden Horde remained on the steppe, with a steppe economy, and their economic interests did not coincide with those of their subjects. There is no evidence to suggest that the Tatars made any effort to bolster any part of the Russian economy, apart from commerce. The segregation imposed by distance and religious hostility also prevented individual Russians from profiting through service in the Mongol bureaucracy.

Russia began its economic recovery about half a century after the conquest (roughly as long as after the Time of Troubles at the turn of the seventeenth century). The increased political activity at this time in new regional power centers like Tver' and Moscow indicates at least moderate prosperity. A surge of urban development beginning in the middle of the fourteenth century, after a hundred years of Mongol rule, shows the Russian economy entering a period of growth. Existing cities grew and new ones were founded. The most successful Russian city was Moscow, whose new walls were material evidence of economic surplus. In Moscow, as in Novgorod and many northeastern Russian cities, churches, including stone ones, began to be built again—a sure sign of improved economic health.

There is every reason to believe that the international commerce the Mongols had fostered was a major cause of Russia's new urbanization and economic recovery.[21] The cities along the oriental trade routes were those that prospered and grew the most. Nizhnii Novgorod, for example, which lay on the main Volga river trade route, from humble beginnings burgeoned within half a century to become the capital of its own principality. Only international commerce, which produced greater profits than any other sector of the economy, could have produced Russia's evident economic surpluses. The Russian princes resumed minting coins, albeit on a small scale. Since Russia produced no silver of its own, the balance of trade was apparently favorable. By promoting trade for their own benefit, the Mongols, who had ravaged Russia and plunged it into economic depression, made possible Russia's recovery and new growth.

As Russia's cities grew, so did their need for the food produced by farmers. Since agricultural technology was essentially static, the increased demand could only be met by an increased number of tillers of the soil in the surrounding countryside. At the same time, the cities were also dependent on rural areas for immigration to sustain and increase the urban populations. Clearly, then, a demographic recovery in Russia's villages and outlying areas was a prerequisite to the urban development and prosperity of the fourteenth and fifteenth centuries.[22] Unfortunately there are no hard data to support this obvious conclusion, and indeed it flies in the face of the well-known fact that the Black Death struck Russia during this period. The growth of the cities cannot be explained by population shifts rather than demographic growth. No evidence suggests that stagnant areas suffered depopulation great enough to account for the growth in the zones of prosperity.[23] The rise of the Russian cities in spite of the undeniable demographic consequences of the plague remains a paradox.

The accepted paradigm of the medieval Russian economy as marginally viable is hard to reconcile with the evidence that Russia paid the tribute and all the other expenses of Mongol rule without starving and in fact went on to new growth. Another difficulty with the traditional view of the Russian economy, as Roublev has discovered, is that the supposedly isolated and autarchic Russian villages paid their share of the tribute in silver. Not only were these hamlets, always presumed to have had subsistence-level natural economies, producing enough of a surplus to pay the tribute, but they were exchanging the surplus for silver from outside Russia and therefore had commercial economies.[24] Indeed the Russian peasants had enough left over to buy the modest oriental goods found in many former villages.

None of this means that the cost of the Tatar yoke was not immense. Evidence from Moscow indicates just how much of a loss to the economy the annual tribute of five to seven thousand silver rubles must have been. When, in 1480, the expected annual tribute fell to only one thousand rubles, the Muscovite princes continued to collect the full amount and kept the difference. Within the next several decades Moscow brought in Italian architects and engineers and built four major cathedrals, several palaces, and new stone walls and towers for the city. Costly political programs were also undertaken; for example, Ivan III imported his bride Sofia Paleologina, niece of the last Byzantine emperor, from Rome along with her suite. Muscovite expansion cannot account for the suddenness of this increase in discretionary income, and no qualitative changes in the economy are apparent. If the tempting inference that these expenditures reflect the savings in tribute is true,[25] one can imagine what the aggregate cost of Mongol rule must have meant for the Russian economy. If Russia was able to sustain such a huge drain on its resources and even go on to new growth, the medieval Russian economy must have been far more resilient than historians have given it credit for.

Another indication of the flexibility of the Russian economy is that it survived the shocks from the Horde's internal unrest and the eventual dissolution of Mongol hegemony. After all, Russia's commerce, and hence prosperity, was closely linked with the Horde's commercial networks, and disasters on the steppe must have had significant repercussions in the Russian economy. Yet Russia seems not to have suffered severe hardships. The consequences of Tamerlane's diversion of the oriental caravan routes away from the Golden Horde were apparently less calamitous for Russia than for the Horde. Until at least the sixteenth century Muscovy remained deeply involved in oriental trade, particularly with Persia, as did Yaroslavl' and the annexed Volga khanates of Kazan' and Astrakhan'. With the collapse of the Golden Horde, the Russian merchants who had frequented Sarai seem simply to have gone to Persia, just as the Persian merchants who had always been active on the Volga came to Russia, or sent their Jewish or Armenian intermediaries. The Golden Horde was gone, but the international trade it had nourished continued.

Examining the large picture of the Tatar influence on the Russian economy during the Mongol period, we see that they brought both woe and wealth and that both were inequitably distributed. Through political dealings or accidents of geography the effects of the conquest varied from region to region. For example, while Smolensk and the Belorussian cities of Polotsk and Vitebsk escaped most of the damage of the conquest, they also, because of their locations, failed to profit significantly from the Tatars' patronage of trade. Yet Vladimir-Suzdalian *Rus'*, which bore much of the brunt of Mongol destruction and paid tribute for the longest time, also enjoyed the greatest access to the lucrative oriental trade. Even within Vladimir-Suzdalian *Rus'* different principalities suffered and prospered at different times with the changing winds of Mongol favor.

The economic hardships and benefits of the Tatar yoke were distributed as unevenly among Russia's social classes as among its regions. The peasantry, of course, suffered the most from the Mongol campaigns and slave-raiding expeditions and paid the greatest part of the tribute. Though the havoc wrought among their taxpayers hurt the aristocracy, they were also the chief beneficiaries of the commerce with the Orient. Further, the princes, as collectors of the tribute, profited handsomely through embezzlement or manipulation.

The complexity of the Mongols' effects on the Russian economy thus precludes any meaningful list of credits and debits. To calculate whether the benefits of being part of the Mongol hegemony outweighed the costs requires a balance sheet we can never fill out. Perhaps the most difficult question is whether the Russian recovery took place in spite of the Mongols or because of them. It is at least evident that Tatar sponsorship of trade had a positive effect. The Volga river, the artery most under the Golden Horde's control, gave Russia access to the continental caravan routes, and the areas of Russia that thrived were precisely those that participated in the Volga trade.[26]

Since the divergent economic influences of Mongol rule defy tabulation, and we can never know how Russia would have developed if the Mongols had not ridden westward, the opportunity cost to Russia of Mongol rule is beyond calculation. Nonetheless, there is a widespread belief that the barbarian Mongols were responsible for Russia's subsequent "backwardness" and inability to "keep up" with Europe. In fact, the very concept of Russian economic backwardness, at least in early modern Muscovy, has been challenged, and indeed, compared to other Eastern European urban groups, Moscow's merchants did not do badly.[27] Be that as it may, even if sixteenth century Muscovy was backward, the assumption that the Mongols are to blame is dubious. While the overall impact of the Mongol period on the Russian economy probably was negative, the damage was neither as uniform nor as long-lasting as has been supposed. Unquestionably, the conquest was a catastrophe, but a catastrophe need not have permanent effects. The Russian economy recovered from the devastating campaigns of 1237–1240 and survived the harsh regimen of taxation and exploitation that followed. Furthermore, by fostering international trade, especially with the Orient, the Golden Horde fostered the resurgence of the Russian economy and the subsequent growth of Russian power.

VIII

The Mongols and the Muscovite Autocracy

IN THE SIXTEENTH CENTURY, FOLLOWING THE DISINTEGRATION OF MONGOL POWER, Moscow's hereditary grand princes became autocratic rulers, stripping the other princely families of their autonomy and limited sovereign rights. With Muscovy's power in Russia by then unchallenged, the new rulers, after 1547, bore the title *tsar'*, or emperor. Conservative Russian historians of the Imperial period of the eighteenth, nineteenth, and early twentieth centuries regarded this development with approval. However, their liberal and radical contemporaries did not see the evolution of an autocratic regime as progress, and the modern Soviet attitude is somewhat ambivalent (since the autocracy, though "progressive" and historically necessary, oppressed the masses). The autocracy has found few defenders among Western scholars, particularly in the twentieth century, or among Russian emigré scholars. In any case, critics of all times and political persuasions have attributed the direction of Russian politics after the Mongol period to the Golden Horde. Certainly the Mongol influence on Muscovy's political development was immense. The Mongols played a role in Moscow's emergence as the unifying force in medieval Russia, provided some of the institutions that made Moscow strong, and influenced Moscow's imperial vision. Still, these elements alone did not determine Moscow's political future. The Mongols facilitated rather than caused the appearance of that Muscovite autocracy which endured, in one form or another, until modern times. To see how this was true, we must begin by analyzing the importance of the Golden Horde in Moscow's rise to preeminence in Russia.

At different times during the Mongol period, Moscow was both allied with and at odds with the Golden Horde, yet managed to profit from both situations. In the earlier decades of the fourteenth century, Moscow made common cause with the Tatars and gathered its strength in safety while Mongol raiders deliberately weakened rival Russian cities like Tver'. Moscow's power swelled with the influx of refugees from the ravaged lands outside of Muscovy. Then, in the later decades of that century, Moscow emerged as the leader of Russian resistance, strong enough to best Tver' again, despite that city's newly formed alliance with the Golden Horde. Donskoi's victory over Mamai at Kulikovo Field in 1380 raised Moscow's prestige to a new high. Moscow had allied itself with the Mongols when the Golden Horde was strongest and then seized more autonomy when the Horde faltered. Muscovite opportunism was unique only in its superior timing. All the other Russian principalities and Russia's neighbors sought alliances with the Tatars at one time or another. Moscow came out on top not because its princes were more ruthless or craven but because they were shrewder politicians.

Historians have not reached a consensus on precisely how the Golden Horde affected Moscow's rise to power.[1] One school argues that Moscow's ascendence was the direct result of its alliance with the Horde and the political and military support that came with it. This thesis originated in the early nineteenth century with the conservative monarchist N. Karamzin (presumably most of its subsequent adherents do not share his view of the merits of the Muscovite autocracy).[2] Another school of thought points out that Mongol policy was designed specifically to prevent the creation of a dangerous power center like Moscow. In this view, internal rather than external forces brought Moscow to the fore, where it was able to take advantage of its position as leader of Russian opposition to Tatar rule. The conservative nineteenth-century historian S. Soloviev promulgated this theory, and it is widely held today.[3]

Actually neither of these views can stand alone as an explanation for the growth of Muscovite power. If Moscow's expansion was dependent on the Horde's active intervention in Russian politics, Muscovy's boundaries should have shrunk when the Mongols weakened. Instead the expansion continued during the Mongol civil wars of the 1360s, and Moscow sustained its powerful position after the Horde fragmented in the middle of the fifteenth century. The durability of Muscovite power cannot be explained by the early years of collaboration. Moscow's ability to hold territory once acquired is a reflection of its own social, economic, and political strength. If we analyze Muscovite institutions to fathom how Moscow was able to control and administer its new domains,[4] we see that Mongol military assistance was not the cause of Muscovite power. Yet it would be a mistake to assert that the Mongols played no role in creating it. Muscovite power was based on internal strengths, but these strengths arose from Tatar influences.[5]

Roublev has argued that one of the most significant Mongol contributions to the rise of Moscow was administrative. It is probable that when Moscow assumed responsibility for collecting the tribute and delivering it to Sarai, it also borrowed the Mongols' assessment and collection apparatus. The Mongol taxation system was far more exploitative than any known in Russia before. By adopting the Tatar model the Muscovite grand princes were able to extract more revenue than ever before and integrate and exploit acquired lands to yield maximum income, and hence power. Moscow continued to collect the full amount of tribute from Russia even after they stopped passing it on to the Golden Horde.

The Muscovite grand princes replaced the Mongol *baskaki* with officials called *danshchiki* (the Russian *dan'* displaced the term *vykhod* for the Mongol tribute). Though no Russian tax collector ever bore the title *baskak*[6] (doubtless a hated word), the *danshchiki* could not have replaced the *baskaki* and done the same job unless they had the same expertise and authority. How Russian princes in other principalities collected the tribute before Moscow annexed their lands is not known. By the same line of reasoning, their tax-collection apparatus was probably also modeled on the *baskak* system and Mongol administrative practices. Hence one may speculate that a similar system for extracting revenue might have been imposed on northeastern Russia regardless of which political center finally united Vladimir-Suzdalian *Rus'*.

The Golden Horde's contribution to the rise of Moscow thus was twofold. Initially, during the heyday of the Horde's alliance with Moscow in the early fourteenth century, Tatar raids in the regions around Moscow weakened that city's rivals and augmented its population. Later, an administrative system on the Mongol model enabled Moscow to capitalize on its territorial acquisitions and consolidate its gains. Though the Mongols had sought above all to prevent the emergence of a single Russian principality strong enough to seriously annoy the Golden Horde, in the end they helped to produce one.

It would be misleading, however, to attribute Russian unification and Muscovite dominance entirely to Tatar policies and influences. The Mongols did not create the impetus for national unification in Vladimir-Suzdalia, and this goal was realized through the grand principality of Vladimir, an autochthonous political entity. Russia's essential political structure predated the conquest, and the centripetal forces that eventually brought the feuding Russian principalities together into a single state derived from the internal processes of Russian history. (It is possible that Russian unification was sped up, compared, for example, to France, because the Muscovites were able to borrow the administrative structures needed for an expanded realm rather than having to evolve them.) Moscow triumphed over its rivals because it took better advantage of the Mongol presence and used Mongol administrative techniques more effectively than other power centers such as Tver'. Examining Moscow's history, it is not possible to separate Mongol contributions from internal factors or to know whether Moscow would still have become the most powerful city in Russia, if the Tatars had never come.

Whatever the role of Mongol administrative models in the growth of Moscow's hegemony, the Muscovite autocracy of the sixteenth century relied on numerous political, military, and social institutions borrowed from the now defunct Golden Horde.[7] These included taxes and the treasury, the organization and armament of the army, bureaucratic language, diplomatic forms, the postal service, and some aspects of criminal punishment and liability. The Mongol influence on Russian society lived on.

The financial workings of the Muscovite state owed more to the Golden Horde than just the mechanisms of tribute-collection. Indeed, though minted specie coinage existed in Russia before the conquest, the Russian word for money or coinage, *den'ga*, comes from the Tatar term. The Russians also adopted the Mongol word for treasury, *kazna*, creating from it the Muscovite word *kaznachei*, treasurer. The Tatar word *tamga* referred to the Mongol customs tax, the official who collected it, and the stamped seal or statement verifying that it had been paid. The Muscovites borrowed the Mongol customs tax system and all three usages of the term *tamga.* The Russian word *tamozhnia,* or customs house, derives from *tamga* and may reflect another institutional borrowing. Whether the Mongols were responsible for bringing the abacus to Russia is not known. Taxation was the lifeblood of the Golden Horde, and as a consequence the Muscovites had a source of sophisticated models at hand when they needed them.

Since armed conflict was a common feature of Russian dealings with the Tatars, Mongol military practices were naturally familiar to the Russians. The Muscovites put this knowledge to work in defending themselves against the Mongols. The site Moscow's generals chose in 1380 for the Battle of Kulikovo Field shows their awareness of the Mongols' style of fighting essential to the survival of Russian troops. The Muscovites precluded the Tatar cavalry's favorite flanking maneuver by positioning themselves with rivers at their backs and forests on both sides.[8] The Muscovites also used their knowledge of Mongol equipment and tactics no matter who they were fighting. European travelers mistakenly identified their accoutrements as Ottoman Turkic, but sixteenth-century depictions of the typical Muscovite cavalryman show him in a Mongol saddle with Mongol stirrups, wearing a Mongol helmet, and armed with a Mongol compound bow with a Mongol quiver. In the field Mongol armies were arranged into an advance guard, a main regiment, left and right regiments, and a rear guard. Because of the superiority of the right in shamanist tradition, the right guard was ranked above the left. Muscovite armies took the field in the same formation, even to the point of having the right guard dominant.

None of this, of course, made the Muscovite cavalryman the equal of his Tatar counterpart. The nomads practically lived in the saddle, and the Russians could not equal their skill in cavalry maneuvers or using the bow from horseback. Princes of the Kievan period faced with this problem hired nomadic auxiliaries. Moscow was able to use Mongols from its client khanate of Kasimov in the same way.[9] In the sixteenth century, however, Moscow's military needs began to change. Increasingly, warfare involved the siege of Eastern European cities rather than battles between mounted archers in the steppe. Moscow began to use its Tatar contingents as scouts and field cavalry in a more western style of warfare. Although the continuing need to defend itself against Mongols from the steppe slowed Moscow's development in gunpowder warfare (Moscow's artillery was better than its handguns), eventually nomadic auxiliaries became obsolete.[10]

Both taxation and warfare were dependent on the Muscovite bureaucracy, but to what extent this was based on Tatar models is not clear.
Claims that the Muscovite bureaux, the *prikazy,* were of Mongol origin
have not been substantiated. Any borrowings would have been of models
from before the Golden Horde adopted Islam and with it the Persian
diwan system. The *diwan* was an expressly Islamic form of government,
and Moscow adopted none of its practices. The Muscovites did use
scrolls called *stolbtsy* or *stolby,* that is, documents sewn together in rolls
rather than stored in files. This custom seems to have originated in Central Asia, and may indicate bureaucratic influences from or through the
Golden Horde.[11]

It has been suggested that the language of the Muscovite bureaucracy was a kind of meta-Turkic, a hyperliteral calque of Turco-Tatar for-
mulae and forms which is often linguistically meaningless without
recourse to the Tatar originals. Supposedly Muscovite bureaucratic paper
followed Mongol formats.[12] All bureaucratic language is stylized, of
course, but there is no question of the awkwardness and obscurity of
Muscovite bureaucratic jargon. As yet the evidence that its syntactical,
morphological, and lexical features derive from Turco-Tatar models remains suggestive rather than conclusive, but the connection is worthy of
further research. Since the chancellery language of the Golden Horde
was Turkic written in Uighur script, it might be fruitful to explore the
dissemination of Uighur script among Russian scribes. Other features of
Moscow's bureaucracy may yet prove to be of Mongol origin.

Given the importance of Russia's relations with its oriental neighbors, it is natural that Muscovy drew upon Tatar diplomatic practices in
establishing its own.[13] Accordingly, Muscovite diplomatic protocol was
essentially Asian. Rulers communicated and exchanged gifts through envoys who were supported by the host country and allowed to engage in
tax-free trading to supplement their subsistence. The envoy presented
himself on his knees and left his weapons outside (a serious problem for
sword-bearing Western nobles). Negotiations were preceded by lengthy
greetings, questions about the journey and the rulers' health, and a ceremonial meal eaten without silverware. Not all the elements of the elaborate diplomatic etiquette were uniquely Asian. Still, it was sufficiently un-
European that in the sixteenth and seventeenth centuries Muscovy and
the Ottomans communicated with a facility neither could achieve in
dealing with Europeans.[14]

Communications within Russia after the Mongol period also depended on Tatar models. The Mongol postal system, or *yam,* was the fastest communications system across the Eurasian continent that had ever been known. It was not surpassed until the development of modern technology. Essentially the *yam* was a network of stations and horses and riders linking all corners of the Mongol Empire. It carried not only news and messages but also officials and ambassadors, all at the expense of the state.[15] The Mongols established the *yam* in all the countries they conquered, but because of Chinese record-keeping traditions it is best known in China, where it developed into a huge bureaucracy. In China, as elsewhere, the Mongols adapted the *yam* to local conditions, using runners in terrain unsuited to horses.[16] In Russia in the late fifteenth century the *yam* ceased to function as the Great Horde became unable to maintain a bureaucracy. To manage its holdings, Moscow needed a postal system of its own. Since the Russian peasantry had already paid a special *yam* tax for centuries, this was simply transformed into an obligation to provide horses and supplies for a Russian system on the Mongol model.[17] This network served Moscow as effectively as it had the Mongols.

One sector of the Golden Horde's social order could not be of help to the developing Muscovite state. Before the Horde's conversion to Islam in the early fourteenth century, its legal system was Mongol customary law, the traditional nomadic laws codified, allegedly by Chingis Khan, in the *Yasa.* After the Golden Horde became an Islamic federation, it obeyed the *Shar'iat,* Muslim religious law. Neither of these had any future in a sedentary, Christian state. Nomadic custom was irrelevant and Islamic law sacrilegious. There is a possibility that the Mongols did influence medieval Russian concepts of legal liability. The practice of *poruka,* collective responsibility for the behavior of members of a sworn group, became more common in Russia during the Mongol period, perhaps because the Mongols used the idea of collective responsibility widely.[18] The Tatars may also have brought from China the practice of beating on the shins. In Russia this punishment *(pravezh)* was the penalty for nonpayment of debts. Since this peculiar punishment appeared in Russia during the Mongol period and is not widespread in the world, the Tatars may have transmitted it. It is also possible that Russians who visited China in Mongol service brought it back with them.[19]

Capital punishment also appeared in Russia for the first time after the conquest, but it is extremely doubtful that Russia adopted it from the Golden Horde. Execution was commonplace among peoples with whom the Russians had already had extensive contacts. The custom could have entered Russia from the German Hanseatic cities through Novgorod and Pskov or from Byzantium, where it was also standard practice. Capital punishment appears frequently in Russian translations of Byzantine secular and canon law in such miscellaneous collections as the *Kormchaia kniga* (Pilot's Book). There is also a chance that it arose in Russia through internal evolution.[20] Some have claimed that harsher criminal penalties like capital punishment became necessary to maintain civil order because the rigors of Mongol rule produced a crime wave. In fact, the impression of increased violence under the Tatar yoke reflects the relative number of records surviving from the Kievan and Mongol eras.[21]

One final aspect of the Golden Horde's social and governmental apparatus that might have been expected to leave traces in the new Muscovite state was the census. Muscovite officials could hardly have been unaware of the advantages of a Mongol-style universal enumeration of the population. Yet as it turns out, Muscovite cadastres and censuses from the end of the fifteenth century show nothing in common with Mongol census practice. It is possible that Muscovy simply lacked the necessary bureaucratic resources for such an undertaking. On the other hand, the Muscovite elite may have rejected the idea of an institution which did not discriminate between the aristocracy and the peasantry (in Russia only the thirteenth-century clergy had been exempt from the Mongol census).[22] The British historian D. Obolensky suggested that Russians, like other Orthodox Slavs, did not adopt the Roman-Byzantine principle of granting all citizens equality before the law because the aristocracy rejected any form of egalitarianism.[23] The same feelings may have prejudiced Moscow's aristocrats against any census in the Tatar mold.

Nearly all of the evidence of the many Mongol forms the Muscovites did find useful in building their state comes from the late fifteenth and sixteenth centuries. Paradoxically, the institutions Muscovy borrowed were characteristic less of the Golden Horde proper than of the world Mongol Empire of the thirteenth century. Probably for religious reasons, the Muscovites never adopted any of the models that arose in the Golden Horde through the influence of the Muslim Near East. The demonstrable superiority of the *diwan* to the chaotic *prikazy* of Muscovy was not enough to overcome the religious barrier. Thus when the Muscovites began adopting Mongol institutions near the end of the fifteenth century, they included ones no longer used by the Mongols of the Golden Horde. How Moscow was able to revive some of these complex obsolete practices is not known.[24] It is possible, of course, that Russians were using these systems earlier but without leaving traces in the surviving records. However, it is safer to argue that Muscovy would not have implemented a full-scale administrative bureaucracy until the unification of the Russian lands created the need for one. As the Muscovite autocracy took control of Russia, it turned to the Mongol legacy for inspiration as it improved and expanded its bureaucratic apparatus.

The Muscovite state, though it depended heavily on institutions borrowed from the Tatars, did not come to resemble a Mongol state. Russian society, after all, was Christian and agricultural. The Russian sense of identity is apparent in the importance of religion in determining which institutions might be made to serve Russian needs and which could not be drawn upon. Predictably, Russian sources never acknowledge the origin of the many governmental structures they did adopt from the Tatars. This would have been inconsistent with Muscovy's self-image as an Orthodox Christian state and out of keeping with the literary etiquette that treated Mongols exclusively as deadly religious foes without any possible redeeming merits. Pragmatism moved the Muscovites to use Mongol models as needed, but their commitment to them was not open-ended. Eventually the time came when those forms no longer suited Russian needs, and they were abandoned.

We have seen that the Mongols were both directly and indirectly involved in Muscovy's becoming the most powerful Russian principality and that the Muscovite autocracy that developed in the sixteenth century relied on many institutions inherited from its former overlords. None of this is to say that this Mongol influence brought autocratic rule to Russia. A centralized bureaucracy does not require a monarch with absolute power or indeed any monarch at all. The Mongol forms were effective tools for the autocracy but not the reason for its existence. Nonetheless, some historians have argued that the Tatars had specific effects on Russian society that did lead directly to the establishment of a Russian autocracy.

One of these theories holds that the Mongols brought absolutism to Russia by removing the two major obstacles to it, the *veche,* or democratic town meeting, and the social power base of the *boyarstvo,* the Russian nobility. Karamzin was the first to propose that the Tatars did away with the *veche* because of its role in Russian resistance, and that the Russian princes, who also found it a nuisance, voluntarily collaborated. Just how democratic the Kievan *veche* was is open to question,[25] but be that as it may, the *veche* as such does not seem to have been a threat to the Golden Horde. The Tatars punished the *veche* uprisings in Rostov in 1289 and Nizhnii Novgorod in 1305 and the 1327 Tver' rebellion, but not the *veche* expulsions of Muslim tax-farmers from the northeastern Russian cities in 1262. The *veche* in Novgorod flourished during the centuries of the Tatar yoke because, despite the trouble over the census in 1259, it never challenged Mongol authority. The Golden Horde acted decisively when problems arose, but did not interfere in domestic Russian politics when their own interests were not affected. There is no evidence that the Mongols found the *veche* as an institution a danger.[26]

Little is known of the history of the *veche* outside of Novgorod during the Mongol era. But while *veche* meetings do not seem to have been common, the concept did not disappear. When Tokhtamysh threatened Moscow in 1382 while Donskoi was away gathering troops, a *veche* was convened to see to the defense of the city. It was apparently still a viable institution in Vladimir-Suzdalian *Rus'* after a century and a half of Mongol rule. How and when the *veche* finally fell into disuse is unknown, but it was not the result of any deliberate Tatar policy.[27]

Karamzin also believed that the Golden Horde paved the way to autocratic rule in Muscovy by breaking the power of the Russian nobility *(boyarstvo)*. In fact the Mongols clearly did nothing to restrict the privileges or influence of the Russian aristocracy. The Muscovite nobility in the fifteenth century formed a small elite group of largely interrelated and intermarried families who monopolized, sometimes on a hereditary basis, the highest offices of government. Indeed, this has been described as something of a Golden Age for the *boyarstvo*.[28] Whether or not the nobility were one of the obstacles to the development of the Muscovite autocracy, their power was not crippled by the Golden Horde.

A vaguer and more pervasive theory blames Muscovite autocracy on the example set by the Tatars. This view holds that the absolute and arbitrary nature of Mongol rule had a debilitating effect on Russian political morality, inculcating expectations of naked power and utter subservience in the elite and the masses respectively. The result was a political culture conducive to autocratic rule. These attitudes survived the passing of the Golden Horde as Muscovy's autocrats assumed the manner of Mongol khans, and the Russian people obeyed the new "khans" with the same servility.[29] This theory of the Mongol influence on Russian behavior is explicit in Harrison Salisbury's remark that modern-day Russia "still struggles against the legacy of backwardness, ignorance, servility, submissiveness, deceit, cruelty, oppression and lies imposed by the terrible Mongols."[30]

The assumption that Russians learned wickedness from the Tatars is predicated on a rather generous vision of Russian behavior in the Kievan period. Sviatopolk's murder of his brothers Boris and Gleb, the blinding of Vasil'ko, the sack of Kiev in 1169 by Andrei Bogoliubskii, and many other examples indicate that the Riurikid princes indulged in unsavory practices long before the Mongols were around to teach them how. As for the alleged submissiveness of the common people, the recurrent urban uprisings suggest that the Mongols did not succeed in breaking the spirit of the Russian masses.

This theory also presumes that the Mongols' political behavior was significantly more heinous than that of other medieval cultures that might otherwise have influenced Russian conduct. Yet the French crusaders showed the meaning of European chivalry to the Albigensians, the Jews on the Rhine, the Muslims of Jerusalem, and the inhabitants of Constantinople. Byzantine and Chinese emperors were no less cruel and devious than the Tatar khans. Nor was Machiavelli, that early product of the slightly more fastidious Renaissance, a Mongol. Though the Tatars were vilified by their enemies, their behavior was in accordance with the standards of the age.

Thus the Muscovite autocracy did not arise because of a political morality acquired from the Mongols, uniquely conducive to absolutism. The Mongols did not destroy the institutional and social obstacles that would have prevented the emergence of an autocratic regime in Russia's most powerful principality. Another claim, that the autocracy arose from the need to overthrow the Golden Horde, is hard to credit, since the first signs of autocratic rule do not appear in Muscovy until after the Horde was dissolved.[31] The Mongol influence on Muscovite governmental forms was immense, and the borrowed Mongol institutions contributed much to the power and efficiency of the Muscovite state, but the Golden Horde neither directly nor indirectly determined how those models were used. Autocracy evolved in medieval Russia, as in most of medieval and early modern Europe, as the result of internal processes.

Muscovy's conception of an Orthodox Christian Empire naturally came from Byzantium, and the ideology of the medieval Russian autocracy was, in its theories and symbols, overwhelmingly Byzantine. Nonetheless, Michael Cherniavsky showed that the Muscovites also drew upon the Mongol imperial tradition, adopting and adapting it for their own uses.[32] The following discussion owes much to Cherniavsky's ideas.

Before the Mongol conquest, the only imperial ruler in Russian experience was the Byzantine emperor, the basileus. After the conquest the Tatar khan dwelt in the steppe, and the Russians referred to this monarch, too, as the *tsar'*. They applied this terminology consistently, referring to the khan's wife as the *tsaritsa,* and to Chingisid heirs as *tsarevichi.* (Familiar with the workings of Mongol succession, the Russians never referred to anyone not of the Golden Kin as more than a *kniaz',* prince.) The khan was not called *tsar'* out of ignorance. The term khan, in the form *kagan,* was familiar from Kievan times.[33] Narratives of the battle on the Kalka river, *sub anno* 1223, refer to "Chingiz kan," with *kan* as part of the personal name.[34] Records of princes' journeys to Karakorum refer to that city as "Kanovi," "Kanovich," or "Kanovichi," all Russianized derivatives of *kan.*[35] (The bookmen could not call Karakorum "Tsar'grad," city of the *tsar',* since that was already the name of Constantinople, city of the other *tsar'.*) Russian derivatives of *kan* also appear in the *vita* of Mikhail of Chernigov[36] and in the Galician-Volhynian chronicle.[37] Nonetheless, the usage of *tsar'* for khan was so thoroughly entrenched by the time the Mongols' *yarliki* to Russian metropolitans were translated into Russian, probably in the late fourteenth century, that even Chingiz kan was rendered Chingis tsar'.[38]

Not only were the khan and the basileus subsumed under a common title, but the images of the two different *tsars* became mingled. In the dyptychs (commemorative lists) the khan is accorded the liturgical prerogatives of the basileus. Pictures of the khan even portray him in the regalia of the Byzantine emperor. Using the same title for the khan and the basileus, with the concomitant blurring of the distinctions between them, implicitly accorded the infidel khan the same legitimacy as the Christian emperor. This helped lead to the limited but significant use of the Mongol imperial tradition apparent in the writings of Moscow's bookmen and the political pretensions of her autocrats.

The Muscovite bookmen of the Kulikovo era consistently manipulated the Chingisid principle for their own purposes. This precept, the overriding factor in Mongol politics, was that khans could only come from among the Golden Kin, the direct descendents of Chingis Khan. The Russians were acutely aware of this essential feature of their rulers' politics. In the tale of the battle on the river Vozha in 1378, the author attacks emir Mamai, who was not a Chingisid, for ruling the Horde illegitimately and dishonoring the *tsar'*. The "Chronicle Tale" of 1380, in the same vein, accuses Mamai of usurping the title khan *(tsar')*. This was untrue and the Muscovites knew it; Mamai used a Chingisid puppet-khan. At the conclusion of this tale the true Chingisid Tokhtamysh defeats Mamai and informs the Russians that he has triumphed over their mutual foe. This obvious ploy depended on a mutual perception of Mamai as a usurper. The tale of Tamerlane's attack on Russia, *sub anno* 1395, accuses him too of trying to usurp the title *tsar'*, though not one of the Golden Kin.

Muscovite writers used the Chingisid principle not only as ammunition for attacks on Russia's enemies but to justify Russian actions. After Tokhtamysh sacked Moscow in 1382, the bookmen sought to explain Donskoi's timely absence as an act of respect for Chingisid legitimacy. Thus Donskoi, who had met and defeated the usurper Mamai in battle, did not want to "raise his hand" against the true *tsar'* Tokhtamysh, or left Moscow when he learned that the "tsar' himself" was riding against the city. Actually strategic considerations rather than legitimist qualms motivated the departure. Once the Mongols arrive at the city, Horde dignitaries trick the inhabitants into opening the gates by invoking an image of the khan consistent with the *philanthropia,* the divine lovingkindness, of the Byzantine basileus.

The chronicles recount emir Edigei's siege of Moscow without castigating him as an usurper, but with considerable attention to Chingisid details. Edigei has the *tsar's* permission to attack; four *tsarevichi* serve in his army; he abandons the siege to defend the *tsar'* against a coup d'état at Sarai. The Muscovite writings from the Kulikovo era show a remarkable concern for the Chingisid principle considering that from the Orthodox Christian point of view all infidel rulers were equally illegitimate. Moscow's bookmen were thoroughly familiar with the ramifications of Mongol succession and used them imaginatively for a variety of ideological purposes.[39]

It is perhaps not surprising that the ideologues of a major Russian city that had constant dealings with the Golden Horde should concern themselves so seriously with the Chingisid principle. However, there is evidence to suggest that this awareness permeated Russia to a much greater degree. This appears in the *vita* of Peter, a *tsarevich* of the Horde who converted to Christianity. The line of Chingisid descent is traced carefully through four generations of Peter's descendents, and the bonds of Chingisid origin are decisive in the plot.[40] This text from the fourteenth century was written in a provincial monastery in the political backwater of Rostov. Appreciation of the special importance of the Golden Kin seems to have been widespread.

Russian consciousness of the Chingisid principle is of interest because after the overthrow of the Great Horde in 1480, Moscow's grand princes, despite the thoroughly Byzantine cast of Muscovite ideology, played upon their status as the conquerors, and hence the successors, of the Horde khans. Cherniavsky's imaginative interpretation of the imagery on a coin minted in honor of the Stand on the Ugra River illustrates this stance. One side of the coin shows a mounted hero, probably St. George. The other has, in place of the name of the Mongol khan, Ivan III's name in Arabic. The symbolism of the coin suggests that it commemorates not a liberation, but one dynasty succeeding another, as the House of Moscow replaces the Golden Kin.

Moscow continued to propagate this aspect of its imperial status for several centuries. In the sixteenth century Muscovy justified its imperial claims to European powers by invoking its conquest of the khanates of Kazan' and Astrakhan'. As late as the seventeenth century, the emigré Muscovite bureaucrat Gregorii Kotoshikhin explained that the ruler of Muscovy was a *tsar'* by virtue of Ivan IV's conquest of Kazan'. It is even possible that the system of icons and frescos in the Archangel cathedral of the Kremlin was inspired by the concept of the Chingisid clan.[41]

There were practical advantages as well to having the Muscovite *tsar'* considered as the heir to the khans of the Golden Horde. For example, as *belii tsar'* (White Tsar), the Muscovite ruler was entitled to the *yasak,* the fur tribute, from the nomadic and sedentary Inner Asian tribes formerly ruled by the Golden Horde. Thus it was profitable for Muscovy to foster its image as the successor state to the Golden Horde and to remain sensitive to steppe traditions of rule.

Comparison of the Mongol legacy in Russia with that in China and Persia reveals a curious paradox. At first glance it would seem that both the Chinese and the Persians assimilated the Chingisid tradition more thoroughly than the Russians. The Chinese retained the "Secret History of the Mongols," with its detailed history of the Chingisid clan, as the basis for their own dynastic histories. The Persian historian Juwaini also recorded a version of the "Secret History" and paid meticulous attention to genealogical questions in his account of the career of Chingis Khan. Nothing of the kind entered Russian literature. Medieval Russian historical writing could not adopt a text like the "Secret History" which was an obviously infidel work. In any case, it would never have fit into the

Russian annalistic format. Yet in Russia the status of the Golden Kin remained high for centuries after the end of Tatar rule, whereas in China and Persia respect for Chingisids largely evaporated once the Mongol dynasties were overthrown. Indeed, even among some Inner Asian nomads the importance of the Golden Kin faded quickly with the collapse of Mongol hegemony. In Russia, remarkably, respect for the Chingisid principle was as well established as among those nomadic peoples who had become incorporated into the Mongol Empire. Ivan IV even abdicated in favor of a Chingisid, Symeon Bekbulatovich, in 1575–1576, and Chingisid descent remained important in Russia until the seventeenth century and Peter the Great's westernization.[42] Members of the Golden Kin could still demand noble status in the Russian Empire as late as the nineteenth century. The Chingisid principle was kept alive in Russia at least in part because the Muscovite *tsars* had assumed the mantle of the khans.

Needless to say, while the use of the Mongol imperial tradition by Moscow's bookmen and *tsars* solved some problems, it created others. Useful as the Chingisid principle was for justifying Russian actions and defaming enemies, it constituted a de facto recognition of the legitimacy of Mongol rule and revealed an unseemly appreciation of infidel ideology. As a consequence, the Muscovite authors' recognition of their own practice is clouded. There was a profound difference, however, between this ideological misdemeanor, openly engaged in but not analyzed, and the idea of a Christian emperor claiming legitimacy as the heir of the khans of the Golden Horde. The latter, made explicit, amounted to a betrayal of Russian Orthodox Christianity and the very concept of a Christian Empire, embodied in the Byzantine trappings, ceremonial, and idiom of the Muscovite court. Hence, despite the evident use the Muscovite autocrats made of the Mongol imperial tradition and the idea of Muscovy as the successor state of the Golden Horde, it is hardly ever referred to in contemporary sources.[43]

There is, of course, a second and even greater paradox, the question of how the Russians could have so thoroughly assimilated the Mongol imperial tradition when Russia's bookmen had not addressed intellectually the fact of their own conquest. The answer lies, at least in part, in the nature of the Tatars' administration of Russia. When writing history Russian intellectuals were able to pretend that Russia was still independent because the Russian princes continued to sit on Russia's thrones and Tatars were seen only intermittently in the Russian forests. Damage from

Mongol raiding parties was evidence only of attacks, not of alien rule. Physical reminders of the true political situation were few.

The bookmen knew better, of course. They were among the elite, the princes, nobles, and ecclesiastics, who commonly visited Sarai and dealt with Mongol officials and rulers. Facing Russia's Tatar monarch in person amid the imperial splendor of the Golden Horde, Russia's political elite felt directly the impact of the Mongol imperial tradition and realized its possibilities. When the Russian princes incorporated the Chingisid principle into their own political ideology, the bookmen who were their spokesmen preferred to leave missing the link between Russian acceptance of Chingisid dynasticism and Mongol sovereignty. The Russian elite found this contradictory stance both viable and beneficial.

The imprint of this heritage on the Muscovite autocracy was not indelible, though it lasted some time. It was useful diplomatically in the sixteenth century for Muscovy to defer to the Chingisid principle in its dealings with the Kazan' and Astrakhan' khanates, the Nogai Tatars, and the client khanate of Kasimov. Even after Moscow annexed Kazan' and Astrakhan', which correspondingly decreased the importance of Kasimov, it still had to contend with the Crimean khanate, which remained a powerful factor in Russian and Eastern European politics despite its status as an Ottoman protectorate. Through the seventeenth century Moscow continued to play upon its tentative status as the Horde's successor in dealings with Inner Asian peoples, and, less often, European powers, although, of course, Muscovy could hardly assert any Chingisid-type claims in its contacts with genuine Chingisid khans in the sixteenth or seventeenth centuries. Eventually, in the seventeenth and eighteenth centuries, even the Crimea declined, as its integrity was subverted by the Ottomans. As Russia's military superiority over all the nomads of the Eurasian steppe became absolute, Russian concern with steppe traditions and principles dwindled. Russia needed neither to invoke its claims as the Horde's successor nor to maintain any expertise in the Chingisid lineages of its neighbors. Westernization all but eliminated Russia's interest in the Golden Kin. Imperial Russian colonial administrators of the eighteenth century manipulated nomadic confederations without regard for the traditional framework of Russian relations with the steppe.

The Muscovite autocracy that arose in the sixteenth century was greatly indebted to its former Tatar overlords, both for Moscow's rise to preeminence and for much of the governmental apparatus that made the autocracy strong. Yet the Tatars had little to do with the movement toward national unification in Russia or with the autocratic character of the Muscovite regime. Absolutism in Russia arose from domestic considerations, and drew its theory and symbolic manifestations from Byzantium rather than Sarai. Still, just as Moscow availed itself of Mongol institutions, Muscovite autocrats made the Mongol imperial tradition serve their purposes. Since Muscovy could not present itself as a new khanate in the Chingisid mold without undercutting its Christian ideology, this stance was rarely made explicit. Christianity determined the fate of Tatar institutions in the Muscovite state, screening out the Islamic forms of the Golden Horde and constraining Moscow's role as the Golden Horde's successor state. Because of the Orthodox Christian foundations of Russian society, Muscovite borrowing of Mongol political forms was significant but not wholesale, with profound but not permanent effects on Russian history.

IX

The Mongols
and Russian Society

HISTORIANS HAVE USUALLY TAKEN THE RUSSIAN BOOKMEN AT THEIR WORD AND accepted their picture of the Tatars as an alien race, whose ways the Russians neither understood nor wished to understand. On religious grounds alone, the Mongols were hateful as infidels, and on top of this they had plundered and burned the Russian cities, ravaged the Russian countryside, and then stayed on as Russia's overlords. Russian writers of the age naturally heaped abuse on their conquerors, using hostile epithets when discussing them as a matter of course and as a matter of duty. In this literary atmosphere of religious and political hatred, any expressed familiarity with the Tatars and Tatar customs carried a suggestion of both blasphemy and treason. Yet for three centuries the Mongols were an integral, unavoidable fact of Russian existence, and Russians, whether they wanted to or not, became intimately familiar with them, both as individuals and as a society. Despite the heavy emphasis in the sources on military encounters, contacts between the two peoples took a variety of forms, including diplomacy, trade, and even intermarriage. Orthodox Christianity dictated that the only proper context in which Russian and Tatar could meet was mortal combat, but the exigencies of real life dictated otherwise. As a consequence, it would be a mistake, when considering the Mongol impact on Russian society and social history, to accept at face value, as many have done, the medieval Russian writers' literary pose.

One of the most immediately apparent indications that the Russian bookmen knew the Mongols better than they were willing to admit is that they not only call the Tatars names, they call them by name. The records name virtually every Tatar prince, grandee, and official with whom the Russians dealt, and the chronicles are replete with the names of military commanders, envoys, and courtiers. The Galician-Volhynian chronicle, for example, in its account of the 1240 sack of Kiev, records the words of Tovrul, a captured informant. He identifies the captains of the Mongol host besieging the city as Urdu, Baidar, Birui, Bechak, Mengu, Kuyuk, Sebedia (Subudai) *bogatyr'*, Burundai *bogatyr'*, and of course Batu.[1] The sources record the genealogy or at least Chingisid status of every khan and emir. One incomplete list of the khans of the Golden Horde *(ordyns- kie tsari)* runs: Batii Sain, Sartak, Berke, Mengu-temer, Nogai, Telebuga, Tokhta, Ozbiak, Zhenebek, Berdebek, Kuplia, Navrus, Khidyr, Timur- Khozia (the last four are ephemeral khans of the civil war period), *u* Mamae Avdula (emir Mamai's puppet-khan Abdul outside Sarai), Umurat (in Sarai at that time), Azia (another of Mamai's puppets), Mamak Saltan, Takhtamysh, Temir-Aksak, Temir-Kutlui, Shadibek, Bulat-Saltan, and Zedi-Saltan, to which should be added Ulu-Mehmed and Akhmed.[2] The Russian chronicles contain more details about the careers of the transient khans during the "Great Troubles" of the late fourteenth century than the Arabo-Persian sources.[3]

The lists of monarchs are less remarkable than the innumerable refer- ences by name to Mongols of lesser rank. It is evident from the matter-of- fact way the names are used that the chroniclers expected their elite Russian audiences to be familiar with these Tatars and their individual attributes. Many Russians were probably also familiar with the Tatar lan- guage and the geography of the Horde's lands.[4] In this and other ways, despite the pervasive hostility to the Mongols that characterizes the Rus- sian sources, the medieval chronicles, tales, and documents themselves betray considerable familiarity with Russia's oppressors. Impressive amounts of information about the Tatars have survived in contemporary sources, which of course represent only a portion of the original material. Clearly, the Russian bookmen's posturing notwithstanding, the Mongols were anything but an unknown and unknowable people. The Tatars, as an abstraction, were loathed on principle, but to the Russian elite their

Tatar counterparts were far from being nameless, faceless enemies. Indeed, Russian aristocrats were probably more familiar with the higher levels of Mongol society than with the society of the Russian peasantry. The Mongol presence did not alter Russian social structure,[5] yet it strongly influenced Russian social life during the Mongol period, which was lengthy. Recognizing that the medieval Russian bookmen, adhering to the ideology of silence, did their best to misrepresent the Tatar role in Russian society is the first step toward determining what that role actually was.

The Mongol impact on Russian society was enormously different at different social levels. The great bulk of the Russian population, the peasantry, had far less contact with the Mongols than did the aristocracy, and what contacts they did have were probably uniformly very unpleasant. Apart from suffering Mongol attacks, the Russian peasants' only contacts with the Tatars would have been as slaves or forced labor. Russians exposed to Tatar society in this way would have been unlikely to adopt Tatar folk customs and introduce them into the Russian countryside, so it is not surprising that no Russian folk customs appear to have originated in the steppe.[6] Doubtless the lot of the Russian peasant worsened as a result of the heavier taxation that began, but did not end, with the Mongol period. The increase in the wealth and influence of the Russian Orthodox Church under the Tatar aegis and the accompanying spread of Christianity in rural Russia must also have affected peasant life.

On the reaction of the Russian "people" to the Tatar yoke, two schools of thought prevail. One group of historians argues that the Mongol invasions traumatized and scarred the collective consciousness of the masses.[7] They present as evidence texts like the sermons of Serapion of Vladimir, which bewail the horror of the invasions and the wretched state of the Russian people since. Not only were the experiences of the elite not those of the peasantry, but these lamentations are couched in Christian rhetoric which would have been irrelevant, possibly incomprehensible, in the Russian countryside, still largely pagan in the thirteenth century. We cannot assume that such texts reflect either the experiences or the responses of peasants.

Adherents of the other school take a more optimistic view, contending that the Russian people never lost hope of eventual liberation and citing the Russian folk epics (byliny) as proof of enduring Russian courage and love of freedom.[8] Unfortunately their evidence is subject to the same objections as before. The byliny very probably originated among the aristocracy, and have as little to do with the real responses of the Russian masses as the aristocratic lamentations.[9] Even if this were not the case, the *byliny* have evolved into the realm of fantasy. In them, allegory and symbolism have transformed the Tatars into mythical beast-men who always fall before Russian heroes. According to the *byliny,* the Mongol siege of Kiev failed. These tales may have warmed Russian hearts on cold winter nights, but the creative process has distorted any historical *realia* beyond the reach of historical analysis.[10]

Both conclusions about the Mongol impact on peasant society, besides resting on shaky arguments and missing data, make the fallacious assumption that there was even such a thing as the "Russian people" during the Mongol period. With no Russian nation existing in the Middle Ages,[11] there could be no cohesive national response. Aristocratic Russians did indeed respond uniformly to Tatar rule, but we cannot assume that the same was true of the common people in different parts of the Russian forest zone. In any case, neither argument addresses the question of the social aftermath of the conquest among Russian peasants more seriously than to conjecture about their morale. There is no evidence to go further.

The Russians who had direct social contact with the Mongols were of the upper classes: rulers, nobles, officials, ecclesiastics, and merchants. Any of them who spent time in the Horde learned perforce the rules of Mongol etiquette. None, for example, would ever have stepped on the threshold of a Tatar tent (at least not more than once). For the Russian princes in particular, a detailed knowledge of Tatar ways was an absolute prerequisite to survival and success. Honoring infidel customs may have been a trial for Russian Christians, but they had little choice. Breaches of courtesy or custom could have fatal consequences. However, though a certain number of Russians thus became proficient in Mongol etiquette and well-versed in the workings of Mongol society, the cosmopolitanism they acquired had no place at home. As Vasilii II learned to his sorrow, any perceived partiality for Tatars or Tatar ways could be dangerous. Similarly, Mongols who immigrated to Russia had to shed their Tatar customs as they entered the forests. Orthodox Christianity screened out Mongol influences from Russian society, so that the forced social accommodation of the upper classes left no permanent effects.

To say that the Russian aristocracy adopted no Mongol social customs is not to deny that the Mongols were a major factor in their social history. To get an idea of the variety and complexity of both the social intercourse between the two peoples and Russian perceptions of the Tatars we must turn in part to the monuments of old Russian literature in the discussions that follow. There are, of course, methodological objections to literary evidence for social history which can neither be dismissed nor adequately resolved here. The historian must make allowances for genre and tendentiousness, for literary aesthetic and political bias. Even the extended narrative "tales" incorporated in the Russian chronicles are literary enough to be unreliable. Nonetheless, the concept of fiction did not exist in medieval Russia; all the works of Old Russian literature were meant to be taken literally. Thus, while we cannot take the episodes in literary works at face value, we can at least be assured that they were considered credible by their aristocratic audiences, within the range of conceivable situations and actions. This in itself provides valuable information for social history.

Old Russian literary texts from the Tatar period are naturally littered with battles and atrocities, but though the torture of Mikhail of Chernigov or the 1382 sack of Moscow are dramatic and pathetic human events and though death and destruction were commonplaces of the time, these accounts are not germane to our interests here. The horrors of the Mongol conquest and subsequent oppression have been amply dwelt upon. Through the occasional breaches in the ideology of silence in the form of tales and documents, with the aid of other standard historical sources, we can catch glimpses of other dimensions of Russo-Tatar relations.

Even in accounts of warfare recognition that the Mongols were not always beasts can show through. The "Tale of the Destruction of Riazan' by Batu" *(Povest' o razorenii Riazani Batyem)* contains a story, usually considered of oral, folkloric origin, about the Russian noble Evpatii. Following the sack of Riazan', Evpatii gathers his retinue and launches a ferocious but hopeless attack on Batu's forces. Frightened and amazed, Batu interrogates several of Evpatii's men who have been wounded and captured. Instead of begging for mercy, they tell Batu they have come to honor him (a traditional metaphor for doing battle). Impressed, Batu summons his counselors and declares that among all the hordes and warriors he has fought, he has never seen such bravery. He resolves to take Evpatii alive, sending out his own brother-in-law as his champion, but this plan fails when Evpatii hews the man in two. The Tatars eventually resort to using catapults, finally knocking the Russian from the saddle, mortally wounded. In spite of the havoc Evpatii has wrought, Batu's admiration for him is so great that he allows the surviving members of the hero's retinue to carry him off the field that he may die with honor. Batu's respect for his enemy falls in the tradition of mutual understanding among military men common along the medieval frontier. This story probably contains only the tiniest grain of truth, but it shows that Russians did consider it plausible that a Tatar might exhibit chivalric courtesy.[12]

The epic *Zadonshchina* about the Battle of Kulikovo Field[13] presents the same picture of chivalric behavior between warring Russians and Mongols as the Evpatii episode but goes a step further. Here, far from being the devils of the standard accounts, the beaten Mongol troops lament that they will never again kiss their wives or fondle their children. When the defeated Mamai seeks refuge with the Genoese at Kaffa, they taunt him, telling him that since he has lost all his men and horses, he must winter in the steppe alone. The Russians obviously knew that this was tantamount to a death sentence.[14] The *Zadonshchina* shows the humanity of the Tatar troops and expresses genuine sympathy for a grief that Russian and Tatar alike could understand. It recognizes the pathos of even the hated Mamai being driven into the steppe, dishonored and forlorn.

Nor were all military interactions between the two societies hostile. Military alliances between the Mongols and various Russian principalities were a constant feature of Russian politics in the Mongol period. We can have no idea of what the Russian nobles fighting side by side with Mongol contingents thought of their infidel allies, but several surviving documents associated with the Moscow-Kasimov relationship suggest the ambience of such alliances. Though this alliance came after the Golden Horde's heyday, it probably resembles earlier ones in many respects, though by this time the balance of power had changed, with the Russians the stronger party.

The Kasimov Tatars were in fact the vassals of the Muscovite grand prince, and Kasimov *tsarevichi* were assigned Russian cities and districts, called *kormlenie* (feedings), for their sustenance. *Kormlenie* were normally equivalent to governorships, but these grants were for revenue only, since no Muslim could be awarded the administration of an Orthodox Christian population. The *tsarevichi* were expected to live elsewhere. A surviving grant of a city in *kormlenie,* Serpukhov, contains rigid provisions protecting the rights of the Russian citizenry from Mongol *tsarevichi, ulany, mirzas,* and princes.[15]

The Kasimov Tatars served the Muscovite state primarily as nomadic auxiliary troops. In an oath, or *shert'* (the Turco-Tatar term), made to

Vasilii III, Abd-ul-latif of Kasimov swore to serve the grand prince loyally and to refrain from robbing or killing Mongol envoys (presumably from Kasimov's enemies Kazan' and the Crimea) or any merchants traveling among the various hordes or to take prisoners (presumably for ransom or as hostages) or commit other crimes. He also swore not to abuse the Muscovite *yam* by using it for anyone except his envoys, to accept as servitors only Tatars from the four leading clans (the Shirins, Baryns, Argyns, and Kipchaks), not to make war on Kazan' without permission, and to remain in his assigned Yur'ev (i.e., Gorodets, Kasimov) unless authorized to leave.[16] The Kasimov Tatars were Russia's allies and servitors but had to be handled with due caution. This sixteenth-century contract from the years when Mongol power was greatly in decline reflects conditions different from those of the Mongol period proper, but its specific prohibitions are clearly a list of the kinds of breakdowns in cooperation that had occurred in earlier alliances between Russians and Mongols.

The *vita* of prince Fedor Rostislavovich of Smolensk and Yaroslavl' and his two sons shows military cooperation growing thoroughly intertwined with personal relationships. The account of Fedor's adventures was written in the late fifteenth century when his wonder-working relics were discovered and survives in several sixteenth-century redactions.[17] According to this story, the handsome Fedor dwelt in the Horde at khan Mengu-Timur's right hand as his cup-bearer. Struck by his beauty, the khansha resolves to have him as a son-in-law. The khan and Fedor both refuse, the khan because Fedor is an *ulusnik* and a *sluzhebnik* (servitor), Fedor because he already has a wife and son in Russia. When news arrives that Fedor's wife has died he asks and is refused permission to return to Russia to look after his patrimony. The khan does consent, however, to Fedor's marriage to a converted Chingisid princess who has taken the name of *tsaritsa* Anna,[18] and the khansha's wishes are gratified. Mengu-Timur treats his new son-in-law with great honor *(tsarska chest')* and gives him thirty-six cities to rule.[19] Eventually Fedor learns that his son Mikhailo by his first wife has died, leaving Yaroslavl' without a ruler. This time the khan allows Fedor to go to Russia along with his two sons by his Tatar wife and sends Mongol regiments with him to coerce the reluctant inhabitants of Yaroslavl' to admit their prince. Fedor and Mengu-Timur have taken pains to assure that the Tatar troops do not harm Fedor's coreligionists, and they leave the city peacefully after reinstalling Fedor on his throne. Fedor rules in tranquility for the rest of his days. In the world of this tale, Mongols and Russians can not only look after each other's political interests but can feel deep respect and affection for one another. However little truth there may be in Fedor's *vita,* it at least shows that such relations were considered plausible.

The historical Fedor Rostislavovich did, in fact, marry a Tatar princess in the thirteenth century, as did Yuri Daniilovich in the next. Gleb Vasil'kovich in the thirteenth century not only married into the Horde but spent his entire career among the Mongols in the steppe. However, such dynastic marriages were rare and ceased altogether in the fourteenth century as the obstacles to such unions, already considerable, became insuperable when the Golden Horde adopted Islam. No Muslim khan could have permitted a Tatar princess to convert to Christianity for the sake of a dynastic marriage, nor would the Russian princes have allowed a Christian princess to marry a Muslim. While the khans could have forcibly taken Christian women into their harems like the Ottoman sultans, none did.

Yet beginning in the fifteenth century, marriages between Russians and Mongols began to occur again, though not among the ruling families. The Golden Horde's political fortunes were waning at this time, and a number of Mongol grandees emigrated to Russia, most of them entering the service of the Muscovite grand princes. Since conspicuous Tatars, like the Muslim Kasimov *tsarevichi,* were excluded from the *mestnichestvo*[20] system of family rankings and from Russian society in general, these emigrés converted to Christianity, married into the aristocracy, and became assimilated.

How much Tatar blood entered the Russian aristocracy in this way is open to question. Some estimates have been very high, calculating that 156 aristocratic families (twenty percent) were of Mongol or oriental origin.[21] This is probably excessive. The evidence, drawn from names, heraldry, and contemporary genealogies, has not always been conclusive. The onomastic evidence is ambiguous, for families bearing names of obviously Tatar provenance, like Baskakov, Yarlikov, and Yasak, were not necessarily of Tatar descent.[22] For example, a Mongol nickname for a Russian child might result generations later in an apparently Tatar patronym.[23] Similarly, Mongol families might have thoroughly Russian names adopted when they converted to Christianity.[24] Still other names are of unidentifiable linguistic origin. Heraldic evidence is also questionable. It is tempting to interpret every crescent as a reference to conversion from Islam and every bow and arrow as an allusion to steppe origin, but

coats-of-arms, even considered with onomastic evidence, can be misleading.[25]

Heraldry and the sixteenth-century genealogical books *(rodoslovnye
knigi)* are both suspect, and for the same reason. The first redaction of
these books dates from the 1540s when the *mestnichestvo,* the system for
allocating position and status, and new legends of the foreign origin of
the ruling Riurikid clan (from the brother of Augustus Caesar) made family
origin a matter of widespread concern among the Russian elite. Some
genealogies, and the heraldic devices that accompany them, are
fictitious.[26] Since foreign origin became fashionable among the Muscovite elite, as among aristocracies of other times and places, genealogies
tracing non-Russian descent are particularly suspect. Few of the
genealogies in these books date from earlier than the late fifteenth century, and many of these were based on oral family legends. Most family
histories involving any foreign descent were invented, though there were
some attempts at verisimilitude. For example, nobles from Riazan'
favored Tatar origin, while those from Chernigov and Tver' were more
likely to claim Lithuanian backgrounds. Those genealogies that trace
descent back to Tatars who entered the service of Alexander Nevskii are
intrinsically suspect. In the thirteenth century the flow was of Russians to
the Mongols on the steppe rather than the other way around. Further, the
terms used for the Horde, *Bol'shaia orda* (Great Horde) and *Zolotaia orda*
(Golden Horde) are anachronistic and signs of adulteration. For these
reasons the most famous genealogy showing Tatar origin, that of the
Gudunov clan from prince Chet, is unreliable.[27] Their own claims to the
contrary notwithstanding, the overwhelming majority of the aristocracy
were native Russians.[28]

Only Tatars who converted, married, and became thoroughly Russianized could be assimilated into Russian society, hence it is doubtful
that they, much less their descendents such as Chaadaev, had much of a
Tatar influence on Russian culture. Historians have spoken of the role of
the "infusion of new blood" in describing the absorption of Germanic
peoples into the Roman Empire or Slavs into the Byzantine Empire.
These, however, were massive migrations important in terms of manpower and resources. The metaphor suggests that the genes of an assimilated people can effect cultural changes and borders on racism. It is
fair to say that some noble Russian families had Mongol ancestors and
that some of their descendents made major contributions to Russian cul-

ture and society. Their contributions, however, had nothing to do with their ancestry.

The real significance of the sixteenth-century genealogies, of course, is the remarkable fact that descent from Russia's bitterest political and religious enemies was considered honorable and even desirable. Though hostility toward Islam and the Tatars was actually on the rise at the time the genealogies were written, it is apparent that Mongol ancestry was as prestigious as German, Latin, or Greek. This in itself constitutes social influence of a sort, even long after the overthrow of Tatar rule, and is perhaps most interesting as a reflection of the complex and often contradictory Russian attitudes toward the Mongols. Tatar descent apparently ceased to be fashionable after the Time of Troubles, for it is rarely found in new genealogies from the following century.

Of vastly greater importance than intermarriage were the effects of the Tatar hegemony on the Russian Orthodox Church. The Mongols not only radically altered the fortunes of the Church, but, since the Church was at the heart of Russian life—politics, economics, culture—through it profoundly changed Russian society as a whole. Naturally the Church suffered during the conquest. The metropolitan, a Greek, probably fled Russia altogether, and some hierarchs lost their lives, but more seem to have managed to survive. Once order had been more or less restored, the Church, which had no choice but to protect its spiritual and material interests, began to accommodate itself to the new situation and sought some sort of *modus vivendi* with the Mongol conquerors.

This was less difficult than might be imagined. Chingis Khan's shamanist tolerance for all religions was part of his legacy, and the Golden Horde continued to respect this tradition even after the conversion to Islam in the early fourteenth century. The Mongols required of the Church only that it pray for the health of the khan, and in return they looked after its interests and fostered its growth. A bishopric was even established at Sarai, the bishop not only ministering to the spiritual needs of Russians there and overseeing some missionary work, but serving as a diplomatic intermediary between the Golden Horde and both the Russian Church and Byzantium.[29]

The Church thrived during the Mongol period.[30] The immense tax privileges the khans granted the Church enabled it to recover from the losses suffered during the invasion and subsequent raids and prosper as never before. The preferred economic status of Church lands may have encouraged an influx of peasant settlers which would have strengthened the Church's economic position even further. It was, by most estimates, during the fourteenth century that Christianity first made decisive inroads into the previously largely pagan countryside.

The "Tale of Peter, tsarevich of the Horde" *(Povest' o Petre, tsareviche ordynskom)* gives a sense of the Mongols' protective role. This tale was written in the fourteenth century to enhance the reputation and protect the resources of the Petrov monastery.[31] It recounts how Peter, a converted Mongol of the royal Chingisid clan, founds the Petrov monastery. Generations later the monastery is threatened by the Rostov princes, the neighboring Russian populace, and Russian fishermen intent on usurping the monastery's fishing rights. In desperation Peter's descendents petition the khans for justice. The khans immediately dispatch envoys who justly rule in the monastery's favor.[32] It is true, of course, that in this tale the blood relationship between Peter's descendents and the khans is of great importance. Nonetheless, the khans are unambiguously the source of true justice and the defenders of Russian Christianity against Russian evildoers.

But though the Church flourished under Tatar patronage, ecclesiastics usually excoriated the Mongols in their writings. The chronicles and saints' lives written under Church auspices or for such sponsors as metropolitans, bishops, and monasteries spared no effort in describing the horrors of Tatar violence and oppression. The Russian princes who lost their lives during the conquest or were executed for rebellion became religious martyrs. The sermons of Serapion, bishop of Vladimir, leave little to the imagination in their presentation of the disastrous consequences of the Tatar invasion and the subsequent spiritual slavery of the Russian people. Russian ecclesiastic texts from throughout the Mongol period revile the Tatar conquerors.

The Church's position as both the caretaker of Russian spiritual and patriotic values and the beneficiary of Tatar policies was extremely awkward. It found itself praying simultaneously for the immediate perdition of all Mongols and (by agreement) for the continued good health of the khan. In dealing with these obvious contradictions, the Church did the best that it could. For example, as Cherniavsky observed, since the name of an infidel khan could hardly have been inscribed in the missals, they left a blank space in the dyptychs, and as priests read them aloud they inserted the khan's name orally. Ecclesiastic sources from this period also are careful to distinguish between the khan and the "Tatars."[33] For example, hagiographers sometimes sought to absolve khans from the responsibility for martyring Russian princes. Many texts of the *vita* of Mikhail of Tver' blame his execution on Ivan Kalita of Moscow or on the Tatar general Kavgadii rather than on Khan Uzbek. No such pose, of course, could satisfactorily resolve the conflicting elements of the Church's policy. The dilemma was rooted in the tension between the Mongols' oppression of Russia and their toleration and promotion of the Church.

Despite the advantages it enjoyed under Mongol rule, the Church was glad when the opportunity arose to extricate itself from this situation. As the Horde began to weaken to the point that Russians might seriously attempt to resist its power, the Church gave its full backing to the Russian princes. St. Sergius in 1380 blessed Dmitrii Donskoi in his struggle against Mamai, and in 1480 Bishop Vassian was the most militant advocate of a confrontation between Ivan III and Khan Akhmed. Once the Mongols were no longer in a position to protect the Church, the Russian princes often proved less generous patrons than the khans. The Church had to fight to retain its privileges. The first of the agreements negotiated between the metropolitans and the Muscovite grand princes (in this case probably Kiprian and Vasilii I) enjoined villages on Church lands to pay the Mongol tribute every time the grand prince did so in spite of the khans' exemption.[34] The Church was perfectly willing to invoke the Mongol model as an example of how it should be treated. To further their cause, sixteenth-century churchmen circulated a translation of the Mongol *yarliki* that granted the Church immunity from taxation.

Ecclesiastic support for Russian rebellion even while the Golden Horde was still a formidable power and the Church's chief protector shows that there is no basis for the claim that the Mongols taught the Church subservience to arbitrary political power. Sixteenth-century European critics attacked the Russian Orthodox Church as servile to the Muscovite state, but did so only by forgetting the histories of their own countries.[35] The Russian Church did serve Moscow's imperialist purposes at Perm' and later in Kazan' and Siberia, but this is not extraordinary. The Catholic Church was an institution of colonialism in Crusader Valencia. Both the German crusading knights in Eastern Europe and the Byzantines in their own empire used their churches for political assimilation and integration. Like churches everywhere, the Russian Orthodox Church could not avoid involvement in the political affairs of the time. On the whole though, both during the Mongol period and afterward, the Church probably sought to avoid secular politics,[36] which were, after all, secondary to its sacramental and liturgical functions. The Church strove to fulfill its offices while making the best arrangements it could with the "powers that be" on earth. In its dealings with the Golden Horde, the Russian Church could not escape the difficulties inherent in its status as an institution in this world but not of it.

Historians have blamed the Mongols for all the "failings" of Russian society at one time or another, so it is not surprising that they have been held responsible for three secular social institutions, all of them repressive, characteristic of later Muscovy. First of these is the *terem*, which epitomized the degradation of women in the Muscovite state. The *terem* was a tower or isolated quarter of a palace where the women were kept in seclusion. When this custom evolved is not entirely clear. The word *terem* dates from Kievan times, but whether the palace towers of this period had anything to do with the sequestration of women is not known. The original Byzantine Greek word *teremnon* means special quarters, but no more.[37] In any case, regardless of when the Russians began isolating women, the Mongols had nothing to do with it. There was no *terem* or similar institution among the nomadic Tatars, and indeed women of the Chingisid clan and the wives and widows of khans exercised considerable political power. Khansha Taidula, for example, granted a *yarlik* to metropolitan Alexei, and when Mikhail of Tver' was seeking protection for his son, he sent him to Uzbek's wife.[38] Some have suggested that the threat of Mongol attacks created the need for the *terem* to protect women. However, it is unlikely that Russian women had more to fear from Mongol raiders than from the warriors of the constantly feuding Russian princes.[39] Besides, the Mongols, who were capable of dismantling entire cities, would easily have stormed towers if for some reason they were determined to do so. Thus the Tatars did not contribute to the seclusion of women in Muscovite society either by example or by indirect effect.[40] The *terem* was in all probability an innovation of the sixteenth-century Muscovite elite, a product of the social tensions produced by the new Russian monarchy.

It is possible that the Golden Horde did provide the model for a second oppressive sixteenth-century Muscovite institution, *kabala* bondage *(kabal'noe kholopstvo)*. In this form of debt-slavery, bondsmen sold themselves into bondage for a set sum, presumably to pay off debts, and thereafter were relieved of tax obligations. In some cases, *kabala* bondage was finite, such that one could, at least in theory, work off the debt. The word *kabala* comes from Arabic, and thus may indicate an influence from or through the Horde. However, with little data on such bondage in the Horde, it is impossible to compare Muscovite *kabala* with its putative Mongol prototype. In any event, the *kabala* evolved rapidly in Muscovy, and in its adaptation to an agricultural rather than a nomadic economy would have changed greatly from the original Tatar institution, if any.[41]

Finally, there is a theory that holds that serfdom was the price the Russian people paid for their freedom from the Tatar yoke.[42] However, the Mongol threat was already declining by the time serfdom began to develop in Russia in the middle of the fifteenth century. The *Ulozhenie* (law code) of 1649 imposed serfdom definitively long after Russian foreign policy had refocused on the West.[43]

All three of the institutions just discussed arose as part of the enormous social changes that took place as the Muscovite grand princes asserted themselves as autocratic tsars following the disintegration of Mongol power. The Church and the nobility had to adapt to the altered relationships implicit in that transformation. During this time the state virtually created two entirely new social groups, the gentry *(dvoriane)*, who were military servitors rewarded with grants of fiefs *(pomest'e)*, and the "clerks" *(d'iaki)*, the professional bureaucrats who manned the Muscovite chancelleries. The peasantry sank deeper into serfdom. Centralization, bureaucratization, secularization, mobilization of resources on the model of an early modern European state—all created social tensions which found their outlet in xenophobia, bigotry, heresy, and eventually in the social pathology and total breakdown of the social order in the Time of Troubles in the early seventeenth century, characterized by massive uprisings of peasants, bondsmen, and Cossacks.

All of these complex developments in Russian social history arose from internal processes and do not in any way reflect a lingering Tatar influence. The Mongols did not reduce the masses to craven servility to arbitrary authority, nor did they inspire or necessitate the enserfment of the peasantry. If the Mongols provided the model for *kabala* bondage, it was only one of a variety of types of bondage known in Muscovy.

Thus the Mongol impact on Russian society was temporary (if a period of roughly three centuries may be considered temporary). Nonetheless, this impact was significant. Having conquered Russia, the Tatars became a non-negotiable fixture of Russian life. Russians were compelled to learn their rulers' language, customs, and mores in order to advance their own interests and to avoid accidentally provoking the dangerous infidels. In the process of this adaptation, Russo-Tatar social relations came to include a variety of more or less friendly cooperative interactions, such that a Mongol khan might be the benevolent father-in-law of a Russian prince or the just defender of a Russian monastery. This state of affairs constituted in itself a major phenomenon of medieval Russian social history.

To the medieval Russian bookmen and probably to all of Russian society this phenomenon was unwelcome. Pragmatic social tolerance violated the Russian Orthodox Church's prohibitions against contacts with infidels. Cosmopolitanism could not be reconciled with the unquestioned superiority of Christian life and ethics. The bookmen's response was to simplify a complex multicolored social reality by viewing it through a monochromatic lens of religious animosity. Of course, as the sources cited in this chapter show, an occasional ray showing the true diversity of social relations between the two peoples slipped through, revealing individual Tatars as perhaps capable of nobility, honesty, or simply humanity. Yet such lapses could be explained as the mysterious workings of the Christian God, and were never allowed to interfere with the fact that Tatars were still Tatars and their ways an abomination. The pragmatic social dealings across the ethno-religious frontier were veiled in religious prejudice and covered over with the ideology of silence. When the frontier disappeared, the social relations that so conflicted with religious hostilities were abandoned.

One last text, though it does not specifically treat the Tatars, is most revealing of the Russian attitude toward the infidels. This is the "Voyage Beyond Three Seas" (Khozhenie za tri moria) by the Tverian merchant Afanasii Nikitin. This remarkable memoir records his travels in Persia and India in the latter half of the fifteenth century and is the richest and fullest account by a contemporary Russian of life among the infidels of the Muslim East.[44] Nikitin only passed through the Golden Horde on his way to more exotic locales, but his response to the Muslims he dwelt among nicely captures the essence of the larger Russian response to their more immediate infidel neighbors. Thus, through a small sleight of hand, we can conclude our discussion with Nikitin's adventures.

The voyage Nikitin describes in his travelogue, though probably his longest, was not his first to the Orient. Indeed, his knowledge of the East was so great that he was able to pass undetected as a Khorassani Muslim. This entailed speaking, dressing, behaving, and even praying like his hosts, ignoring Easter and fasting for Ramadan. So complete was his assimilation that even while writing his memoirs in Russian, he slips in and out of an oriental patois of Persian, Turkic, and Arabic. Yet despite his extraordinary familiarity with and integration into Muslim society, Nikitin retained an awareness of himself as an outsider. He had abandoned his native language, customs, and even perhaps his religion by necessity rather than choice, and his knowledge of the Muslim world did not erase his contempt for it or for himself. Accusing evil Muslim merchants of manipulating commercial regulations to prevent non-Muslims from profiting from trade in India, he warned Russian merchants who wished to trade there to leave their faith at home. The ambivalence and contradictions in Nikitin's feelings toward Muslim society gave him no rest, and the troubled man died on his way home in a monastery where he was compiling his memoirs and trying to expiate his sins.

In significant ways, Nikitin's reactions reflect the larger experience of Russian society as it was forced into contact with infidel culture. Certainly few, if any, Russians became as thoroughly assimilated into Tatar society as Nikitin did among the Muslims of the East, yet large numbers of Russian princes, nobles, clergy, artisans, and merchants did come into intimate contact with the Golden Horde in pursuit of their own political, ecclesiastic, or financial ends. Like Nikitin, they did so in direct violation of some of the strongest proscriptions of their culture and religion, and at the expense of great philosophical difficulties. Like Nikitin, Russian society learned as much as it needed to about the infidels and made whatever adjustments were necessary, all without ever overcoming its deeply rooted prejudices. As a result, Mongol social influence ended with the Mongol period.

X

Cultural Life

IF ONLY FOR ECONOMIC REASONS, THE INITIAL IMPACT OF THE MONGOL CONQUEST on Russia's cultural life, on its literature, arts, and architecture, was severe. The destructive campaigns of 1237–1240 and the rigorous taxation that followed drastically depleted the wealth of the land, and much of Russian cultural activity dried up as a result. Not surprisingly, its most visible and expensive manifestation, church construction, virtually came to a halt for a hundred years. (There may have been regional exceptions, as in Novgorod and Rostov, both of which escaped the brunt of the Mongol onslaught, and in Galicia-Volhynia.[1]) Many crafts traditions foundered, some of them disappearing forever, as those craftsmen not impressed into Mongol service found that patrons had fallen upon hard times. Nor was the damage to Russian cultural life limited to the effects of a vanished economic surplus. Nearly every major library of Kievan *Rus'* perished as the Mongols systematically razed the cities of the Dnepr' valley (Novgorod, again, constituting the significant exception). The consequences of this loss for Russian cultural development cannot be estimated, but the disappearance practically overnight of the manuscripts containing hundreds of years of cultural achievement may well have left in its wake a serious cultural lag.

Yet despite the gravity of the losses suffered during the conquest, they were not irreversible, and the prospects for Russian cultural life were

120

not uniformly bleak. A noteworthy indication of this is that Russian book-men remained active. Typically conquests are followed by a decline in literacy as a delayed response, the already-educated generation of the conquest period finding no successor. Such was the pattern within the Roman Empire following the Germanic invasions. In Russia, however, literacy did not decline,[2] and literary production never faltered, either during the conquest or afterward.

Nor did the quality of Russian literature deteriorate.[3] Judgments to the contrary rest too heavily on the evidence of a single text, the sparse and laconic Laurentian Chronicle. This text, surviving in a single, defective manuscript, is the only extant chronicle of Vladimir-Suzdalian *Rus'* from the half century following Batu's campaigns. Compared to the vivacious chronicles of Kievan times, it is undeniably meager and unimpressive, but the quality of Russian literature in the latter thirteenth century cannot be judged by the Laurentian Chronicle alone.[4] Indeed, many of the most interesting works of Old Russian literature date from this period. Other northeastern Russian cities continued to produce chronicles; textual analysis has revealed the remains of some of them, particularly those of Vladimir and Rostov, in the Laurentian Chronicle. Chronicle-writing also continued unabated in Galicia-Volhynia and Novgorod. All three of the major chronicles of the thirteenth century (Laurentian, Galician-Volhynian, and Novgorodian) incorporate contemporary literary tales recounting events of the Mongol campaigns of 1237–1240. Other texts from the latter part of the century include the *Slovo o pogibeli russkoi zemli* (Tale of the destruction of the Russian Land), the *vita* of Mikhail of Chernigov, the *vita* of Alexander Nevskii, the sermons of Bishop Serapion of Vladimir, and some sections of the *Povest' o razorenii Riazani Batyem* (Tale of the destruction of Riazan' by Batu). Russian authors in all parts of the country were in fact displaying admirable literary qualities in a variety of genres.

Russian literature of Kievan times, despite the active contacts between Russia and Catholic Europe, had never owed much to Russia's western neighbors. Original Russian works of the eleventh and twelfth centuries betray no French or Italian influences,[5] and Scandinavian and German Latin literature never entered the Russian literary stream. Thus even if the Mongols had isolated Russian literature (or for that matter, Russian culture), the effect would have been negligible.

Russia's cultural inspiration throughout the Middle Ages came instead from Byzantium. Contacts weakened for a time in the thirteenth century, not because of the Mongols but because in 1204 the French and Italians of the Fourth Crusade sacked Constantinople and partitioned the Empire. The patriarch had fled to Nicea in Asia Minor, and the Golden Horde later actually fostered communication between Russia and the Nicene Patriarchate, delegating the newly appointed bishop of Sarai as an intermediary between all three parties. With the restoration of the Byzantine Empire in 1261, Russia's contact with its spiritual and cultural mother city revived. For reasons never fully understood, the Orthodox Slavs uniformly rejected, during both the Kievan and Mongol periods, the secular elements of Byzantine culture, that is, the heritage of classical Greece. Having received the Christian liturgy in Old Church Slavonic, a sacred language, they had no need to learn Greek and seem to have eschewed classical Greek works without religious significance.

Pushkin's remark that the Mongols made Russia "miss" the Renaissance cannot be reconciled with the fundamental facts of medieval Russian culture.[6] Russia had never been part of the Roman Empire and was neither Catholic nor within the sphere of medieval Latinity. Indeed, a general prejudice against Latin Catholics obtained even in those parts of Russia in closest contact with the West, as the animosity manifest in the Novgorodian Chronicle makes clear.[7] Russian intellectuals could hardly have participated in the revival of a classical Latin heritage that was not their own. The Renaissance was intrinsically a phenomenon of the Latin West. The widespread notion that the Mongols cut off Russian Christianity from the rest of European civilization, holding Russia in the Dark Ages while her western neighbors leapt forward, need not be taken seriously.

When the Russian "renaissance" did arrive, the models came from the Byzantines, the Orthodox South Slavs (Serbs and Bulgarians), and the Kievan past.[8] This period of cultural revival had begun by the middle of the fourteenth century. Church construction resumed everywhere, most particularly in the cities directly involved in the oriental trade fostered by the Mongols—Moscow, Tver', Novgorod, and Nizhnii Novgorod. In the northeast many princes, cities, and ecclesiastical institutions (such as the metropolitanate) sponsored new chronicles. These regional chronicles, continuing a trend begun in the twelfth century, reflect a certain provincialism of outlook. Even the thirteenth-century chronicle of Novgorod, for all that city's western contacts, exhibits little interest in events outside Novgorodian territory. Still, in spite of the provincial character of the chronicles[9] and the regional stylistic variations, the cultural efflorescence of the fourteenth and fifteenth centuries was a phenomenon of Russia as a whole.

Russian literature saw the revival of a purer Church Slavonic, with a linguistic inventiveness, literary extravagance, and more humanistic conception of human nature which found their highest expression in the works of the hagiographer Epifanii *Premudrii* (the Wise). In art the incomparable frescoes and icons of Andrei Rublev brought out the evocative mystical and lyrical elements of Byzantine and Slavic Hesychasm (a monastic movement). Stagnating cultures do not produce geniuses of their stature.[10]

Although the Golden Horde was enormously influential in Russian political life during this period, the culture of the Russian renaissance was conspicuously free of Tatar influence. This does not mean, as historians of the past have assumed, that Mongol culture was inferior or nonexistent. On the contrary, Mongol culture was rich and complex, both after their conversion to Islam and earlier when their culture was characteristic of Inner Asian nomads. Unfortunately, artifacts of the earlier culture are few. Nomadic existence demands a portable culture; tents leave no traces on the landscape, and oral literature, when a people undergoes a cultural transformation, can disappear quickly if not recorded in writing. Still, though medieval nomadic art, apart from Scythian goldwork, has not found favor with modern critics,[11] nomadic culture was anything but backward. The Inner Asian nomads developed a written literature earlier than the Slavs, the Orkhon river inscriptions predating the first Slavic alphabet (the Glagolithic, invented by Saints Cyril and Methodius) by a century. The "Secret History of the Mongols" is a rich mixture of history, folklore, and mythology and certainly not inferior to the Laurentian Chronicle.

When the Golden Horde converted to Islam in the early fourteenth century, the Mongols also became the inheritors of the ancient and sophisticated Muslim cultural traditions. In their great city of Sarai on the Volga, they developed a complete "high" Muslim culture. Sarai itself, with its paved streets, mosques, medresses, and caravansarais, was worthy of comparison with the great cities of the Muslim East. (Archaeological evidence shows the strongest influences to have been Egypt and Khwarizm in Central Asia.) The Mongols were surely writing in Arabic in the fourteenth century—literature, poetry, religious expositions—but unfortunately none has survived. Tatar writers in the fifteenth century began producing literature in a new dialect, Chagatai Turkic.

Certainly it was not the poverty of the Golden Horde's culture that kept Russian culture free of Mongol influences. Partly, of course, the Russian simply were not looking for better ways to build mosques or for new interpretations of the Koran. Whereas they had needed new administrative and bureaucratic forms and were able, unobtrusively, to adopt them, in cultural life the Mongol models were in many cases inapplicable and in almost all cases unavailable. The arts in medieval Russian society were inextricably bound to religious faith and functions, making them proof against infidel influences. In the more secular realms of government, Mongol models were fair game, if discretion was used, but in architecture and the arts religious taboos made the integration of Mongol forms almost impossible. A few decorative motifs whose religious elements were insignificant did find their way into Russian handicrafts, but Orthodox Christianity kept Russian cultural life for the most part free of influence from the Golden Horde.

The most noteworthy exception to this pattern occurred in a manner which actually confirms and illustrates Russia's fastidious religious sensibilities rather than the reverse. A number of Old Russian texts prove to have Armenian, Georgian, Turkic, Persian, and Arabic originals. All of these, however, entered Russia only in intermediary translations into acceptable languages like Greek, Latin, and (South) Slavic, and after having been thoroughly reworked into Christian idiom. Thus Alexander in the Alexandriad and even Buddha in the tale of Barlaam and Joasaph appear as Christian saints. The Russian bookmen were probably entirely unaware that these stories originated among the infidels.

If Russian intellectuals failed to avail themselves of Eastern literary traditions in other than "sanitized" form, it was because they were unwilling rather than unable. Russians who dealt regularly with infidels could master oriental languages as needed (Afanasii Nikitin is a prime example). Further, Russians showed considerable ability in preparing acceptable texts for Russian consumption. (A good example is the Byzantine epic "Digenis Akritas." Though this work's depiction of life on the Greek and Arab frontier must have struck familiar chords in Russia, the Russian "translation" is best described as an adaptation.[12]) Still, the bookmen were not inclined to expend their talents adapting recognizably oriental texts. Perhaps as a result of the conquest, Russian audiences developed a taste for tales with "oriental" settings,[13] but the real thing was, for religious reasons, unacceptable.[14]

In the late fifteenth century, as the flow of tribute from Russia to the steppe slackened, the Muscovite elite embarked upon more ambitious cultural projects. Churches built during the Mongol centuries, doubtless for reasons of expense, had been small compared to those of Kievan times. Now free Muscovy began to sponsor monumental architecture on a grandiose scale and to seek new cultural inspiration. The many Russians who had visited Khwarizm or Sarai knew Central Asian and Horde Muslim architecture at first hand, and architecturally Tamerlane's tomb, for example, ranks with Renaissance churches. Yet Muscovy turned instead to Christian, albeit Catholic, Europe. Ivan III proved that Russia was not isolated by importing Fioravanti and other architects from Italy.[15] This choice was, of course, inevitable, the natural continuation of the Russian tradition of rigorously excluding from their arts infidel elements, regardless of merit.

The Mongols had laid waste the Russian economy, destroyed the Kievan libraries, and stayed on as a dominant factor in Russian life. Yet because of Russia's faith, while the Mongols' effect on Russia's cultural life was great, their influence was small.

XI

Conclusion

DURING THE MONGOL PERIOD, MEDIEVAL RUSSIA CHANCED TO BE AT THE interface of two vast and irreconcilable worlds. Considered from the West, Russia lay at the distant rim of European Christendom, on the most remote reaches of the frontier. Contemplated from the East, Russia was the westernmost of the huge Mongol dominions stretching all the way from the China Sea. It is part of the conundrum of medieval Russia that it was part and yet not a part of both realms. Tied culturally to Byzantium and the West, politically to the pagan and later Muslim East, Russia under the Golden Horde was from either perspective an anomaly.

Medieval Russia was, furthermore, a conquered land whose conquerors were often not in evidence. The enormous pastures of the Pontic and Caspian steppe supported large nomadic armies close enough to Russia that the Mongols found direct occupation unnecessary. The consequences of this, both for Russian history and for the writing of it, were profound. Elsewhere, in both the Christian-Muslim conquest societies of Europe and the Middle East and in the Mongol realms, conquerors dwelt as aristocratic minorities amid their subjects. These resident overlords tended in time to adopt some of the cultural traits of the people they ruled. But while the Mongols of the Yüan dynasty in China, for example, were learning calligraphy and an appreciation of Chinese poetry, most of the Mongols of the Golden Horde were still spending their days in the

126

saddle and their nights in tents. The result for Russia was prolonged subjugation to Mongols whose cavalry remained as deadly as ever, and when cultural borrowing occurred, the Russians were influenced by their masters rather than the other way around.

Another effect of Russia's position within the Golden Horde is less immediately apparent. Thoroughly devastated by the wars of conquest, harried by raids both punitive and recreational, straining to pay a heavy tribute, Russia nonetheless was left, to a degree, to its own devices. This made possible its unique variation of the ideology of silence. Russia was already part of this pervasive intellectual tradition of the medieval ethno-religious frontier, in which the realities of profitable cooperation with unbelievers were not allowed to impinge upon religious ideology. Another part of the Kievan heritage was a vocabulary for describing interactions with steppe peoples which had never involved changes of suzereignty. Thus when the Mongols, after adding Russia to the Mongol Empire, largely withdrew, the Russian bookmen had a unique opportunity to avoid confronting the awesome ideological problem of their defeat. Already adept at ignoring reality when it endangered the religious foundations of their society, the Russian writers recorded the history of their servitude in an idiom that implicitly denied that any substantive change had taken place. With few Mongols actually living in the Russian forests, the bookmen were able to maintain the fiction that Russia retained its independence.

Throughout this book I have stressed this theme of Russia's intellectual reluctance to face facts for two reasons. First, the ideology of silence is a historical phenomenon of considerable interest, worthy of study in its own right. Second, its influence on the historical record has been immense, especially in Russia where the ideology of silence may be said to have achieved its most baroque development. It is more than an interesting sidelight on the history of Russia and the Golden Horde. Analyzing and keeping in mind this peculiar intellectual posture is in fact an absolute prerequisite to a meaningful reading of those medieval Russian texts which remain our major source of information about Mongol Russia. Unless we know the prescription of the lens through which our medieval authors viewed the world, we ourselves can see that world only distortedly.

That all written records from the past must be interpreted with care and accepted with caution does not need, or should not need, restatement here. Yet the fact remains that the medieval Russian sources are, as a result of a deliberate and sustained policy, particularly misleading and that subsequent historians, through either bias or indifference, often have been particularly willing to be misled. No historian is without cultural bias, and many historians of Russia have been reluctant to admit that the society of Russia, bulwark of Christianity and inheritor of Byzantine civilization, could have been affected, except possibly for the worse, by homeless nomads. An unfortunate combination of circumstances involving the nature of the historical record and centuries-old prejudices has led many historians to dismiss this period as one in which Russian society was in a state of suspended animation or of cultural and economic decay. The intellectual climate has been especially conducive to uncritical acceptance of evidence which is not only almost entirely from the Russian perspective, but is, as I have been at some pains to show, highly deceptive.

The tenacious picture of Russian existence as part of the Golden Horde that has survived is the one that medieval Russian intellectuals could reconcile with Christian ideology—a simplistic vision of brutal oppression and bitter resistance. Further, excessive reliance on Russian texts taken at face value has inevitably led historians to interpret the events of the Mongol period almost exclusively in terms of Russian motivations and abilities. This approach commits the error of ignoring the varying power and motives of the Golden Horde—something medieval Russians were never able to do. The Horde's bureaucratic evolution, foreign policies, and internal politics all had enormously important consequences for Russia and must be part of any coherent vision of the times.

It has been the aim of this book to seek a truer picture of Russian life during the Mongol period, and to consider it realistically as a complex, multifaceted, and long-term relationship between two peoples who were often but by no means always hostile. The Russian princes showed ample courage but for the most part did not indulge in empty heroics. Thus we find the Russian principalities not even united in their opposition to the Tatars. What emerged instead was a "fluid mosaic," with the various princes alternately rebelling against the Tatars when circumstances seemed propitious and collaborating when they did not. Each principality was at the center of a web of constantly shifting alliances linking it to others of the constantly feuding Russian polities and very possibly to the Golden Horde or even to a faction within the Horde.

Other aspects of Russia's relationship with the Mongols were equally complex and equally at odds with the demands of Orthodox Christianity.

Though the Russian bookmen tried methodically (though, as we have seen, not always successfully) to conceal it, it is abundantly clear that a variety of peaceful interactions were commonplace. Russian and Mongol warriors often rode into battle side by side, Russian princes brought home Tatar wives, great trading expeditions traveled between Sarai and the Russian forests, and so on. In addition, the Golden Horde's effect on Russia's development, though hard to measure, was clearly very great. The destruction of the conquest is beyond calculation, but so too is the importance of the rich commerce that arose later, carefully nurtured by the Golden Horde. Under Mongol patronage the Russian Orthodox Church grew immensely in wealth and influence. The precise role the Horde played in the rise of Moscow and the unification of Russia is difficult to assess, but it is clear that Muscovy availed itself of a number of Tatar institutions as it consolidated its power and during its later expansion. In brief, the Mongol impact on medieval Russia was diverse, complicated, and powerful.

The pieces of this puzzle have not been easy to find, much less to assemble. Consider, for example, the *baskak* system. It was clearly of major importance in Russian life and doubtless among the most galling and persistent reminders of alien rule. Yet we must assemble a picture of *baskak* administration from scarce and often cryptic allusions, a name here, a dark deed there, that crept as if by accident into the Russian chronicles. Indeed, much of the information in this book from contemporary sources was gleaned in spite of rather than because of the medieval Russian bookmen. Evidence of this kind often comes from reading between the lines, and from noting what is consistently *not* said. It also comes from searching for the chinks left in the wall of concealment the bookmen have so carefully constructed, the occasional tales, anecdotes, or documents that give the game away. Perhaps the bookmen's ingrained intellectual habit of not recording the contradictions between the realities of their lives and the ideological foundations of their society sometimes made them careless. Accustomed to ignoring contradictions, they sometimes became unable to perceive them, or, in their zeal to record events of importance, preserved evidence whose significance, if explored, would have been most unwelcome. Thus the bits of light slip through, the tale of a Russian prince with a Tatar wife, oaths of alliance between Tatars and Muscovy, the records of trading expeditions to and from the Horde. From these we can reconstruct a realistic image of Russo-Tatar relations.

Parts of this image are necessarily speculative, for in many areas the evidence remains scanty. Increasingly, however, scholars have been motivated to return to the medieval Russian texts for a second look, and archaeologists and philologists are bringing to light new evidence. The findings of these researchers demand a thorough rethinking of the Mongol period of Russian history. What is needed is a reappraisal of the depth and complexity of the Tatar impact on the lives of medieval Russians of all classes in peace as well as in war, in government and commerce, in society and economics. This book is part of such an undertaking, an attempt to raise the curtain on the years when the princes of Russia bent the knee to the khans of the Golden Horde.

NOTES

I. The Medieval Ethno-Religious Frontier

1. Charles J. Halperin, "The Ideology of Silence: Prejudice and Pragmatism on the Medieval Religious Frontier," *Comparative Studies in Society and History* 26:3 (July 1984), pp. 442–466.

On Spanish Catholics and Moors consult Robert Ignatius Burns, S.J., *Islam under the Crusaders: Colonial Survival in the Thirteenth-Century Kingdom of Valencia* (Princeton, 1973), and idem, "Spanish Islam in Transition: Acculturative Survival and Its Price in the Christian Kingdom of Valencia," in Speros Vryonis, ed., *Islam and Cultural Change in the Middle Ages* (Wiesbaden, 1975), pp. 97–105. On Byzantium and its Muslim neighbors, see Speros Vryonis, Jr., "The Byzantine Legacy and Ottoman Forms," *Dumbarton Oaks Papers* 23–24 (1969–1970), pp. 253–308 and idem, "Byzantium and Islam, Seventh–Seventeenth Centuries," *East European Quarterly* 2 (1968), pp. 205–240. On the French Crusaders in Palestine and Muslims, see Joshua Prawer, *The Latin Kingdom of Jerusalem. European Colonialism in the Middle Ages* (London, 1972).

2. Charles J. Halperin, "Russia in the Mongol Empire in Comparative Perspective," *Harvard Journal of Asiatic Studies* 43:1 (June 1983), pp. 239–261.

II. Kievan *Rus'* and the Steppe

1. Compare the standard works by George Vernadsky, *Kievan Russia* (volume 2 of *A History of Russia,* New Haven, 1948) and B. D. Grekov, *Kievan Russia* (tr. Y. Sdobnikov; Moscow, 1959) for Western and Soviet views. The most reliable history of Kievan *Rus'* is now the monograph by Harmut Rüss, "Das Reich von Kiev," in Manfred Hellmann, ed., *Handbuch der Geschichte Russlands,* Band 1, *Von der Kiewer Reichsbildung bis zum Moskauer Zartum,* Lieferung 3–6 (Stuttgart, 1979–1980), pp. 199–429.

2. V. V. Alin, "Rus' na bogatyrskikh zastavakh," *Voprosy istorii* 1968 #12, pp. 99–115, 1969 no. 1, pp. 136–152. For a recent (but tendentious) review of Soviet historiography on Kievan *Rus'* and the steppe see R. M. Mavrodina, "Rus' i kochevniki," in *Sovetskaia istoriografiia Kievskoi Rusi* (Leningrad, 1978), pp. 210–221.

3. No evidence exists for many theories of Khazar–East Slavic relations. See for example Vladimir Parkhomenko, "Kievskaia Rus' i Khazariia (Rol' khazarskogo torgovogo kapitala v istorii Kievskoi derzhavy)," *Slavia* 6 (1927), pp. 380–387 and George Vernadsky, *Ancient Russia* (volume 1 of *A History of Russia;* New Haven, 1943). The great sceptic on this question, not necessarily for the right

reasons, is B. A. Rybakov, "Rus' i Khazariia (k istoricheskoi geografii Khazarii)," in *Akademiku B.D. Grekovu ko dniu 70-letiiu. Sbornik statei* (Moscow, 1952), pp. 76–88.

4. See Charles J. Halperin, "Now You See Them, Now You Don't: A Note on the First Appearance of the *Rus (Ros)* in Byzantium," *Canadian-American Slavic Studies* 7:4 (Winter, 1973), pp. 494–497; Lüdolf Müller, *Das Metropoliten Ilarion, Lobrede auf Vladimir den Heiligen und Glaubensbekenntnis* (Wiesbaden, 1962); and N. K. Gudzii, ed., *Khrestomatiia po drevnei russkoi literatury,* 7th ed. (Moscow, 1962), pp. 58–71.

5. V. V. Bartol'd, *Sochineniia,* IX, p. 357; Vernadsky, *Kievan Russia,* p. 174, although Vernadsky ascribes the title to a ruler in Tmutorokan' (e.g., pp. 44, 77). Now see Peter B. Golden, "The Question of the Rus' Qağanate," *Archivum Eurasiae Medii Aevi* II (1982), pp. 77–97.

6. The Khazar ruler retained this title after the conversion of the upper classes to Judaism.

7. B. D. Grekov, "Volzhskie bolgary v IX–X vv.," *Istoricheskie zapiski* 14 (1945), pp. 3–37; Iu.A. Limonov, "Iz istorii vostochnogo torgovli Vladimiro-Suzdal'skogo kniazhestva," in *Mezhdunarodnye sviazi Rossii do XVII v. Sbornik statei* (Moscow, 1961), pp. 55–63; Thomas S. Noonan, "Suzdalia's Eastern Trade in the Century before the Mongol Conquest," *Cahiers du monde russe et soviétique* XIX (4) (1978), pp. 371–384; and Ellen S. Hurwitz, *Prince Andrej Bogoljubskij: The Man and the Myth* (Firenze, 1980), pp. 15, 46, 60–68.

8. *Povest' vremennykh let,* ed. V. P. Adrianova-Peretts, 2 vols. (Moscow-Leningrad, 1950), v. I, Tekst, s.a. 968, p. 47.

9. I am indebted to Peter Voorheis for this observation.

10. In the fourteenth century Vitovt, grand prince of Lithuania, settled his serving Tatars in exactly the same regions and for the same reason. A. E. Presniakov, *Lektsii po russkoi istorii. Tom II: Zapadnaia Rus' i Litovsko-russkoe gosudarstvo* (Moscow, 1939), p. 83.

11. See the comments of D. S. Likhachev, *Chelovek v literature drevnei Rusi,* 2nd ed. (Moscow, 1970), pp. 41–42, and Charles J. Halperin, "The Concept of the *ruskaia zemlia* and Medieval National Consciousness," *Nationalities Papers* VIII:1 (Spring, 1980), p. 80, on this passage.

12. D. A. Rasovskii, "O roli Chernykh Klobukov v istorii drevnei Rusi," *Seminarium Kondakovianum* I (1927), pp. 93–109. See also his "Pechenegi, Torki i Berendei na Rusi i v Ugrii," ibid., VI (1933), pp. 1–66. Cf. S. A. Pletneva, "Pechenegi, torki i polovtsy v iuzhnorusskikh stepiakh," *Trudy Volgo-Donskoi Arkheologicheskoi ekspeditsii. Materialy i issledovaniia po arkheologii SSSR,* #62 (Moscow-Leningrad, 1958), pp. 151–226.

13. The best study of the Polovtsy is the unfinished series of articles by D. A. Rasovskii: "K voprosu o proiskhozhdenii Codex Cumanicus," *Seminarium Kondakovianum* III (1929), pp. 193–214; "Polovtsy. I. Proiskhozhdenie Polovtsev," ibid., VII (1935), pp. 245–262; "Polovtsy. II. Razselenie Polovtsev," ibid., VIII (1936), pp. 161–182; "Polovtsy. III. Predelia 'polia polovetskago'," ibid., IX (1937), pp. 71–88, X (1938), pp. 155–178; "Polovtsy. IV. Voennaia istoriia Polovtsev," ibid., XI (1939), pp. 95–128; and "Rus', Chernye Klobuky i Polovtsy v XII v.," *Bulgarsko Istorichesko Drushtvo. Izvestiia* 16/18. *Sbornik v pamet na Prof. N. Nikov* (Sofia, 1940), pp. 369–378.

14. Rasovskii, "O roli Chernykh Klobukov v istorii drevnei Rusi," passim, and D. A. Rasovskii, "Rol' polovtsev v voinakh Asenei s vizantiiskoi i latinskoi

imperiiami v 1186–1207," *Spisanie na B''lgarskata Akademiia na Naukite*, kn. 58 (Sofia, 1939), pp. 203–211.

15. D. A. Rasovskii, "Rus' i kochevniki v epokhu Vladimira Sviatago," *Vladimirskii sbornik, v pamiati 950-letiia kreshcheniia Rusi (988–1938)* (Belgrade, 1938), pp. 149–154.

16. *Povest' vremennykh let*, I, pp. 160–161, 194.

17. K. V. Kudriashev, *Polovetskaia zemlia: ocherk istoricheskoi geografii (Geograficheskoe obshchestvo SSSR. Zapiski*, novaia seriia, t. 2; Moscow, 1948), pp. 91–95, 112–122.

18. Most notably by Kudriashev (see n. 17) and more recently by S. A. Pletneva, "Polovetskaia zemlia," in *Drevnerusskie kniazhestva v X–XIII vv.* (Moscow, 1975), pp. 260–300.

19. See Peter B. Golden, "The *Polovci Dikii*," *Harvard Ukrainian Studies* III/IV (1979–1980) (Eucharisterion—Pritsak Festschrift), Part 1, pp. 296–309.

20. This analysis belongs to Larry W. Moses.

21. The Alans were an Iranian people living north of the Caucasus.

22. Kudriashev, pp. 103–111; G. A. Fedorov-Davydov, *Kochevniki Vostochnoi Evropy pod vlast'iu zolotoordynskikh khanov. Arkheologicheskie pamiatniki* (Moscow, 1966), pp. 202–203; Vernadsky, *Kievan Russia*, pp. 110–111, 118, 121.

23. G. A. Fedorov-Davydov, *Obshchestvennyi stroi Zolotoi Ordy* (Moscow, 1973), pp. 68–70. Cf. L. N. Gumilev, "Udel'no-lestvichnaia sistema u tiurok v VI–VIII vv. (k voprosu o rannykh formakh gosudarstvennosti)," *Sovetskaia etnografiia* 1959 #3, pp. 21–23.

24. D. S. Likhachev, *Velikoe nasledie: Klassicheskie proizvedeniia literatury drevnei Rusi* (Moscow, 1975), p. 158. The chronicles, of course, do not mention this phenomenon.

25. According to the chronicle, Vsevolod "Big Nest" (*Bolshoe gnezdo*, so named for his numerous progeny) studied five languages at home. Vernadsky, *Kievan Russia*, pp. 191–192, repeated the speculation that one was Turkic. This suggestion had already been rejected by Bartol'd, *Sochineniia*, IX, pp. 534–536, who argued that Vsevolod could not literally have *studied* Turkic at home. The chronicle passage might be no more than hyperbole.

26. Vernadsky, *Kievan Russia*, pp. 245, 249–250, 251–252, 263, 272–273, 307, makes many assertions but supplies no evidence to corroborate them.

27. *Povest' vremennykh let*, I, s.a. 972, p. 253.

28. V. A. Pakhomenko, "Sledy polovetskogo eposa v letopisiiakh," *Problemy istochnikovedeniia* III (1940), pp. 391–393 (although his discrimination of folkloric genres is not rigorous); D. S. Likhachev, *Razvitiia russkoi literatury X–XVII vv. Etiudi i stili* (Leningrad, 1973), p. 48; Likhachev, *Chelovek v literature drevnei Rusi* (Moscow, 1958), p. 49. Scholars invariably entitle Otrok a "khan," although the text reads "prince" *(kniaz')*.

29. Kudriashev, pp. 42–90; Likhachev, *Chelovek v literature drevnei Rusi*, p. 37; Likhachev, *Velikoe nasledie*, pp. 132–204.

For an allegorical interpretation of the Tale of the Host of Igor' see L. N. Gumilev, "Les Mongoles au XIIIe siècle et la *Slovo o polku Igoreve*," *Cahiers du monde russe et soviétique* VII:1 (January–March 1966), pp. 37–57 and his *Poiski vymyshlennogo tsarstva (Legenda o "Gosudarstve presvitra Ioanna")* (Moscow, 1970), pp. 305–346.

30. A. N. Nasonov, ed., *Novgorodskaia pervaia letopis' starshego i mlad-*

shego izvodov (Moscow-Leningrad, 1950), pp. 61, 264.

31. V. V. Kargalov, "Polovetskie nabegi na Rus'," *Voprosy istorii* 1965 #9, pp. 68–73.

32. Werner Philipp, *Ansätze zum geschichtlichen und politischen Denken in Kiewen Russland* (Breslau, 1940), pp. 48–55.

33. S. V. Ikonnikov, *Opyt' russkoi istoriografii,* 2 vols. (Kiev, 1891–1908), v. II part 1, p. 275; Grekov and Iakubovskii, p. 234.

III. The Mongol Empire and the Golden Horde

1. For a literary translation of the "Secret History" see Arthur Waley, *The Secret History of the Mongols and Other Pieces* (London, 1963), pp. 217–291. The most informative critical studies are probably W. Hung, "The Transmission of the Book Known as *The Secret History of the Mongols,*" *Harvard Journal of Asiatic Studies* 14:3–4 (December 1951), pp. 433–492; F. W. Cleaves, "The Historicity of the Baljuna Covenant," ibid., 18 (1955), pp. 357–421; and Igor de Rachewiltz, "Some Remarks on the Dating of the *Secret History of the Mongols,*" *Monumenta Serica* 24 (1965), pp. 185–206.

2. Despite its popular nature, Owen Lattimore, "Chinghis Khan and the Mongol Conquests," *Scientific American* 209 (August, 1963), pp. 54–68, best makes this point. Cf. his "The Social History of Mongol Nomadism," in W. G. Beasley and E. G. Pulleybank, eds., *Historians of China and Japan* (*Historical Writing on the Peoples of Asia,* v. 3; London, 1961), pp. 328–343.

3. Igor de Rachewiltz, "Some Remarks on the Ideological Foundations of Chinghis Khan's Empire," *Papers on Far Eastern History of the Australian National University* 7 (1973), pp. 21–36.

4. E. Voegelin, "The Mongol Orders of Submission to European Powers, 1245–1255," *Byzantion* 15 (1941), pp. 378–413; W. Kotwitcz, "Les Mongoles, promoteurs de l'idée de paix universelle au début du XIII siècle," in *La Pologne au VIIe Congrès International des Sciences Historiques* (Warsaw, 1933) and "Formules initiales des documents mongoles au XIIIme et XIVme siècles," *Rocznik Orientalistyczny* 10 (1934), pp. 131–157.

5. Larry W. Moses, "A Theoretical Approach to the Process of Inner Asian Confederation," *Études Mongoles* 5 (1974), pp. 113–122.

6. L. S. Puchkovskii, "Mongol'skaia feodal'naia istoriografiia," *Uchenye zapiski Instituta Vostokovedeniia* VI (1953), pp. 131–166.

7. Henry Surruys, "Mongol Altan 'Gold' = Imperial," *Monumenta Serica* 21 (1962), pp. 357–378; Surruys, "A Mongol Prayer to the Spirit of Cinggis-qan's Flag," in Louis Ligeti, ed., *Mongolian Studies* (*Bibliotheco Orientalis Hungarica,* XIV; Amsterdam, 1970), pp. 527–535; N. P. Shastina, "Obraz Chingiskhana v srednevekovoi literature mongolov," in S. L. Tikhvinskii et al., *Tataro-Mongoly v Azii i Evrope. sbornik statei* (Moscow, 1970), pp. 435–454.

8. For two interpretations of "the" *Yasa,* see Valentin A. Riasanovsky, *Fundamental Principles of Mongol Law* (1937; Bloomington, 1965) and George Vernadsky, "The Scope and Contents of Chinghiz Khan's *Yasa,*" *Harvard Journal of Asiatic Studies* III (1938), pp. 337–360. Now see David Ayalon, "The Great *Yāsa* of Chinghiz Khan: A Reexamination," *Studia Islamica* 33 (1971), pp. 97–140, 34 (1971), pp. 151–180.

The *yarliki* from the khans of the Golden Horde to the metropolitans of the Russian Orthodox Church also allude to the *Yasa.*

9. See Larry William Moses, *The Political Role of Mongol Buddhism* (Bloomington, 1977), pp. 1–82.

10. Cf. such sources as Christopher Dawson, ed., *Mission to Asia. Narratives and Letters of the Franciscan Missionaries in Mongolia and China in the Thirteenth and Fourteenth Centuries* (New York, 1955, 1966; originally *The Mongol Mission*); John Andrew Boyle, tr., *al Juwaini, The History of the World Conqueror*, 2 vols. (Manchester-Cambridge, Mass., 1958); Arthur Waley, tr., *The Travels of an Alchemist: The Journey of the Taoist Ch'ang-ch'un from China to the Hindukush at the Summons of Chinghiz Khan, Recorded by his Disciple Li Chih-ch'ang* (London, 1931; rpt. Westport, Conn., 1976); and Igor de Rachewiltz, "The *Hsi-yu lu* of Yeh-lü Ch'u-ts'ai," *Monumenta Serica* 21 (1962), pp. 1–128.

11. B.Ia. Vladimirtsev, *Obshchestvennyi stroi Mongolov: Mongol'skii kochevoi feodalizm* (Leningrad, 1934). Cf. A.Iu. Iakubovskii, "Kniga B.Ia. Vladimirtseva 'Obshchestvennyi stroi mongolov' i perspektivy dal'neishego izucheniia Zolotoi Ordy," *Istoricheskii sbornik* (Instituta istorii A.N. SSSR), t. V (Moscow-Leningrad, 1936), pp. 293–313 and Iakubovskii, "Iz istorii izucheniia mongolov perioda XI–XIII vekov," *Ocherki po istorii russkogo vostokovedeniia*, sb. 1 (Moscow, 1953), pp. 82–88.

12. Soviet scholars adhere to a unilinear conception of social development in which clan-tribal and feudal formations are successive and antagonistic stages. Thus the retention of clan-tribal elements in the feudalizing Mongol Empire is considered a source of disorder and weakness. The imperial-bureaucratic social and institutional structures are subsumed, apparently, under the rubric of feudalism.

13. Tikhvinskii et al., *Tataro-Mongoly v Azii i v Evrope* is a prime example; it contains no chapter on the structure of the Mongol Empire, its institutions or bureaucracy.

14. Berthold Spuler, *Die Goldene Horde. Die Mongolen in Russland* (2nd ed.; Wiesbaden, 1965), pp. 274–280, or M. G. Safargaliev, *Raspad Zolotoi Ordy* (Saransk, 1960), pp. 26–28.

15. Spuler, pp. 300–312; George Vernadsky, *The Mongols and Russia* (New Haven, 1953), pp. 121–130, 214–232; Grekov and Iakubovskii, pp. 122–140; V. L. Egorov, "Gosudarstvennoe i administrativnoe ustroistvo Zolotoi Ordy," *Voprosy istorii* 1972 #2, pp. 32–42.

16. See the comparative study of A. P. Grigor'ev, *Mongol'skaia diplomatika XIII–XV vv. (Chingizidskie zhalovannye gramoty)* (Leningrad, 1978), on internal documents.

17. The basic publication remains M. D. Priselkov, *Khanskie yarliki russkim mitropolitam* (Zapiski Istoriko-filologicheskago fakul'teta Imp. Petrogradskago universiteta, v. 133; Petrograd, 1916). For differing interpretations of Mongol taxation see Herbert Franz Schurmann, "Mongolian Tributary Practices of the Thirteenth Century," *Harvard Journal of Asiatic Studies* 19 (1956), pp. 304–389 and John Masson Smith, "Mongol and Nomadic Taxation," ibid., 30 (1970), pp. 46–85.

18. H. A. R. Gibb, tr., *Ibn Batuta, Travels in Asia and Africa 1325–1354* (New York, 1929), pp. 142–152.

19. See G. A. Fedorov-Davydov, *Obshchestvennyi stroi Zolotoi ordy*, for a summary of his numerous articles on Horde society.

20. G. V. Vernadskii, "Zolotaia orda, Egipet i Vizantiia v ikh vzaimootnosheniiakh v tsarstvovanii Mikhaila Paleologa," *Seminarium Kondakovianum* 1

(1927), pp. 73–84; Spuler, pp. 346–361; and the most extensive treatment, Salikh Zakirov, *Diplomaticheskie otnosheniia Zolotoi Ordy s Egiptem (13–14 vv.)* (Moscow, 1966).

21. In his review of Zakirov (and his original publications) M. A. Usmanov argues that the Golden Horde composed diplomatic correspondence in Mongol *script,* i.e., Uighur script, not the Mongol language, which would require reinterpreting the expertise of the "Mongolist" in the Mameluke chancellery. See *Narody Azii i Afriki* 1968 #1, pp. 210–212.

22. Janet Martin, "The land of darkness and the Golden Horde. The fur trade under the Mongols. XIII and XIV centuries," *Cahiers du monde russe et soviétique* XIX (4) (1978), pp. 401–422.

23. John Meyendorff, *Byzantium and the Rise of Russia. A Study of Byzantine-Russian Relations in the Fourteenth Century* (Cambridge, England, 1981), ascribes great influence in East European politics to the Genoese.

24. Spuler, pp. 10–209. Vernadsky, *The Mongols and Russia* and Grekov and Iakubovskii, *Zolotaia orda i ee padenie* also provide extensive narratives.

25. Recognized by John J. Saunders, *The History of the Mongol Conquest* (New York, 1971), p. 118.

26. Fedorov-Davydov, *Obshchestvennyi stroi Zolotoi ordy,* pp. 28–29, 94–103; Egorov, passim; less clearly in Grekov and Iakubovskii and barely if at all in Spuler or Vernadsky. The implications of this fact have never been fully explored.

27. Fedorov-Davydov, *Obshchestvennyi stroi Zolotoi ordy,* pp. 43–44, 118.

Fedorov-Davydov informed me that in his opinion at least the Muscovite and other northeastern lands under the control of Dmitrii Donskoi and his successors must have been part of the *ulus,* since these princes issued coinage with the name of the khan of the Golden Horde. However, the position of *Rus'* in the *ulus* was special, since it was not Muslim, was not in the steppe, and retained its own princes. See G. A. Fedorov-Davydov, *Monety Moskovskoi Rusi (Moskva v bor'be za nezavisimoe i tsentralizovannoe gosudarstvo)* (Moscow, 1981). Fedorov-Davydov's argument begs a number of questions: how does one prove Russia's inclusion in the *ulus* before the reign of Dmitrii Donskoi? Were territories outside the realm of Muscovite coinage, such as Riazan' or Tver', outside the *ulus?*

Medieval Russian bookmen attribute descriptions of *Rus'* as the *tsarev ulus* (*ulus* of the khan) to Russian princes and nobles, and even to Tatars. See Charles J. Halperin, "*Tsarev ulus:* Russia in the Golden Horde," *Cahiers du monde russe et soviétique* 23:2 (April–June, 1982), pp. 257–263.

See the remarks on the relationship of *Rus'* to the Horde in V. L. Egorov's review of Fedorov-Davydov, *Obshchestvennyi stroi Zolotoi ordy,* in *Voprosy istorii* 1974 #1, pp. 173–175, especially pp. 173–174.

28. For a synthesis of his research see G. A. Fedorov-Davydov, *Kochevniki Vostochnoi Evropy pod vlast'iu zolotoordynskikh khanov. Arkheologicheskie pamiatniki.*

29. On Horde culture compare the views of Grekov and Iakubovskii, pp. 160–176, or Spuler, pp. 423–438, with the more pessimistic evaluation of Safargaliev, pp. 72–100.

30. Perry Anderson, *Passages from Antiquity to Feudalism* (London, 1974), p. 227.

IV. The Mongol Administration of Russia

1. I am inclined to follow I. Vásáry, "The Origin of the Institution of Basqaqs," *Acta Orientalia Academiae Scientiarum Hungaricae* 32:2 (Budapest,

1978), pp. 201–206, in identifying Karachanid, Karakhitan, and Seljuk antecedents to the Mongol *baskak* rather than A. A. Semenov, "K voprosu o zolotoordynskom termine 'baskak'," *Izvestiia Akademii nauk SSSR, otdelenie literatury i iazyka*, tom VI vyp. 2, pp. 137–147, in trying to show that the origin was Polovtsian, since the Polovtsy never administered sedentary areas.

2. Dawson, p. 40.

3. *Troitskaia letopis'*, ed. M. D. Priselkov (Moscow-Leningrad, 1950), pp. 326–327.

4. I have benefitted greatly in preparing this chapter from access to Chapter III, "Aspects of the New Order," of Michel Roublev's manuscript, "The Scourge of God."

5. *Polnoe sobranie russkikh letopisei* [hereafter *P.S.R.L.*] II. Ipat'evskaia letopis' (Moscow, 1962), col. 829.

6. *Pamiatniki russkogo prava* III (Moscow, 1955), p. 467.

7. *Novgorodskaia pervaia letopis' starshego i mladshego izvodov*, p. 319.

8. *P.S.R.L.* X (St. Petersburg, 1885), p. 147. I would not accept this entry as readily as Roublev.

9. *P.S.R.L.* X, p. 130, a new prologue to the *vita* found in the Nikon chronicle.

10. *P.S.R.L.* X, p. 117.

11. *Akty sotsial'no-ekonomicheskoi istorii severo-vostochnoi Rusi kontsa XIV–nachala XVI vv.* III (Moscow-Leningrad, 1964), p. 373.

12. The earliest extant version is in *Novgorodskaia pervaia letopis'*, p. 298, although I am sceptical that the Mongols conducted a census in the south so soon. Martin Dimnik, *Mikhail, Prince of Chernigov and Grand Prince of Kiev, 1224–1246* (Toronto, 1981), does not discuss the problem of the Mongol census in southern *Rus'*. Thomas T. Allsen, "Mongol Census-Taking in *Rus'*, 1245–1275," *Harvard Ukrainian Studies* V:1 (March, 1981), pp. 32–53, treats all chronicle entries, regardless of date of composition, equally; his study's value lies in its comparison of Mongol techniques and purposes from evidence about the entire Mongol empire.

13. *P.S.R.L.* I. Lavrencheskaia letopis' (Moscow, 1962), cols. 474–475; *Novgorodskaia pervaia letopis'*, pp. 82–83.

14. Nasonov, *Mongoly i Rus' (Istoriia Tatarskoi politiki na Rusi)* (Moscow-Leningrad, 1940), pp. 15–21. Michel Roublev and Janet Martin accept Nasonov's argument.

Nasonov also suggested that the Muslim tax-farmers overthrown in 1262 were employed by the grand Mongol Empire, not the Golden Horde. The khan of the Horde was feuding with the Empire at the time. This situation would explain why neither Karakorum nor Sarai dispatched a punitive expedition in the wake of the 1262 rebellion. Safargaliev, *Raspad Zolotoi Ordy*, p. 51, rejects this interpretation.

15. V. V. Kargalov, "Sushchestvovali li na Rusi 'voenno-politicheskaia baskacheskaia organizatsiia' mongol'skikh feodalov?" *Istoriia SSSR* 1962 #1, pp. 161–165; Kargalov, *Vneshnepoliticheskie faktory razvitiia feodal'noi Rusi*, pp. 154–160, 162–163; and Kargalov, "Baskaki," *Voprosy istorii* 1972 #5, pp. 212–216.

Kargalov follows A. A. Zimin, "Narodnye dvizheniia 20-kh godov XIV v. i likvidatsiia sistemy baskachestva v severo-vostochnoi Rusi," *Izvestiia Akademii nauk SSSR, seriia istorii i filosofii*, t. IX no. 1, 1952, pp. 61–65, in interpreting both the establishment and elimination of the *baskak* system in northeastern *Rus'* as a Mongol response to Russian opposition to Tatar rule.

16. *P.S.R.L.* IV, p. 52.

17. Fedor's princely status is quite doubtful, and his lineage unknown. In connection with this incident Presniakov invokes the analogy of the *boyar* Fedor, offered the throne of Chernigov if he did not follow the example of his martyred lord Mikhail in refusing to walk between the two fires, as evidence that the Mongols would make a non-Riurikid a prince in Russia. Presniakov, *Lektsii po russkoi istorii,* II, pp. 18–21. This is uncharacteristically credulous of Presniakov, since the Mongol offer to *boyar* Fedor of Chernigov is certainly fictitious. On prince Fedor of Kiev in 1331 cf. M. Grushevskii, *Ocherki istorii Kievskoi zemli ot smerti Yaroslava do kontsa XIV stoletiia* (Kiev, 1891), pp. 465–470 and Safargaliev, p. 67.

18. Zimin, "Narodnye dvizheniia 20-kh godov XIV v. i likvidatsiia sistemy baskachestva v severo-vostochnoi Rusi," p. 63, cites an unpublished manuscript.

19. The Laurentian chronicle is missing the folia which should have contained the beginning of this tale, but the Trinity and Simeon chronicles, based on the Laurentian, do retain the full story. We may therefore assume that the Laurentian chronicle's missing folia did have the beginning of the tale as it was preserved in later chronicles. The extant mutilated Laurentian chronicle does narrate the end of the tale. See *P.S.R.L.* I, cols. 481–482; *Troitskaia letopis',* pp. 340–342; and *P.S.R.L.* XVIII (St. Petersburg, 1913), pp. 79–81.

20. For example, V. V. Mavrodin, "Levoberezhnaia Ukraina pod vlast'iu tataro-mongolov," *Uchenye zapiski Leningradskogo gosudarstvennogo universiteta,* #32, vypusk 2 (1939), pp. 57–61.

21. For various opinions on the provenance of the tale of *baskak* Akhmad cf. A. N. Nasonov, *Mongoly i Rus',* pp. 70–71, and his "Lavrent'evskaia letopis' i Vladimirskoe velikokniazheskoe letopisanie pervoi poloviny XIII v.," *Problemy istochnikovedeniia* XI (1963), p. 450; M. D. Priselkov, *Istoriia russkogo letopisaniia,* p. 109; and V. A. Kuchkin, *Povesti o Mikhaile Tverskom. Istoriko-tekstologicheskoe issledovanie* (Moscow, 1974), p. 4.

22. George A. Perfecky, *The Hypatian Codex. Part II. The Galician-Volynian Chronicle. An Annotated Translation* (Munich, 1973), pp. 68–69 and notes, does not ameliorate the confusion over the Milei episode.

23. *P.S.R.L.* I, col. 528. No historian has ever questioned the provenance of this fact, recorded not in the Laurentian manuscript of the Laurentian chronicle, but in its continuation, the Academic manuscript.

24. *P.S.R.L.* X, p. 211.

25. *Pamiatniki drevne-russkago kanonicheskago prava,* ch. 1. *Pamiatniki XI–XV vv.* (= *Russkaia istoricheskaia biblioteka,* t. VI) (St. Petersburg, 1908), nos. 18, col. 164 and 19, col. 167; *Dukhovnye i dogovornye gramoty velikikh i udel'-nykh kniazei XIV–XVI vv.,* ed. L. V. Cherepnin (Moscow-Leningrad, 1950), #10, p. 29 [hereafter *DDG*].

26. Roublev and Kargalov footnote this assertion with a reference to *P.S.R.L.* XXVI (Moscow-Leningrad, 1959), p. 157, the "chronicle redaction" (*letopisnaia redaktsiia*) of the *Skazanie o Mamaevom poboishche* preserved in the *Vologodsko-Permskaia letopis',* recorded *sub anno* 1380. Although datings of this narrative tale of the battle of Kulikovo of 1380 vary, the *Vologodsko-Permskaia letopis'* is certainly of sixteenth-century origin, and the "chronicle redaction" of the *Skazanie o Mamaevom poboishche* is a derivative, secondary redaction. It would be preferable to quote this accusation from the "Expanded Redaction" of the so-called *vita* of Dmitrii Donskoi, recorded *sub anno* 1389, the year of his

death, in the Novgorod Fourth Chronicle, which derives from the hypothetical "compilation" *(svod)* of 1448 and dates to the middle of the fifteenth century, *P.S.R.L.* IV, Appendix, p. 350, thus closer in time to the battle of Kulikovo. I suspect that the "Chronicle Redaction" of the *Skazanie o Mamaevom poboishche* borrowed the accusation from the *vita* of Dmitrii Donskoi.

On these various texts see Charles J. Halperin, "The Russian Land and the Russian Tsar: The Emergence of Muscovite Ideology, 1380–1408," *Forschungen zur osteuropaischen Geschichte* 23 (1976), pp. 23–27, 69–78.

27. Kargalov, *Vneshnepoliticheskie faktory razvitiia feodal'noi Rusi*, p. 165, cites Tatishchev to the effect that a *baskak* denounced Roman Ol'govich of Riazan' in 1270 and Karamzin that another did the same to the martyred Mikhail of Tver' in 1318. Chronicle entries for both events do not identify any individual as a *baskak.*

28. István Vásáry, "The Origin of the Institution of *Basqaqs*," passim, and his "The Golden Horde Term *Daruga* and Its Survival in Russia," *Acta Orientalia Academiae Scientiarium Hungaricae* XXX:2 (1976), pp. 187–197.

29. Larry W. Moses once suggested to me that the paucity of references to *baskaki* in the Russian sources could be explained by the fact that they were primarily absentee officials.

30. *P.S.R.L.* XVIII, p. 224.

31. Ibid., pp. 171–172, 188–190.

32. *Troitskaia letopis'*, pp. 401–402.

33. *Novgorodskaia pervaia letopis'*, p. 82.

34. *Troitskaia letopis'*, p. 327. Nasonov, *Mongoly i Rus'*, p. 30 n. 3, identified him with Quibilai Khan, although he is called a Muslim; cf. Spuler, *Die Goldene Horde*, p. 36.

35. *P.S.R.L.* II, cols. 876–878.

The mid-fifteenth-century Sofiiskii I chronicle calls Ivrui (Nevrui) *s.a.* 1296 a *posol* (*P.S.R.L.* V, p. 202), although earlier chronicles do not. Probably this is an unreliable interpolation by a later scribe.

36. S. M. Soloviev, *Istoriia Rossii s drevneishikh vremen* (Moscow, 1953), II, pp. 488–489.

37. In the following list, *TL* = Troitskaia letopis', *NPL sm* = Novgorodskaia pervaia letopis' starshego i mladshego izvodov, and *PSRL* = Polnoe sobranie russkikh letopisei.

Envoys to Rus' *in the Fourteenth Century*

```
1314  Arachii (TL, pp. 354–355)
1315  Tiatemer (TL, p. 355)
1317  Kavgadii (TL, p. 355)
1318  Konchia (TL, p. 356)
1322  Sevenchug buga (TL, p. 357)
      Akhmyl (NPL sm, p. 96)
1327  Shevkal (NPL sm, p. 98)
1338  Kondyk and Avdul' (TL, p. 362)
1347  Koga (TL, p. 368)
      It'kar (PSRL XVIII, p. 100)
1357  Iryn'chei (PSRL XV, col. 65)
      Koshak (PSRL IV, p. 63)
      Chechklia and Alachi (PSRL XXVII, p. 241)
```

1360 Zhukotnitsa (*TL*, p. 377)
      Akhmiiadva (*PSRL* XX, p. 189)
1361 Osan (*PSRL* IV, p. 65)
1363 Iliaka (*PSRL* XI, p. 2)
1364 Urus'mandy (*PSRL* XV, col. 77)
1365 Baran Khoza, Osan [the same as 1361?] (*PSRL* IV, p. 65)
1368 Korach', Ovdar', Temerkat (*TL*, p. 386, *PSRL* XI, p. 10)
1370 Achikhoza (*TL*, p. 389)
1371 Sarykhoza (*PSRL* XV, col. 95)
1374 Saraik (*TL*, p. 396)
1382 Karach, Shikhmat (*TL*, p. 425)
1382 Adash (*TL*, p. 427)
1389 Shikhmat (a rare return appearance; *TL*, pp. 434–435)
      Ulan (*PSRL* IV, p. 97)
1399 El'cha and Bekshchii Satkin (*TL*, pp. 450–451)

Although I have tried to cite the earliest reference in each case, I have made no attempt to rationalize the contradictions among the chronicles concerning which envoy participated in which event in which year.

38. For explanations of abbreviations, see n. 37.

Envoys to Rus' in the Fifteenth Century

1400 Sofria (*TL*, p. 454)
1403 Entiak (*TL*, p. 456)
1405 Mirza (*TL*, p. 466)
1408 Mamant Derbysh (*PSRL* XV, col. 473)
1433 Mansyr Ulan *tsarevich* (*PSRL* V, p. 202)
1445–1446 Bigika, *kniaz'* Seit Asan, Utesha Karaisha, Dylkhozia, Aidar (*PSRL* XVIII, pp. 193–195)
1474 Karakuchiuk (*PSRL* IV, p. 151)
1476 Bochiuka (*PSRL* XVIII, p. 252)

The data in nn. 37 and 38 should not be construed as exhaustive; I have probably failed to locate some envoys' names in the Russian sources.

39. N. M. Karamzin, *Istoriia gosudarstva Rossiiskago* (St. Petersburg, 1892), IV, p. 121, V, p. 55, castigates the envoys as murderers, bandits *(razboiniki)*, and blood-suckers *(krovopiitsy)*. The chronicles apply all these terms to the Tatars in general, but rarely if ever directly to a *posol*.

40. Nasonov, *Mongoly i Rus'*, p. 109 n. 2 (continues to p. 110). Nasonov also observes that the chronicles may not have noted all the Mongol envoys to *Rus'*.

41. *P.S.R.L.* XV, vyp. 1, col. 68.

42. *P.S.R.L.* XXII, p. 431.

43. *DDG*, #40, p. 119. I am not entirely confident of this reading of the phrase.

44. The classic study of Tverian chronicle-writing is A. N. Nasonov, "Letopisnye pamiatniki Tverskogo kniazhestva. Opyt rekonstruktsii tverskogo letopisaniia s XIII do kontsa XV v.," *Izvestiia Akademii nauk. otdelenie gumanitar-nykh nauk*, VII seriia, 1930, #9, pp. 707–738, #10, pp. 739–773.

45. There is now a consensus in favor of the revisionist conclusions on the

dating of the *Khronograf* of 1512 proposed by B. M. Kloss, "O vremeni sozdanii russkogo Khronografa," *Trudy otdela drevnerusskoi literatury* XXVI (1971), pp. 244–255.

46. Charles J. Halperin, "The Defeat and Death of Batu," *Russian History* 10:1 (1983), pp. 50–65.

47. *Akty, otnosiashchiesa k istorii Zapadnoi Rossii,* t. II (St. Petersburg, 1848), nos. 6, pp. 4–5, and 200, pp. 362–364, cited from Roublev.

48. For an excellent presentation of the impact of the Golden Horde on the Crimean Khanate see the works of Alan W. Fisher: *The Russian Annexation of the Crimea* (Cambridge, England, 1970), pp. 1–18; "Les Rapports entre l'Empire Ottoman et le Crimée: l'aspect financier," *Cahiers du monde russe et soviétique* III/3 (1972), pp. 368–381; "Crimean Separatism in the Ottoman Empire," in William W. Haddad and William Ochsenwald, eds., *Nationalism in a Non-National State: The Dissolution of the Ottoman Empire* (Columbus, 1977), pp. 57–76; *The Crimean Tatars* (Stanford, 1978), pp. 1–47; "The Ottoman Crimea in the Mid-Seventeenth Century: Some Problems and Preliminary Considerations," *Harvard Ukrainian Studies* III/IV (1979–1980) (Eucharisterion-Pritsak Festschrift), Part 1, pp. 215–226; and "The Ottoman Crimea in the Sixteenth Century," *Harvard Ukrainian Studies* V:2 (June, 1981), pp. 135–170.

On Crimean charters see M. A. Usmanov, *Zhalovannye akty Dzhuchieva ulusa XIV–XVI vekov* (Kazan', 1979), which summarizes his numerous articles.

Cf. A. A. Novosel'skii, *Bor'ba moskovskogo gosudarstva s Tatarami v pervoi polovine XVII veka* (Moscow-Leningrad, 1948), p. 419.

49. Cf. Nasonov, *Mongoly i Rus',* pp. 98–99.

50. In 1371 Dmitrii Donskoi ransomed the hostage Ivan Mikhailovich of Tver' from the Horde for *"t'mu rublev"* (*Troitskaia letopis',* p. 393); in 1315 a combined Muscovite-Tatar army attacking Torzhok was bought off with five times *"tem griven srebra"* (silver *grivny*) (*P.S.R.L.* IV, p. 48). The accuracy of these astronomical financial amounts is not at question here, only the use of *t'ma* to mean ten thousand.

51. For example, Batu attacked Kozel'sk in 1237 with three sons of *temniki* (*P.S.R.L.* II, col. 781), which would suggest instant Russian adoption of the Russianized term; Shchelkan brought five *temniki* to Tver' in 1327 (*Troitskaia letopis',* pp. 358–359); and Mamai is called a *temnik* (*P.S.R.L.* IV, p. 64), although he was probably a beylerbey/emir. I know of no instance where the Russian sources mention a *t'ma*/tumen commanded by a *temnik* which was garrisoned in the Russian forest zone.

V. The Mongol Role in Russian Politics

1. *Novgorodskaia pervaia letopis',* pp. 264–266, 61–63.

2. Thomas T. Allsen, "Prelude to the Western Campaigns: Mongol Military Operations in the Volga-Ural Region, 1217–1237," *Archivum Eurasiae Medii Aevi* III (1983), pp. 5–24.

3. The three basic chronicle accounts of the campaign of 1237–1238 in Russia are *Polnoe sobranie russkikh letopisei,* I, cols. 460–468, II, cols. 778–782, and *NPL,* pp. 286–289, 74–77. The full tale of the sack of Kiev is in *P.S.R.L.* II, cols. 784–787.

4. Denis Sinor, "Horse and Pasture in Inner Asian History," *Oriens Extremis* 19 (1972), pp. 171–183.

5. Mikhail of Chernigov earned martyrdom for refusing to perform a shamanist purification ritual. Only a later redaction of his *vita* records a Tatar offer to give his throne to his *boyar* Feodor if he did what his prince had not. Compare the earliest redaction in *NPL*, pp. 298–303 with the sixteenth-century Voskresensk chronicle *P.S.R.L.* VII, pp. 152–156.

6. John L. I. Fennell, *The Emergence of Moscow, 1304–1359* (Berkeley and Los Angeles, 1968), pp. 25–26, 36–42.

7. I. M. Kataev, "Tatary i poraboshchenie imi Rusi," in M. V. Dovnar-Zapol'skii, *Russkaia istoriia v ocherkakh i stat'iakh* (Moscow, 1909), p. 574.

Ukrainian publicists often began with thirteenth-century evidence when they compared the "servile" behavior of the Great Russians toward the Tatars with the "freedom-loving" and brave reactions of the Ukrainians, a contrast of nationalist stereotypes which has not entirely disappeared. On the most prolific nineteenth-century proponent of this theory, the historian and publicist N. Kostomarov, see N. L. Rubinshtein, *Russkaia istoriografiia* (Moscow, 1941), pp. 421–440, especially pp. 434–435.

8. *P.S.R.L.* II, cols. 805–808.

9. Dimnik, *Mikhail, Prince of Chernigov and Grand Prince of Kiev,* exaggerates Mikhail's opposition to the Tatars and does not deal at all with how a political execution became a martyrdom.

10. In his early Eurasian works George Vernadsky argued that Nevskii was saving the Russian soul from Catholic aggression by submitting to the Mongols: see G. Vernadskii, "Dva podviga sv. Aleksandra Nevskogo," *Evraziiskii vremennik* 4 (1925), pp. 318–337. In a recent series of articles John L. I. Fennell has been debunking the Nevskii mythology; see his "Andrej Yaroslavovič and the Struggle for Power in 1252: An Investigation of the Sources," *Russia Mediaevalis* I (1973), pp. 46–73, and "The Struggle for Power in North-East Russia, 1246–1249: An Investigation of the Sources," *Oxford Slavonic Papers* 7 (1974), pp. 112–121. For a balanced view cf. Walter Leitsch, "Einige Beobachtungen zum politischen Weltbild Aleksandr Nevskijs," *Forschungen zur osteuropaischen Geschichte* 25 (1978), pp. 202–216. No purpose would be served in citing the verbal gymnastics of Soviet scholars on the question of Nevskii's dealings with the Horde.

11. Because Nevskii fought the Teutonic Knights in winter, the season the Mongols preferred for warfare, and used archers, Michael Cherniavsky suspected that his archers were Mongols, and that Nevskii received Mongol military support in defending a Mongol dependency against hostile intruders.

12. *P.S.R.L.* I, col. 476. Nasonov, *Mongoly i Rus',* pp. 50–51, tried to show that Nevskii played a role in the uprisings, although the evidence suggests otherwise. If, as Nasonov argued, the tax-farmers were from the grand Mongol Empire, with whom the Horde was feuding, perhaps Nevskii would not have had to dissuade the Horde from a punitive expedition.

13. *NPL*, s.a. 1257, pp. 82–83.

14. Ibid., s.a. 1269, pp. 88–89.

15. *P.S.R.L.* V, p. 228; *Gramoty Velikogo Novgoroda i Pskova,* ed. S. N. Valk (Moscow-Leningrad, 1949), #15, p. 26 [hereafter *GVNP*].

16. *GVNP* #3, 1270, p. 13, is the first instance; with some fluctuations, the formula is repeated through the 1471 treaty of Novgorod with Ivan III, ibid., #26–27, p. 48.

17. The most nationalistic Great Russian historiography argued that the entire population of Kievan *Rus'* had moved to the northeast; therefore, the Great

Russians were the heirs of Kievan *Rus'*, and the Ukrainians the descendents of Poles et al. who moved into the Dnepr' river valley after the Mongol conquest. In refuting this exaggerated view, M. Grushevskii (Hrushevsky), *Ocherki po istorii Kievskoi zemli ot smerta Yaroslava do kontsa XIV stoletiia*, pp. 427–497, advanced an idealized and unsubstantiated theory that the Mongols had a "democratizing" influence, since the elite migrated and what was left in the Kievan region were lordless, self-governing peasant communes. Cf. Presniakov, *Lektsii po russkoi istorii*, II, pp. 18–20, for a comment on Grushevskii's conclusions.

18. *P.S.R.L.* I, s.a. 1300, col. 485. See Charles J. Halperin, "The Tatar Yoke and Tatar Oppression," *Russia Mediaevalis*, in press. The chronicler was probably thinking of Tatar oppression of Russia, not of any specific Tatar actions against the officially tolerated Orthodox Church.

19. Michael Zdan, "The Dependence of Halych-Volyn Rus' on the Golden Horde," *Slavonic and East European Review* 35:85 (June 1957), pp. 505–522, minimizes Mongol influence on Galicia-Volhynia.

20. The Galician-Volhynian Chronicle describes the princes as being in the "will" *(volia/nevolia)* of the Tatars for participating in these campaigns.

21. This realization is one of the virtues of I. B. Grekov, *Vostochnaia Evropa i upadok Zolotoi ordy (na rubezhe XIV–XV vv.)* (Moscow, 1975) as of his earlier *Ocherki po istorii mezhdunarodnykh otnoshenii vostochnoi Evropy XIV–XVI vv.* (Moscow, 1963). This is also true of Vernadsky's volumes.

22. Nasonov, *Mongoly i Rus'*, pp. 71–77; *Troitskaia letopis'*, s.a. 1297, pp. 347–348.

23. *P.S.R.L.* IV, p. 249, and V, p. 202. This seems to be a new reading in the hypothetical "compilation" *(svod)* of 1448, from which both the Novgorod Fourth and Sofia First chronicles, cited here, derive.

24. The earliest chronicle redaction of the *vita* of Mikhail of Tver' is in *P.S.R.L.* V, pp. 207–215. See V. A. Kuchkin, *Povesti o Mikhaile Tverskom. Istoriko-ekstologicheskoe issledovanie.*

25. *NPL*, s.a. 1325, p. 97.

26. *P.S.R.L.* XV, col. 42–44. See, e.g., L. V. Cherepnin, "Istochniki po istorii antimongol'skogo vosstaniia v Tveri v 1327 g.," *Arkheograficheskii ezhegodnik za 1958* (1960), pp. 37–53, and in his *Obrazovanie russkogo tsentralizovannogo gosudarstva v XIV–XV vv.: Ocherki sotsial'no-ekonomicheskoi i politicheskoi istorii Rusi* (Moscow, 1960), pp. 475–496.

John Fennell has argued that Chol khan was sent to Tver' to provoke Russian opposition in his "The Tver Uprising of 1327: A Study of the Sources," *Jahrbücher für Geschichte Osteuropas* 15 (1967) pp. 161–179 and in his *The Emergence of Moscow, 1304–1359*, pp. 105–110 et passim.

27. *Troitskaia letopis'*, s.a. 1348, p. 369.

28. Because Fennell's *The Emergence of Moscow, 1304–1359*, concludes at this point, he does not discuss the second phase of the rise of Moscow when it fought the Tatars.

29. *Troitskaia letopis'*, s.a. 1362, 1363, p. 378.

30. Failure to realize the limits of Horde centralized policy making toward Russia during the period of civil wars is one of the flaws of I. B. Grekov's *Vostochnaia Evropa i upadok Zolotoi ordy.*

31. *Dukhovnye i dogovornye gramoty*, #9, p. 26, is the provision of the 1375 treaty between Tver' and Moscow in which Tver' agreed to a defensive-offensive military alliance against the Tatars. Moscow decided which policy to

follow. Vel'iaminov was later captured by Muscovite forces and publicly executed in Red Square in Moscow.

32. See Halperin, "The Russian Land and the Russian Tsar," p. 39.

33. Ibid., pp. 39–44, et passim, pp. 7–82. See Charles J. Halperin, "The Six-Hundredth Anniversary of the Battle of Kulikovo Field, 1380–1980, in Soviet Historiography," *Canadian-American Slavic Studies,* in press.

34. Halperin, "The Russian Land and the Russian Tsar," pp. 44–48. I am unconvinced that the use of deceit and surprise by the Tatars in 1382 indicates that the Horde was weaker than before 1380 and knew it could not meet Muscovite forces in a fair, open battle.

35. In his famous lecture on the rise of Moscow, V. O. Kliuchevskii cited its geographic immunity from Tatar attack as a contributing factor in Moscow's political rise. Kliuchevskii seems to have been extrapolating from that period of the fourteenth century when Moscow was a Tatar ally, during which the Tatars did not try to attack the city. The Tatars did sack Moscow in 1237–1238 and in 1382, besiege it in 1408, and reach its gates in 1439. In 1571 the Crimean Tatars virtually burned the city to the ground, although they did not take the Kremlin.

36. Halperin, "The Russian Land and the Russian Tsar'," pp. 48–52. It has been suggested that Tamerlane was afraid of making war on the victor of Kulikovo Field in 1380, as if the sack of Moscow of 1382 had not altered Moscow's reputation! Tamerlane was not easily dissuaded from a campaign by the likelihood of opposition.

37. Ibid., pp. 52–53.

38. Ibid., pp. 53–57.

39. *P.S.R.L.* XVIII, p. 168.

40. Ibid., pp. 171–172.

41. Ibid., pp. 193–196. The role of the Tatars in the Muscovite civil war and the presentation of the debates over Muscovite succession in the Horde deserve additional and fresh analysis.

42. Ibid., pp. 267–268.

VI. The Russian "Theory" of Mongol Rule

1. Robert Blake and Richard Frye, "The History of the Nation of Archers (Mongols) by Grigor of Akanc," *Harvard Journal of Asiatic Studies* XIII: 3–4 (December, 1949), p. 297.

2. Ihor Ševčenko, "The Decline of Byzantium Seen Through the Eyes of Its Intellectuals," *Dumbarton Oaks Papers* XV (1961), pp. 167–176.

3. Hok-lam Chan, "Liu Ping-chung (1216–1274). A Buddhist Taoist Statesman at the Court of Kubilai Khan," *T'oung Pao* 53 (1967), pp. 98–146; John Dardess, "Ming T'ai-tsu on the Yüan: An Autocrat's Assessment of the Mongol Dynasty," *Bulletin of Sung-Yüan Studies* 14 (1978), pp. 6–11.

4. Halperin, "Russia and the 'Tatar Yoke': Concepts of Conquest, Liberation, and the Chingissid Idea," *Archivum Eurasiae Medii Aevi,* II (1982), pp. 97–107, represents a very early phase of my study of this problem. Now see Halperin, *The Tatar Yoke* (Columbus, Ohio), forthcoming.

5. Gian Andri Bezzola, *Die Mongolen in abenländischen Sicht (1220–1270). Ein Beitrag zur Frage der Volkerbegegnung* (Bern, 1974).

6. I. I. Sreznevskii, *Materialy dlia slovaria drevnerusskogo iazyka,* 3 vv. (St. Petersburg, 1893–1912), v. II col. 976: *pleniti = vziat' v plen* (to take prisoner),

zavoevat' (to defeat), *pokorit'* (to conquer), *uvlich'* (to capture), *soblaznit'* (to seduce?).

7. In 1251 Nevrui was responsible for the "plundering" *(plenenie)* of the Suzdalian Land (*Novgorodskaia pervaia letopis'*, p. 304). In 1258 the Tatars "took" *(vziasha)* the Lithuanian land (ibid., p. 82). In 1402 the Tatars "plunder" *(popleniv)* Nizhnii Novgorod (ibid., p. 402). In 1399 the Russians "plunder" *(plenisha)* the Tatar Land (*Troitskaia letopis'*, p. 453). In 1357 khan Amurat threatens to "plunder" *(pleniti)* the Russian Land if metropolitan Alexei does not come to the Horde to cure his wife (*P.S.R.L.* XV, cols. 422—428). According to mid-fifteenth-century chronicles, in 1293 *tsar'* Diuden "took" *(vziasha)* Vladimir, Pereiaslavl', Moscow, Volok, and fourteen other cities, and "captured" *(plenisha)* many Christians (*P.S.R.L.* IV, p. 44). The Muscovite army in 1375 is said to have "captured and taken" *(plenisha i vziasha)* many cities in the Tverian principality (*P.S.R.L.* XXIV, pp. 130–131). In 1471 the Viatchane (men of Viatka) "took" *(vziasha)* Sarai (*P.S.R.L.* XXVII, p. 135). The sixteenth-century Nikon chronicler writes that in 1405 the bishop of Turov invited khan Shadibek to "plunder" *(pleniti)* the city of Kiev and all of Volhynia (*P.S.R.L.* XI, p. 192). In 1340 the Novgorodian lower classes *(chern')* "plundered" *(plenisha)* the villages of the *boyare* of the Novgorodian border city of Torzhok (*P.S.R.L.* X, p. 212).

8. *Voinskie povesti drevnei Rusi,* pp. 9–19.

9. This very sentiment is also recorded *sub anno* 1238 in the *Troitskaia letopis'*, p. 219.

10. Laurentian chronicle, *P.S.R.L.,* I, cols. 460–468. The Hypatian account, *P.S.R.L.* II, cols. 778–782, contains one serious innovation: the princes in Vladimir do not wish to become the "servitors" *(poruchniki)* of the Tatars, a perhaps anachronistic and certainly very idiosyncratic use of a term denoting mutual responsibility *(poruka)*. The entirely different Novgorod First Chronicle account, *Novgorodskaia pervaia letopis'*, pp. 286–289, 74–77, uses the standard vocabulary. The same pattern holds for descriptions of the "taking" of Kiev in 1240: *P.S.R.L.* I, col. 470, *P.S.R.L.* II, cols. 784–787.

The extant fragment of the *Slovo o pogibeli russkoi zemli* (Tale of the Destruction of the Russian Land) breaks off without naming the Tatars. See Begunov, *Pamiatnik russkoi literatury XIII v. 'Slovo o pogibeli russkoi zemli'*, pp. 187–194 et passim.

11. *P.S.R.L.* II, cols. 871–874, 881–882, 888, 891–895, 897. "Will" can also be used to connote a Diktat, a dictated peace. In 1269 the great *baskak* Argaman forced the Germans to accede to a peace treaty entirely according to his "will" *(volia)* (*Novgorodskaia pervaia letopis'*, pp. 88, 319).

12. Kargalov, *Vneshnepoliticheskie faktory razvitiia feodal'noi Rusi,* pp. 135–136.

13. The word *yarlik* does not occur in thirteenth-century chronicles. Until the Golden Horde became autonomous, its rulers would neither have taken the title khan nor issued *yarliki*, a prerogative of the khan. Rather they would have issued charters, which would accurately be translated by the Russian *gramota*. Thirteenth-century Russian sources do refer to *gramoty* from the Horde (e.g., *Gramoty Velikogo Novgoroda i Pskova*, p. 13). See A. P. Grigor'ev, "K rekonstruktsii tekstov zolotoordynskikh iarlykov XIII–XIV vv.," *Istoriografiia i istochnikovedeniia istorii stran Azii i Afriki* V (Leningrad, 1980), pp. 16–17. It is possible that the thirteenth-century Russian princes received *yarliki* from the Great Khan in Karakorum through the ruler of the Golden Horde or that the ruler

in Sarai issued a confirmation of a grant by the Great Khan.

14. *Novgorodskaia pervaia letopis'*, pp. 62–63.

15. The *vita* of Mikhail of Chernigov, written after the taking of the census in the northeast, perhaps invented a census in the south. The full text of the *vita* is found only in the younger recension of the Novgorod First Chronicle, not in the Laurentian, Hypatian, or older recension of the Novgorod First Chronicles.

16. Cherniavsky, "Khan or Basileus," p. 465.

17. Ibid., pp. 465–466.

18. Text in Begunov, *Pamiatnik russkoi literatury XIII veka 'Slovo o pogibeli russkoi zemli'*, pp. 187–194.

19. *P.S.R.L.* II, cols. 805–806.

20. E. V. Petukhov, *Serapion Vladimirskii, russkii propovednik XIII v.* (Zapiski istoriko-filologicheskago fakul'teta St. Peterburgskago Universiteta, ch. XVII; St. Petersburg, 1888), Appendix, pp. 2, 5, 8, 12, 14. Serapion never mentions the name "Tatars," which no scholar has ever found significant.

21. See Halperin, "The Russian Land and the Russian Tsar," passim. The patriotic interpretation of the sources about the battle of Kulikovo Field, now common in Soviet and Western studies, originated in Imperial Russian scholarship.

22. *Troitskaia letopis'*, pp. 419–421, and *P.S.R.L.* IV, pp. 75–87.

23. *Povesti o Kulikovskoi bitvy*, ed. M. N. Tikhomirov, V. F. Rzhiga, and L. A. Dmitriev (Moscow, 1959), pp. 9–16.

24. Ibid., pp. 43–76.

25. *P.S.R.L.* IV, Appendix, pp. 350–351.

26. *P.S.R.L.* XXV, pp. 327–328, and XVIII, pp. 627–628, for example.

27. *P.S.R.L.* XXII, pp. 500–502.

The significance, indeed meaning, of the so-called *yarlik* of Akhmad remains controversial. See K. V. Bazilevich, "Yarlik Akhmeda-khana Ivanu III," *Vestnik Moskovskogo Gosudarstvennogo Universiteta*, 1948 #1, pp. 29–46. Edward L. Keenan, "The *Yarlik* of Axmed-Khan to Ivan III: A New Reading—A Study in Literal *Diplomatica* and Literary *Turcica*," *International Journal of Slavic Linguistics and Poetics* no. 11 (1967), pp. 33–47, claims a seventeenth-century origin, which I do not find convincing. Cf. M. A. Usmanov, "Ofitsial'nye akty khanstv Vostochnoi Evropy XIV–XVI vv. i ikh izucheniia," *Arkheograficheskii ezhegodnik za 1974* (1975), p. 131 and A. P. Grigor'ev, *Mongol'skaia diplomatika XIII–XV vv.*, p. 28.

28. *P.S.R.L.* XX, pp. 339–345 and VIII, pp. 207–213.

29. Cherniavsky, "Khan or Basileus," pp. 459–476.

30. Ibid., pp. 472–473. I have deleted a footnote.

31. During his lifetime Batu was not entitled khan/*tsar'*, in part because he may have been illegitimate (fathered by Chingis' enemy, Jamuga, who raped Chingis' wife), in part because the Golden Horde did not yet claim independence from the world Mongol Empire. By the end of the thirteenth century, however, no Russian bookman would have questioned his retroactive right to the title *tsar'*.

32. D. P. Golokhvastov and archimandrite Leonid, "Blagoveshchenskii ierei Sil'vestr' i ego poslaniia," *Chteniia v Obshchestve istorii i drevnostei rossiiskikh pri Moskovskom universitete*, #88 (1974), kniga 1 (January–March), pp. 70–72.

33. Despite its limitations as a text publication, I have used G. N. Moiseeva, ed. & intro., *Kazanskaia istoriia* (Moscow-Leningrad, 1954), here pp. 45, 55–57.

34. Despite Edward L. Keenan, Jr., "Coming to Grips with the *Kazanskaya*

istoriya: Some Observations on Old Answers and New Questions," *Annals of the Ukrainian Academy of Arts and Sciences in the United States,* v. 31–32 (1967), pp. 143–183, who of course relegates it to the seventeenth century.

35. Although close in meaning, the words *yarmo* (burden) and *igo* (yoke) should be distinguished. I have seen no commentary on the earliest passage to use *igo* as a political concept, rather than in a Scriptural quotation. The *Kazanskaia istoriia* applies the term to the relationship between Novgorod and the grand principality of Vladimir/Moscow! (*P.S.R.L.* XIX, p. 6 and *Kazanskaia istoriia,* ed. Moiseeva, pp. 54–55).

VII. Economic and Demographic Consequences

1. The most thorough discussion is Kargalov, *Vneshnepoliticheskie faktory razvitiia feodal'noi Rusi,* pp. 173–217 passim; on rural population pp. 179–218, and his "Posledstviia mongolo-tatarskogo nashestviia XIII v. dlia sel'skikh mestnostei Severo-Vostochnoi Rusi," *Voprosy istorii* 1965 #3, pp. 53–58. The standard treatment of artisans is B. A. Rybakov, *Remeslo drevnei Rusi* (Moscow-Leningrad, 1948), pp. 525–538 passim. Soviet historians have concluded that the effect of the Mongol conquest on the Russian economy was not only negative but regressive, setting back economic development by destroying the productive forces.

2. Robert E. F. Smith, *The Origin of Farming in Russia* (Paris, 1959); M. N. Tikhomirov, *Drevnerusskie goroda* (Moscow, 1956).

3. V. V. Kargalov, "Mongolo-tatarskie vtorzheniia i peremeshchenie naseleniia severo-vostochnoi Rusi vo vtoroi polovine XIII v.," *Nauchnye doklady. Vysshei Shkoly. Istoricheskie nauki* 1961 #4, pp. 134–137, and in his *Vneshnepoliticheskie faktory razvitiia feodal'noi Rusi,* pp. 190–200.

4. Kargalov, *Vneshnepoliticheskie faktory razvitiia feodal'noi Rusi,* pp. 162–172, 185–188.

5. Vernadsky, *The Mongols and Russia,* pp. 228–232, made three fallacious assumptions in trying to calculate the quantity of the tribute: that there was no change over time, so that chronicle entries from the thirteenth to the fifteenth centuries could be integrated into a single calculation; that the demographic family ratios from a nineteenth-century Russian census could be projected onto medieval Russian population per household; and that a *t'ma* meant ten thousand recruits. Vernadsky also invented the number of *t'my* for Tver' and Riazan' and arbitrarily assigned a tribute to Novgorod of 25,000 rubles. Russian boats floating down the Volga river with an amount of silver equivalent to Vernadsky's statistics would have sunk long before they reached Sarai.

6. See Michel Roublev, "Le tribut aux Mongoles d'après les Testaments et Accords des Princes Russes," *Cahiers du monde russe et soviétique* VII (1966), pp. 487–530, translated and reprinted as "The Mongol Tribute According to the Wills and Agreements of the Russian Princes," in Michael Cherniavsky, ed., *The Structure of Russian History* (New York, 1970), pp. 29–64; and Roublev, "The Periodicity of the Mongol Tribute as Paid by the Russian Princes during the Fourteenth and Fifteenth Centuries," *Forschungen zur osteuropaischen Geschichte* 15 (1970), pp. 7–13. The fundamental step in Roublev's analysis is his translation of a key phrase that a certain city or district will pay so much *po* five thousand rubles of tribute not to mean PER five thousand, as Vernadsky argued, but OF THE five thousand, which makes this the aggregate amount of the tribute.

The articles of N. P. Pavlov, "Reshaiushchaia rol' vooruzhenoi bor'by russkogo naroda v 1472–1480 gg. v okonchatel'nom osvobozhdenii Rusi ot tatarskogo iga," *Uchenye zapiski Krasnoiarskogo gosudarstvennogo pedagogicheskogo instituta,* IV, vyp. 1, 1955, pp. 182–195, and "K voprosu o russkoi dani v Zolotoiu ordu," ibid., XIII, vyp. 2, 1958, pp. 74–112, do not cite Vernadsky's calculations, but reach conclusions similar to Roublev's. Pavlov estimates the tribute at 13,000–14,000 rubles per annum before 1380, 5,000–7,000 rubles per annum from 1380 to 1472, 4,200 rubles per annum from 1472 until 1476 when it stopped, and gifts of approximately 1,000 rubles per annum after 1480. Although he does not argue the point as effectively as Roublev, Pavlov must interpret the preposition *po* in the same way. (Pavlov's articles are obscure within Soviet historical scholarship; they were known by but inaccessible to Roublev.)

7. *Troitskaia letopis',* p. 334. This observation comes from Michael Cherniavsky.

8. Kargalov, *Vneshnepoliticheskie faktory razvitiia feodal'noi Rusi,* p. 96.

9. There is an approximate analogy in Arab treatment of formerly Byzantine provinces in the Near East after the Arab conquests. With political stability a selfish concern for the economic well-being of Christian taxpayers induced some restraint on the part of the Muslim administration. See Demetrios J. Constantelos, "The Moslem Conquests of the Near East as Revealed in the Greek Sources of the Seventh and Eighth Centuries," *Byzantion* 42 (1972), pp. 325–357.

10. Michel Roublev, Chapter IV, "The Scourge of God," in his unpublished manuscript, "The Scourge of God."

11. Ibid.

12. Vernadsky, *The Mongols and Russia,* pp. 338–344, deserves credit for posing the question of the economic consequences of the Mongol conquest in balanced terms and for calling attention to the benefits of oriental commerce for Russia.

Soviet specialists in medieval Russian history are somewhat sensitive on the topic of Russian participation in the oriental trade, and criticize any scholar, such as Vernadsky or Bartol'd, who extols it for neglecting the negative impact of the Mongols on the Russian economy.

13. Janet Martin, "The Land of Darkness and the Golden Horde . . . ," passim.

14. *Gramoty Velikogo Novgoroda i Pskova,* #30, p. 57.

15. See M. W. Thompson, compiler, *Novgorod the Great* (New York-Washington, D.C., 1967), for an English-language summary of the archaeological research.

16. Thomas S. Noonan, "Russia's Eastern Trade, 1150–1530: The Archaeological Evidence," *Archivum Eurasiae Medii Aevi* III (1983), pp. 201–264.

17. *Polnoe sobranie russkikh letopisei,* VIII, p. 180.

18. See Herbert Franz Schurmann, *Economic Structure of the Yüan Dynasty: Translation of Chapters 93 and 94 of the Yüan Shih* (Cambridge, Mass., 1956; Harvard-Yenching Institute Studies, XVI); I. P. Petrushevskii in John Andrew Boyle, ed., *Cambridge History of Iran,* v. V. *Saljuq and Mongol Periods* (Cambridge, England, 1968), pp. 505–514; L. O. Babaian, *Sotsial'no-ekonomicheskaia i politicheskaia istoriia Armenii v XIII–XIV vv.* (Moscow, 1969), pp. 119–140.

19. Jung-pang Lo, "The Controversy over Grain Conveyance during the Reign of Qubilai Qaqan, 1260–1290," *Far Eastern Quarterly* 13 (1954), pp. 262–285.

20. I. P. Petrushevskii, *Zemledelie i agrarnye otnosheniia v Irane XIII–XIV vv.* (Moscow-Leningrad, 1960), pp. 170, 173, 203–205, 222–223.

21. For an optimistic assessment of this urban development, see Lawrence N. Langer, "The Russian Medieval Town: From the Mongol Invasion to the End of the Fifteenth Century," dissertation, University of Chicago, 1972; Langer, "The Black Death in Russia: Its Effect Upon Urban Labor," *Russian History* II:1 (1975), pp. 53–67; and Langer, "The Medieval Russian Town," in Michael Hamm, ed., *The City in Russian History* (Lexington, Ky., 1976), pp. 11–33, a précis of the dissertation. Langer does not confront the Mongol question directly. Cf. the Soviet view of A.M. Sakharov, *Goroda severo-vostochnoi Rusi XIV–XV vv.* (Moscow, 1959).

22. For a controversial analysis of agriculture during this period see G.E. Kochin, *Sel'skoe khoziaistvo na Rusi kontsa XIII–XIV v.* (Leningrad, 1965). Unfortunately Robert E.F. Smith has not discussed agriculture during the Mongol period. His earlier monograph dealt with the pre-Mongol Kievan period (see n. 2) and his later work, summarized in *Peasant Farming in Muscovy* (Cambridge, England, 1977), treats the post-Mongol period, largely the sixteenth century.

23. This is my inference from Langer's work, not his own.

24. Roublev, Chapter VI, "Conclusion," "The Scourge of God."

25. Michael Cherniavsky made this point in colloquium.

26. Cherepnin, *Obrazovanie russkogo tsentralizovannogo gosudarstva,* p. 390, reaches an opposite conclusion.

27. Paul Bushkovitch, *The Merchants of Moscow, 1580–1650* (Cambridge, England, 1980). See his "Towns, Trade and Artisans in Seventeenth-Century Russia: The View from Eastern Europe," *Forschungen zur osteuropaischen Geschichte* 27 (1980), pp. 215–232.

VIII. The Mongols and the Muscovite Autocracy

1. The most extensive survey of the historiography on this question remains Cherepnin, "Istoriografiia," *Obrazovanie russkogo tsentralizovannogo gosudarstva,* pp. 15–144.

2. For example, Western scholars such as Fennell, *The Emergence of Moscow.*

3. ·This has been the standard Soviet view since Nasonov, *Mongoly i Rus'.* It is shared by much Russian emigré scholarship, such as Vernadsky.

4. This is not done, for example, by Vernadsky or Fennell.

5. As Roublev suggested, Chapter V, "The New Order Subverted: The Muscovite *Baskaki,*" in "The Scourge of God."

6. The title of Roublev's chapter (see n. 5) is therefore metaphoric.

7. Vernadsky, *The Mongols and Russia,* pp. 127–130, 222–223, 362–363, 387–388, makes the most extensive, if unfortunately scattered, argument for Muscovite borrowing of Mongol institutions.

8. The Russians unwittingly followed the tactical advice of Carpini (Dawson, pp. 43–50).

9. N. P. Pavlov, "Tatarskie otriazi na russkoi sluzhbe v period zaversheniia ob"edineniia Rusi," *Uchenye zapiski Karsnoiarskogo gos. ped. inst.,* t. 9, vyp. 1 (1957), pp. 165–177, minimizes the importance of such Tatar units.

10. Thomas Esper, "Military Self-Sufficiency and Weapons Technology in Muscovite Russia," *Slavic Review* 28:2 (June, 1969), pp. 185–208.

11. Peter B. Brown, "Early Modern Russian Bureaucracy: The Evolution of

the Chancellery System from Ivan III to Peter the Great, 1478–1717," dissertation, University of Chicago, 1977, pp. 12–13, 147 and especially 614–626.

12. Edward L. Keenan, "The *Yarlik* of Axmed Khan to Ivan III: A New Reading," pp. 33–47 passim.

13. N. I. Veselovskii, "Tatarskoe vliianie na posol'skii tseremonial v moskovskii period russkoi istorii," *Otchet Sv. Peterburgskago Universiteta za 1910* (and separate publication, St. Petersburg, 1911), pp. 1–19, based upon Veselovskii's most reliable work (see Bartol'd, *Sochineniia*, IX, pp. 642–664).

14. Alan W. Fisher, "Muscovite-Ottoman Relations in the Sixteenth-Seventeenth Centuries," *Humaniora Islamica* I (1973), pp. 207–217.

15. V. A. Riasanovskii and Nicholas Riasanovsky argue that the *yam* is merely the Kievan *povoz* under another name, perhaps with faster Mongol horses. Grekov and Iakubovskii, *Zolotaia orda i ee padenie,* pp. 224–225, admit some Mongol input. The *povoz* merely provided sustenance to traveling officials; the term is unattested in Muscovite sources. The *povoz* was not in the same universe administratively as the *yam.*

16. Peter Olbricht, *Das Postwesen in China unter den Mongolenherrschaft im 13. und 14. Jh.* (Göttinger Asiatische Forschungen, 1; Wiesbaden, 1954).

17. Gustave Alef, "The Origin and Development of the Muscovite Postal Service," *Jahrbücher für Geschichte Osteuropas* 15 (1967), pp. 1–15.

18. Horace W. Dewey, "Kinship and *Poruka* before Peter the Great," paper, American Association for the Advancement of Slavic Studies Convention, Philadelphia, November 5, 1980.

19. Horace W. Dewey and Ann M. Kleimola, "Coercion by Righter *(Pravezh)* in Old Russian Administration," *Canadian-American Slavic Studies* 9:2 (1975), pp. 156–167.

20. Daniel H. Kaiser, *The Growth of Law in Medieval Russia* (Princeton, 1980), explains the evolution of Russian law during the thirteenth to fifteenth centuries on the basis of internal causation, and does not discuss the Tatars. In his review of this monograph Basil Dmytryshyn, *Canadian Slavonic Papers* XXIII:4 (December, 1981), p. 476, criticizes Kaiser for neglecting the Mongol influence on medieval Russian procedures and practices, including the "liberal resort" to capital punishment, branding, and torture.

21. Cf. Oswald P. Backus III, "Evidence of Social Change in Medieval Russian Religious Literature," in Andrew Blane, ed., *The Religious World of Russian Culture: Essays in Honor of Georges Florovsky,* v. 2: *Russia and Orthodoxy* (The Hague, 1975), pp. 75–100.

22. A Mongol aristocrat could be exempted from taxation by receiving a grant of immunity and becoming a *tarkhan,* a term the Russians also borrowed in this meaning (hence *tarkhannye gramoty,* grants of immunity). In the thirteenth century no Russian prince or noble possessed such a grant; only the Russian Orthodox Church avoided the fiscal obligations of Mongol rule.

23. Dimitri Obolensky, *The Byzantine Commonwealth: Eastern Europe, 500–1453* (New York, 1971), pp. 314–321, especially p. 315.

24. Vernadsky spoke of the "delayed reaction" of Muscovy to Mongol rule, while Wittfogel wrote that the Mongols planted an "institutional timebomb" in Russia which exploded into oriental despotism after the overthrow of the Golden Horde.

Jaroslaw Pelenski, "State and Society in Muscovite Russia and the Mongol-Turkic System in the Sixteenth Century," *Forschungen zur osteuropaischen Ges-*

chichte 27 (1980), pp. 157–167, argues that some Muscovite institutions were borrowed from the khanate of Kazan'.

25. The theory of the democratic nature of the *veche* received its widest credence in the lectures of Kliuchevskii, from whence it made its way to Vernadsky and recently Froianov. Presniakov expressed judicious doubts on the subject three quarters of a century ago.

26. For an opposite view, cf. Vernadsky, *The Mongols and Russia,* pp. 345–346. Klaus Zernack, *Die burgstädtischen Volksversammlungen bei den Ost- und Westslawen. Studien zur verfassungsgeschichtlichen Bedeutung des Večes* (Osteuropastudien des Hochschulen des Landes Hessen. Reihe I. Giessiner Abhandlungen zur Agrar- und Wirtschaftsforschungen der Europaischen Ostens. Band 33; Wiesbaden, 1967), pp. 104–108, 115–116, 126, 165–175, attributes the decline of the *veche* to predatory Mongol destruction of Russian cities rather than an anti-*veche* Mongol policy per se.

27. Cherniavsky once suggested that since the *veche* served the social interests of the aristocracy (as Presniakov implied), the changing structure of medieval Russian princely administration made it more efficient for the *boyare* to function through a *boyar duma.* As a result the *veche* became institutionally obsolete and declined.

28. Nancy Shields Kollmann, "Kinship and Politics: The Origin and Evolution of the Muscovite Boyar Elite in the Fifteenth Century," dissertation, Harvard University, 1980.

29. For example, Berthold Spuler, "Die Goldene Horde und Russlands Schicksal," *Saeculum* VI (1955), pp. 397–406, or Szczesniak, Szamuely, or Richard Pipes.

30. Harrison E. Salisbury, *War Between Russia and China* (New York, 1969), p. 31. Salisbury traces Russian attitudes toward the now fellow-Communist Chinese to medieval Russian attitudes toward the Mongols (pp. 29–38). However, medieval Russian animosity toward the Tatars was religious, whereas modern Russian hatred for Chinese (or other Asiatics) is political and racial.

31. Despite Vernadsky, *The Mongols and Russia,* p. 390.

32. Cherniavsky, "Khan or Basileus," pp. 459–476, also reprinted in Cherniavsky, ed., *The Structure of Russian History,* pp. 65–79. Cherniavsky's use of numismatic, artistic, and iconographic evidence was exhaustive, but his theory can fruitfully be applied to considerably more written evidence.

33. In Turkic and Mongol, kagan evolved linguistically into khan: kagan → ka'an → kan → khan.

34. From the Hypatian chronicle this passage found its way in the middle of the fifteenth century into the northeastern chronicle tradition. See *P.S.R.L.* II, col. 745; V, p. 73; VII, p. 132; XXVI, p. 169.

35. *P.S.R.L.* I, cols. 470, 471, 472, s.a. 1243, 1245, 1246, 1247, 1249.

36. *Novgorodskaia pervaia letopis',* Kommisionyi spisok, s.a. 1245, p. 298 although *tsesar' Batyia,* pp. 299–300.

37. *P.S.R.L.* II, s.a. 1250, col. 806, refers to *Chingiza kan,* and s.a. 1274, cols. 871–874, calls the Mongol khans *"tsari."*

38. Priselkov, *Khanskie yarliki russkim mitropolitam,* p. 56.

39. Halperin, "The Russian Land and the Russian Tsar," pp. 38–57.

40. Charles J. Halperin, "A Chingissid Saint of the Russian Orthodox Church: The 'Life of Peter, *tsarevich* of the Horde'," *Canadian-American Slavic Studies* 9:3 (1975), pp. 324–335.

41. Michael Cherniavsky, "Ivan the Terrible and the Iconography of the Kremlin Cathedral of Archangel Michael," *Russian History* II:1 (1975), pp. 3–28.

42. Cherniavsky drew a contrast between the secular image of the khan and the religious image of the basileus in medieval Russian thought. In Russia the image of the khan was secular because the khan governed Russia by right of conquest and was not subordinate to Christian law. In the steppe, of course, the imperial mandate of the descendents of Chingis Khan was religious, from Tengri, and was later reinforced by Buddhist belief. Cherniavsky did not relate the image of the khan to another secular image of ruler, that of the Renaissance prince. It is possible that the image of the khan was subsumed under that of the Renaissance prince, who was autonomous in function and person.

43. Despite Jaroslaw Pelenski, *Russia and Kazan: Conquest and Imperial Ideology (1438–1560s)* (The Hague-Paris, 1973), p. 299.

IX. The Mongols and Russian Society

1. *P.S.R.L.* II, col. 784.

2. *P.S.R.L.* XXIII, Appendix, p. 168. Cf. M. E. Bychkova, *Rodoslovnye knigi XVI–XVII vv. kak istoricheskii istochnik* (Moscow, 1975), pp. 147–150.

3. Grekov and Iakubovskii, *Zolotaia orda i ee padenie*, p. 272. Iakubovskii also comments on the accuracy of Russian transcription of Tatar names in the chronicles, A. Iakubovskii, "Iz istorii padeniia Zolotoi ordy," *Voprosy istorii* 1947 #2, p. 40, high praise from an orientalist.

4. Charles J. Halperin, "Know Thy Enemy: Medieval Russian Familiarity with the Mongols of the Golden Horde," *Jahrbücher für Geschichte Osteuropas,* 30 (1982), pp. 161–175.

5. This is the conclusion of Vernadsky's chapter on "Social Changes," *The Mongols and Russia*, pp. 366–377, but cf. his views on Mongol causation of serfdom.

6. N. I. Veselovskii, "Perezhitki nekotorykh tatarskikh obychaev u russkikh," *Zhivaia starina* 21:1 (1912), pp. 27–38, finds three Tatar customs among the Russian people: not shaking hands across the threshold, hanging a horseshoe over the threshold, and honoring someone by throwing him in the air. The first is not identical to the Mongol shamanist tabu at stepping on the threshold, which the Christian Russians are unlikely to have copied; the second, like the famous axe on the wall, is undocumented; and the third reflects a Mongol ceremonial for electing a khan, hardly a likely precedent for Russian folk customs, and is independently quite widespread.

7. E.g. Richard Pipes, *Russia under the Old Regime* (London, 1974), p. 55.

8. This is the standard Soviet view, e.g., I. U. Budovnits, "Ideinaia osnova rannikh narodnykh skazanii o tatarskom ige," *Trudy otdela drevnerusskoi literatury* XIV (1958), pp. 170–171 and in his *Obshchestvenno-politicheskaia mysl' drevnei Rusi (XI–XIV vv.)* (Moscow, 1960), pp. 344–347.

Nineteenth-century critics of tsarism, such as the Ukrainian nationalist-populist Kostomarov, contrasted the "servile" Muscovite-Russians with the "freedom-loving" Ukrainians. Evidence from the thirteenth to the fifteenth centuries does not suggest much difference among the East Slavs in this regard.

9. Felix J. Oinas, "The Problem of the Aristocratic Origin of the Russian *Byliny,*" *Slavic Review* 30:3 (September, 1971), pp. 513–522. Also useful in this discussion are Felix J. Oinas and S. Soudakoff, eds., *The Study of Russian Folklore*

(The Hague, 1975) and Alex E. Alexander, *Bylina and Fairy Tale: The Origin of Russian Heroic Poetry* (The Hague, 1973). I am assuming the standard dating of the *byliny,* which holds that they originated in the Kievan period, were revised orally during the Mongol period to substitute Tatar villains for Polovtsians, and then recorded during the seventeenth to nineteenth centuries.

10. B. N. Putilov, "Kontseptsiia, so kotoroi nel'zia soglasit'sia," *Voprosy literatury* 1962 #11, pp. 98–111, and his "Ob istorizme russkikh bylin," *Russkii fol'klor* X. *Spetsifika fol'klornykh zhanrov* (Moscow-Leningrad, 1966), pp. 103–126. I am much indebted to Peter Voorheis for this analysis.

11. Michael Cherniavsky, Chapter V, "Russia," in Orest Ranum, ed., *National Consciousness, History and Political Culture in Early Modern Europe* (Baltimore, 1975), pp. 118–143, and Halperin, "The Concept of the *ruskaia zemlia* and Medieval National Consciousness from the Tenth to the Fifteenth Centuries," pp. 75–86.

Irene Neander, "Die Bedeutung der Mongolenherrschaft in Russland," *Geschichte in Wissenschaft und Unterricht* 5 (1954), pp. 257–270, contends that the Russians would have become more conscious of their identity as Europeans, in contrast to Asians, under Mongol rule. No concept of "Europe" is evident in any medieval Russian source, and Russian perceptions of Catholics had been well-formed during the Kievan era.

12. *Voinskie povesti drevnei Rusi,* pp. 13–14.

13. The *Zadonshchina* may not, as is generally believed, have been written by Sofronii of Riazan'; see R. P. Dmitrieva, "Byl li Sofronii riazanets avtorom Zadonshchiny?" *Trudy otdela drevnerusskoi literatury* XXXIV (1979), pp. 18–25.

14. This "prediction" was academic: Mamai was granted refuge in Kaffa after his defeat by Tokhtamysh and then murdered for his treasure. Mamai is never called a "nomad." As in the Kievan sources, the term "nomad" and its variants, such as "nomadizing," are conspicuous by their rarity in Russian sources of the Mongol period, perhaps because there was no need to identify a Tatar as a nomad to a Russian audience. See *P.S.R.L.* XV, cols. 447–456, s.a. 1395, *kochevishche* = nomadic camp?; *P.S.R.L.* XVIII, p. 235, s.a. 1471, *kocheval* (nomadized), distorted in a later chronicle to *nocheval* (spending the night), *P.S.R.L.* XXVII, Nikanorovskii, p. 135, and misdated to 1469 but correct in the *Ioasafovskaia letopis',* ed. A. A. Zimin (Moscow, 1957), p. 73; K. N. Serbina, ed., *Ustiuzhskii letopisnyi svod (Arkhangelogorodskii letopisets)* (Moscow-Leningrad, 1950), s.a. 1424, pp. 72–73, *kochev'ia* (nomadic camp/grounds?); and *Kazanskaia istoriia,* ed. Moiseeva, *kochevitsa, kachiuiut* = nomadic camp, nomadizes, pp. 147, 48–49. This discussion of the *Zadonshchina* is taken from Halperin, "The Russian Land and the Russian Tsar," pp. 9–22.

15. V. V. Vel'iaminov-Zernov, *Issledovaniia o Kasimovskikh tsariakh i tsarevichakh,* 4 vv. (Trudy Vostochnago otdeleniia Russkago arkheologicheskago obshchestva, tt. 9–12; St. Petersburg, 1863–1887), I, pp. 280–281.

16. Ibid., I, pp. 208–210.

17. *Stepennaia kniga, P.S.R.L.*XXI, pp. 307–311 and the *Kholmogorskaia letopis', P.S.R.L.* XXXIII, pp. 74–75. The text is also found in the *Chet'i Minei.* See S. M. Shpilevskii, *Velikii kniaz' smolenskii i iaroslavskii Fedor Rostislavich Chernyi* (Iaroslavl', 1899), a speech in honor of the anniversary of the discovery of Fedor's relics.

18. The wife of St. Vladimir, baptizer of Russia, was a Byzantine princess and porphyrogenita (born to the purple, i.e., in the Imperial Palace after the

coronation of her father as basileus) who is called tsaritsa Anna in the Kievan sources. Cherniavsky would have found amusing the juxtaposition of two tsaritsa Annas, one Byzantine, the other Chingisid.

19. The list of cities demonstrates typical rhetorical hyperbole: Chernigov, Bolgary, Kumane, Korsun', Turu, Kazan', Aresk, Gormir, and Balamaty. No Russian princes could have been given a governorship over areas in the steppe such as Cherson (Korsun') in the Crimea or wherever Kumane (= Kipchak, Polovtsy) was, and Kazan' had not yet even been founded. I suspect that the approval of Fedor's second marriage by the Patriarch of Constantinople is also fictitious.

20. Ann M. Kleimola kindly answered this question for me.

21. Vernadsky, *The Mongols and Russia*, p. 270, cites Zagoskin's figure.

22. Hence the limited utility for tracing ethnic origin of S. V. Veselovskii, *Onomastikon. Drevnerusskie imena, prozvishcha i familii* (Moscow, 1974).

23. S. V. Veselovskii, *Issledovaniia po istorii klassa sluzhilykh zemlevladel'-tsev* (Moscow, 1969), pp. 228.

24. Veselovskii, *Issledovaniia po istorii klassa sluzhilykh zemlevladel'tsev,* pp. 397–398 (Serkizov), 403–404 (Miachkov), 404–405 (Ozakov).

25. This is Bychkova's critique of N. A. Baskakov, "Russkie familii tiurskogo proiskhozhdeniia," in *Onomastika* (Moscow, 1969), pp. 5–26.

26. This is, again, Bychkova's critique of V. N. Bochkov, "'Legenda' o vyezde dvorianskikh rodov," *Arkheograficheskii ezhegodnik za 1969* (1971), pp. 73–93.

See M. E. Bychkova, "Rodoslovnye knigi serediny XVI veka," *Trudy Moskovskogo Gosudarstvennogo Istoriko-Arkhivnogo Instituta* 16 (1961), pp. 475–480; idem, "Redaktsiia rodoslovnykh knig vtoroi poloviny XVI v.," *Arkheograficheskii ezhegodnik za 1962* (1963), pp. 126–133; idem, "Obzor rodoslovnykh knig XVI–XVII vv.," *Arkheograficheskii ezhegodnik za 1966* (1968), pp. 254–275; idem, *Rodoslovnye knigi XVI–XVII vv. kak istoricheskii istochnik.*

27. Veselovskii, *Issledovaniia po istorii klassa sluzhilykh zemlevladel'tsev,* pp. 162–195. Cf. Bychkova, *Rodoslovnye knigi XVI–XVII vv. kak istoricheskii istochnik,* p. 102.

28. Veselovskii and Nancy Shields Kollmann agree on this conclusion, although the latter has corrected much of the former's data.

The Eurasianists exaggerated the significance of the entrance of Tatar nobles into Muscovite service, asserting that they brought with them concepts of Mongol *gosudarstvennost'* (statehood), also acquired by Muscovite borrowing of Mongol institutions. See I. R. (= N. S. Trubetskoi), *Nasledie Chingis khana. V"zgliad na russkuiu istoriiu ne s Zapada, a s Vostoka* (Berlin, 1925), p. 27.

29. On clerics in the Horde see M. D. Poluboiarinova, *Russkie liudi v Zolotoi orde* (Moscow, 1978), pp. 22–34.

30. Hence the embarrassment of E. Golubinskii, *Istoriia russkoi tserkvy,* II ch. 1 (St. Petersburg, 1900), pp. 1–49, compared to the different emotions of I. U. Budovnits, "Russkoe dukhovenstvo v pervoe stoletie mongolo-tatarskogo iga," *Voprosy istorii religii i ateizma* VII (1959), pp. 284–302.

31. Despite Pelenskii, *Russia and Kazan',* pp. 257–259.

32. Halperin, "A Chingissid Saint of the Russian Orthodox Church," passim. My discussion therein of the literary history of the Tale of *tsarevich* Petr (p. 328) is in error. In the Soviet Union I had the opportunity to examine the following manuscripts of the "separate" or basic redaction: Saltykov-Shchedrin Library,

Manuscript Division, Sofia Collection 1364, ff. 328–338 (published by Skripil'); Sofia Coll. 1389, ff. 493–501^v; Solovetskii coll. 834/944, ff. 497–506^v [which has some slight but insignificant distortions]; Solovetskii Coll. 806/916, ff. 227–238^v; F.I.286, ff. 48–56^v; and Library of the Academy of Sciences, Manuscript Division, 33.9.7, as published in "Skazanie o blazhennom Petre, tsareviche ordynskom," *Pravoslavnyi sobesednik,* January, 1859, chast' pervaia, pp. 356–376, previously inaccessible to me. All are sixteenth-century manuscripts, and none contradicts the analysis of the text presented in my article or here. However, the text in the Novgorod *Cheti Minei,* Saltykov-Shchedrin Library, Manuscript Division, Sofia Collection #1322, ff. 230^v–233^v does contain the second half of the tale, albeit in very distorted form. I was denied permission to verify the redaction in the Moscow *Cheti Minei,* State Historical Museum, Manuscript Division, Synodal Coll. #995, ff. 446–450^v, but David B. Miller kindly informed me that according to his notes it duplicates the Novgorod *Cheti Minei.* The specific changes in the *Minei* redaction cannot be presented here, but they do not alter the major thrust of the text. Since the *Minei* redaction is clearly secondary, it is unlikely the tale was written for inclusion in it rather than separately, probably at a much earlier time.

33. John L. I. Fennell, "The Ideological Role of the Russian Church in the First Half of the Fourteenth Century," in *Gorski Vijenac. A Garland of Essays Offered to Professor Elizabeth Hill* (Cambridge, England, 1970), pp. 105–111, draws conclusions about Russian Church attitudes toward the Tatars from texts which present judgments of the khans.

34. *Pamiatniki russkogo prava* III, pp. 421–423.

35. Charles J. Halperin, "Sixteenth-Century Foreign Travel Accounts to Muscovy: A Methodological Excursus," *The Sixteenth Century Journal* VI:2 (October, 1975), p. 97.

36. Despite G. M. Prokhorov, *Povest' o Mitiae (Rus' i Vizantiia v epokhu Kulikovskoi bitvy)* (Leningrad, 1978), who argues that the Russian Hesychasts pursued a consistent anti-Tatar policy, and that the anti-Hesychast Russian clergy, such as the priest Mitiai, were pro-Tatar. In this conception he is followed by Meyendorff, *Byzantium and the Rise of Russia.*

37. D. N. Ushakov, *Tolkovyi slovar' russkogo iazyka,* IV (Moscow, 1940), col. 689.

Linguistically there is no way to derive *terem* from harem. The Mongols would not have adopted the harem until their conversion to Islam.

38. Grekov and Iakubovskii, *Zolotaia orda i ee padenie,* p. 120.

39. Despite Dorothy Atkinson, "Society and the Sexes in the Russian Past," in Atkinson, Alexander Dallin, and Gail W. Lapidus, eds., *Women in Russia* (Stanford, 1977), pp. 13–14.

40. Suzanne Janosik McNally, "From Public Person to Private Prisoner: The Changing Place of Women in Medieval Russia," dissertation, State University of New York at Binghamton, 1976, pp. 142–148, 253–256, approaches the *terem* this way.

On sixteenth-century social change, see Halperin, "Master and Man in Muscovy," pp. vii–xxi.

41. George Vernadsky, "A propos des origines du servage de 'kabala' dans le droit russe," *Revue historique du droit français et étranger,* 4 ser., 14 (1935), pp. 360–367, is an early study. Of the considerable literature on Muscovite *kabala* bondage see I. I. Smirnov, *Ocherki politicheskoi istorii Russikogo*

gosudarstva 30–50-kh godov XVI veka (Moscow, 1958), pp. 379–385; V. M. Paneiakh, *Kabal'noe kholopstvo v XVI v.* (Leningrad, 1957); V. M. Paneiakh, *Kholopstvo v XVI–XVII vv.* (Leningrad, 1975), pp. 11–27, 105–131, 185–219. I have not seen Richard Hellie, *Slavery in Russia 1450–1725* (Chicago, 1982).

42. Vernadsky, *The Mongols and Russia,* p. 390.

43. Cf. Jack M. Culpepper, "The Legislative Origin of Peasant Bondage in Muscovy," *Forschungen zur osteuropaischen Geschichte* 14 (1969), pp. 162–237, and Richard Hellie, *Enserfment and Military Change in Muscovy* (Chicago, 1971). A further argument against attributing the development of serfdom in Russia to the Mongols is the simultaneous emergence of serfdom, variously the "second serfdom," in Eastern and Central Europe, for which the Mongols can bear no responsibility. In his early, extravagant Eurasian, period Vernadsky traced Russian serfdom not to the military necessity of overthrowing Mongol rule but to the provision of Chingis Khan's Yasa that a warrior could not leave his military unit upon penalty of death, in which Vernadsky saw the essence of the serf system *(krepostnyi ustav).* G. V. Vernadskii, *O sostave velikoi Yasy Chingis khana* (Studies in Russian and Oriental History, ed. G. Vernadsky, #1; Brussels, 1939), pp. 17–18, and George Vernadsky, "The Scope and Contents of Chingiz Khan's Yasa," pp. 347–348. Mongol customary law would not have applied in the Russian forest zone and a military regulation against desertion in battle would have no bearing upon a civilian social institution.

44. Texts in *Khozhenie za tri moria Afanasiia Nikitina 1466–1472 gg.* (Moscow, 1st ed., 1948; 2nd ed., 1958). A number of mysteries about Nikitin's journey still remain. Of the considerable scholarship on the text, see the overlooked studies of Ia.S. Lur'e, "Izdanie bez tekstologa," *Russkaia literatura* 1960 #3, pp. 220–223, and "Podvig Afanasiia Nikitina (K 500-letiiu nachala ego puteshestviia)," *Izvestiia Vsesoiuznogo Geograficheskogo obshchestva* t. 99, 1967, #5, pp. 435–442, and the stimulating recent studies of Gail Lenhoff, "Beyond Three Seas: Afanasij Nikitin's Journey from Orthodoxy to Apostasy," *East European Quarterly* XIII:4 (1979), pp. 431–447; "The Making of the Medieval Russian Journey," dissertation, University of Michigan, 1978, Chapter VI, "Afanasij Nikitin's Journey Beyond Three Seas," pp. 198–248; and "The Case Against Afanasij Nikitin," paper, American Association for the Advancement of Slavic Studies Convention, Philadelphia, November 6, 1980. I am very grateful to Professor Lenhoff for making the relevant chapter of her dissertation and her conference paper available to me.

X. Cultural Life

1. N. S. Borisov, "Russkaia arkhitektura i mongolo-tatarskoe igo (1238–1300)," *Vestnik Moskovskogo Universiteta. Istoriia.* #6, 1976, pp. 63–79.

2. Despite D. S. Likhachev, *Kul'tura Rusi vremeni Andreia Rubleva i Epifaniia Premudrogo (konets XIV-nachalo XV vv.)* (Moscow-Leningrad, 1962), pp. 23–25.

3. Despite John Fennell in John Fennell and Anthony Stokes, *Early Russian Literature* (Berkeley, 1974), pp. 80–81.

4. M. N. Tikhomirov, "Vossozdanie russkoi pis'mennoi traditsii v pervye desiatiletiia tatarskogo iga," *Vestnik istorii mirovoi kul'tury* 1957 #3, pp. 3–13.

5. There are some parallels between twelfth-century Vladimir-Suzdalian architecture and Romanesque architecture.

6. Pushkin declared that the Mongols were not Moors; they brought neither Aristotle nor algebra with them to Russia, as the Moors had to Spain. This comparison is something of a non sequitur, since it is doubtful Russia would have borrowed either from the Mongols if they had.

7. Thomas S. Noonan, "Medieval Russia, the Mongols, and the West: Novgorod's Relations with the Baltic, 1100–1350," *Medieval Studies* 37 (1975), pp. 316–339.

8. For various views of this cultural era, see Likhachev, *Kul'tura Rusi vremeni Andreia Rubleva i Epifaniia Premudrogo;* Riccardo Picchio, "On Russian Humanism: The Philological Revival," *Slavia* 44:2 (1975), pp. 161–171; and Henrik Birnbaum, "Serbian Models in the Literature and Literary Language of Medieval Russia," *Slavic and East European Journal* 23:1 (Spring, 1980), pp. 1–13.

9. The Galician-Volhynian and Vladimir-Suzdalian chronicle traditions were united only in the middle of the fifteenth century, but this time lag, despite D. S. Likhachev, *Kul'tura Rusi epokhi obrazovaniia russkogo natsional'nogo gosudarstva (konets XIV–nachalo XVI vv.)* (Moscow-Leningrad, 1946), pp. 63–64, was a function of Russian political developments, owing nothing to the Mongols.

10. Despite D. S. Likhachev, *Natsional'noe samosoznanie drevnei Rusi. Ocherki iz oblasti russkoi literatury XI–XVII vv.* (Moscow-Leningrad, 1945), pp. 65–67.

11. L. N. Gumilev, *Khunnu. Sredinnaia Aziia v drevnie vremena* (Moscow, 1960), pp. 94–98.

12. Hugh F. Graham, "Digenis Akritas and the *Devgenievo Dejanie*—A Reappraisal," *Studies in Medieval Culture* IV/3 (1974), pp. 483–495; Graham, "The Tale of Devgenij," *Byzantinoslavica* 29 (1968), pp. 51–91; and Graham, "*Digenis Akritas* as a Source for Frontier History," *Actes du XIVe Congrès International des Études Byzantines, Bucarest 6–12 Septembre 1971,* v. 2 (Bucarest, 1975), pp. 321–329.

13. I. Iu. Krachkovskii, *Ocherki po istorii russkoi arabistiki* (= *Izbrannye sochineniia,* t. V; Moscow-Leningrad, 1958), pp. 13–28.

14. D. S. Likhachev, *Poetika drevnerusskoi literatury* (Leningrad, 1967), pp. 11–13, describes the impermeability of Old Russian literature to oriental literature as a paradox, which he explains by a variety of social and cultural factors.

15. See Michael Cherniavsky, "Ivan the Terrible as a Renaissance Prince," *Slavic Review* 27 (1968), pp. 195–211.

BIBLIOGRAPHY

Akty sotsial'no-ekonomicheskoi istorii severo-vostochnoi Rusi kontsa XIV–nachala XVI vv., III. Moscow, 1964.

Alef, Gustave. "Origin and Development of the Muscovite Postal Service." *Jahrbücher für Geschichte Osteuropas* 15 (1967), pp. 1–15.

Alexander, Alex E. *Bylina and Fairy Tale: The Origin of Russian Heroic Poetry.* The Hague, 1973.

Ali-Zade, A. A. *Sotsial'no-ekonomicheskaia i politicheskaia istoriia Azerbaidzhana XIII–XIV vv.* Baku, 1956.

Alin, V. V. "Rus' na bogatyrskikh zastavakh." *Voprosy istorii* 1968 #12, pp. 99–115; 1969 #1, pp. 136–152.

Allsen, Thomas T. "Mongol Census-Taking in Rus', 1245–1275." *Harvard Ukrainian Studies* V:1 (March, 1981), pp. 32–53.

———. "Prelude to the Western Campaign: Mongol Military Operations in the Volga-Ural Region, 1217–1237." *Archivum Eurasiae Medii Aevi* III (1983), pp. 5–24.

Alpatov, M.A. *Russkaia istoricheskaia mysl' i Zapadnaia Evropa XII–XVII vv.* Moscow, 1973.

Anderson, Perry. *Passages from Antiquity to Feudalism.* London, 1974.

Atkinson, Dorothy. "Society and the Sexes in the Russian Past." In Dorothy Atkinson, Alexander Dallin, and Gail W. Lapidus, eds., *Women in Russia.* Stanford, 1977, pp. 3–38.

Ayalon, David. "The Great Yāsa of Chinghiz Khan: A Reexamination." *Studia Islamica* #33 (1971), pp. 97–140; #34 (1971), pp. 151–180.

Babaian, L. O. *Sotsial'no-ekonomicheskaia i politicheskaia istoriia Armenii v XIII–XIV vekakh.* Moscow, 1969.

Backus, Owald P. "Evidence of Social Change in Medieval Russian Religious Literature." In Andrew Blane, ed., *The Religious World of Russian Culture: Essays in Honor of Georges Florovsky.* Volume 2: *Russia and Orthodoxy.* The Hague, 1975, pp. 75–100.

Bartol'd, V. V. *Raboty po istorii vostokovedeniia = Sochineniia*, tom IX. Moscow, 1977.

Baskakov, N. A. "Russkie familii tiurskogo proiskhozhdeniia." In *Onomastika* (Moscow, 1969), pp. 5–26.

Bazilevich, K. V. "Iarlyk Akhmed-khana Ivanu III." *Vestnik Moskovskogo Gosudarstvennogo Universiteta* 1948 #1, pp. 29–46.

Begunov, Iu. K. *Pamiatnik russkoi literatury XIII v. "Slovo o pogibeli russkoi zemli."* Moscow-Leningrad, 1965.

Berezin, I. N. "Ocherk vnutrennogo ustroistva ulusa Dzhuchieva." *Trudy Vostochnago Otdeleniia Russkago arkheologicheskago obshchestva* 8 (1864), pp. 387–494.

Beskrovnii, L. G., et al. *Kulikovskaia bitva. sbornik statei.* Moscow, 1980.

Beyerly, Elizabeth. *The Europocentric Historiography of Russia: An Analysis of the Contributions by Russian Emigre Historians in the USA, 1925–1955.* The Hague-Paris, 1973.

Bezzola, Gian Andri. *Die Mongolen in abenländischen Sicht (1220–1270). Ein Beitrag zur Frage der Völkerbegegnung.* Bern, 1974.

Billington, James. *The Icon and the Axe. An Interpretive History of Russian Culture.* New York, 1966.

Birnbaum, Henrik. "Serbian Models in the Literature and the Literary Language of Medieval Russia." *Slavic and East European Journal* 23:1 (Spring, 1979), pp. 1–13.

Black, J. L. *Nicholas Karamzin and Russian Society in the Nineteenth Century: A Study in Russian Political and Historical Thought.* Toronto, 1975.

————. "Nicholas Karamzin's Scheme for Russian History." *New Review* VIII:4–IX:3 (September, 1969), pp. 16–33.

————. "The *Primechaniia*: Karamzin as a 'Scientific' Historian of Russia." In J. L. Black, ed., *Essays on Karamzin: Russian Man-of-Letters, Political Thinker, Historian, 1766–1826.* The Hague-Paris, 1975, pp. 127–147.

————. "The 'State School' Interpretation of Russian History: A Re-Appraisal of its Genetic Origins." *Jahrbücher für Geschichte Osteuropas* 21 (1973), pp. 509–530.

Blake, Robert and Frye, Richard, trs. "The History of the Nation of Archers (Mongols) by Grigor of Akanc." *Harvard Journal of Asiatic Studies* XII:3–4 (December, 1949), pp. 269–399.

Bochkov, V. N. "'Legenda' o vyezde dvorianskikh rodov." *Arkheograficheskii ezhegodnik za 1969* (1971), pp. 73–93.

Borisov, N. S. "Otechestvennaia istoriografiia o vliianii tataro-mongol'skogo nashestviia na russkuiu kul'turu." *Problemy istorii SSSR* V (Moscow, 1976), pp. 129–148.

————. "Russkaia arkhitektura i mongolo-tatarskoe igo (1238–1300)." *Vestnik Moskovskogo Universiteta. Istoriia,* #6, 1976, pp. 63–79.

Böss, Otto. *Die Lehre der Eurasier: Ein Beitrag zur russischen Ideengeschichte des 20 J.* Veröffentlichungen des Osteuropa-Instituts München, Band XV. Wiesbaden, 1961.

Boyle, John Andrew, ed. *Cambridge History of Iran,* v. V: *Saljuq and Mongol Periods.* Cambridge, England, 1968.

Boyle, John Andrew, tr. & ed. *Juvaini, The History of the World Conqueror.* 2 vols. Manchester-Cambridge, Mass., 1958.

Brown, Peter B. "Early Modern Russian Bureaucracy: The Evolution of the Chancellery System from Ivan III to Peter the Great, 1478–1717." Dissertation, University of Chicago, 1977, 2 vols.

Budovnits, I. U. "Ideinaia osnova rannikh skazanii o tatarskom ige." *Trudy otdela drevnerusskoi literatury* XIV (1958), pp. 169–175.

————. *Obshchestvenno-politicheskaia mysl' drevnei Rusi (XI–XIV vv.).* Moscow, 1960.

————. "Russkoe dukhovenstvo v pervoe stoletie mongolo-tatarskogo iga." *Voprosy istorii religii i ateizma* VII (1959), pp. 284–302.

Burns, Robert Ignatius, S. J. *Islam under the Crusaders: Colonial Survival in the Thirteenth-Century Kingdom of Valencia.* Princeton, 1973.
———. "Spanish Islam in Transition: Acculturative Survival and its Price in the Christian Kingdom of Valencia." In Speros Vryonis, ed., *Islam and Cultural Change in the Middle Ages.* Wiesbaden, 1975, pp. 87–105.
Bushkovitch, Paul. *The Merchants of Moscow, 1580–1640.* Cambridge, England, 1980.
———. "Towns, Trade and Artisans in Seventeenth-Century Russia: The View from Eastern Europe." *Forschungen zur osteuropaischen Geschichte* 27 (1980), pp. 215–232.
Bychkova, M. E. "Obzor rodoslovnykh knig XVI–XVII vv." *Arkheograficheskii ezhegodnik za 1966* (1968), pp. 254–278.
———. "Redaktsiia rodoslovnykh knig vtoroi poloviny XVI v." *Arkheograficheskii ezhegodnik za 1962* (1963), pp. 126–133.
———. *Rodoslovnye knigi XVI–XVII kak istoricheskii istochnik.* Moscow, 1975.
———. "Rodoslovnye knigi serediny XVI veka." *Trudy Moskovskogo Gosudarstvennogo Istoriko-Arkhivnogo Instituta,* 16 (1961), pp. 475–480.
Chan, Hok-lam. "Liu Ping-chung (1216–1274). A Buddhist Taoist Statesman at the Court of Kubilai Khan." *T'oung Pao* 53 (1967), pp. 98–146.
Ch'en, Paul Heng-chao. *Chinese Legal Tradition under the Mongols. The Code of 1291 as Reconstructed.* Princeton, 1979.
Cherepnin, L. V. "Istochniki po istorii anti-mongol'skogo vosstaniia v Tveri v 1327 g." *Arkheograficheskii ezhegodnik za 1958* (1960), pp. 37–53.
———. *Istoricheskie vzgliady klassikov russkoi literatury.* Moscow, 1968.
———. *Obrazovanie russkogo tsentralizovannogo gosudarstva v XIV–XV vv.: Ocherki sotsial'no-ekonomicheskoi i politicheskoi istorii Rusi.* Moscow, 1960.
Cherniavsky, Michael. "Ivan the Terrible and the Iconography of the Kremlin Cathedral of Archangel Michael." *Russian History* 2:1 (1975), pp. 3–28.
———. "Ivan the Terrible as a Renaissance Prince." *Slavic Review* 27 (1968), pp. 195–211.
———. "Khan or Basileus: An Aspect of Russian Medieval Political Theory." *Journal of the History of Ideas* 20 (1959), pp. 459–476. Rpt. in Cherniavsky, ed., *The Structure of Russian History.* New York, 1970. pp. 65–79.
———. "The Old Believers and the New Religion." *Slavic Review* 21 (1966), pp. 1–39.
———. Chapter V, "Russia." In Orest Ranum, ed., *National Consciousness, History and Political Culture in Early Modern Europe.* Baltimore, 1975, pp. 118–143.
———. *Tsar and People. Studies in Russian Myths.* New Haven, 1961, 1970.
———. "What Is a Russian?" Unpublished essay.
Chumachenko, E. G. V. O. Kliuchevskii—istochnikoved. Moscow, 1970.
Cleaves, Francis Woodman. "The Fifteen Palace Poems by K'o Chiu-ssu." *Harvard Journal of Asiatic Studies* 20 (1957), pp. 391–479.
———. "The Historicity of the Baljuna Covenant." *Harvard Journal of Asiatic Studies* 18 (1955), pp. 357–421.
Constantelos, Demetrius J. "The Moslem Conquests of the Near East as Revealed in the Greek Sources of the Seventh and Eighth Centuries." *Byzantion* 42 (1972), pp. 325–357.

Culpepper, Jack M. "The Legislative Origins of Peasant Bondage in Muscovy." *Forschungen zur osteuropaischen Geschichte* 14 (1969), pp. 162–237.

Dardess, John. "Ming T'ai-tsu on the Yüan: An Autocrat's Assessment of the Mongol Dynasty." *Bulletin of Sung-Yüan Studies* 14 (1978), pp. 6–11.

Davis, R. H. C. "William of Tyre," in Derek Baker, ed. *Relations between East and West in the Middle Ages*. Edinburgh, 1973, pp. 64–76.

Dawson, Christopher, ed. & intro. *Mission to Asia. Narratives and Letters of the Franciscan Missionaries in Mongolia and China in the Thirteenth and Fourteenth Centuries.* (Previously published as *The Mongol Mission*, 1955.) New York, 1966.

de Rachewiltz, Igor. "The *Hsi-yu lu* of Yeh-lü Ch'u-ts'ai." *Monumenta Serica* 21 (1962), pp. 1–128.

———. "Some Remarks on the Dating of the *Secret History of the Mongols*." *Monumenta Serica* 24 (1965), pp. 185–206.

———. "Some Remarks on the Ideological Foundations of Chinghis Khan's Empire." *Papers on Far Eastern History* (of the Australian National University) 7 (1973), pp. 21–36.

Dewey, Horace W. "Kinship and *Poruka* before Peter the Great." Paper, American Association for the Advancement of Slavic Studies Convention, Philadelphia, November 5, 1980.

———. "Sentimentalism in the Historical Writings of N. M. Karamzin." In *American Contributions to the Fourth International Congress of Slavists. Moscow, September 1958* (s' Gravenhage, 1958), pp. 41–50.

Dewey, Horace W. and Kleimola, Ann M. "Coercion by Righter *(Pravezh)* in Old Russian Administration." *Canadian-American Slavic Studies* 9:2 (1965), pp. 156–167.

Dimnik, Martin. *Mikhail, Prince of Chernigov and Grand Prince of Kiev, 1224–1246*. Toronto, 1981.

Dmitrieva, R. P. "Byl li Sofronyi riazanets avtorom Zadonshchiny?" *Trudy otdela drevnerusskoi literatury* 34 (1979), pp. 18–25.

Dukhovnye i dogovornye gramoty velikikh i udel'nykh kniazei XIV–XVI vv., ed. L. V. Cherepnin. Moscow-Leningrad, 1950.

Egorov, V. L. "Gosudarstvennoe i administrativnoe ustroistvo Zolotoi Ordy." *Voprosy istorii* 1972 #2, pp. 32–42.

Esper, Thomas. "Military Self-Sufficiency and Weapons Technology in Muscovite Russia." *Slavic Review* 28:2 (June, 1969), pp. 185–208.

Evans, Bergan. *Dictionary of Quotations*. New York, 1968.

Fedorov-Davydov, G. A. *Kochevniki Vostochnoi Evropy pod vlast'iu zolotoordynskikh khanov: Arkheologicheskie pamiatniki.* Moscow, 1966.

———. *Monety Moskovskoi Rusi (Moskva v bor'be za nezavisimoe i tsentralizovannoe gosudarstvo)*. Moscow, 1981.

———. *Obshchestvennyi stroi Zolotoi Ordy*. Moscow, 1973.

Fennell, John L. I. "Andrej Jaroslavovič and the Struggle for Power in 1252: An Examination of the Sources." *Russia Mediaevalis* I (1973), pp. 49–63.

———. *The Emergence of Moscow, 1304–1359*. Berkeley and Los Angeles, 1968.

———. "The Ideological Role of the Russian Church in the First Half of the Fourteenth Century." In *Gorski Vijenac. A Garland of Essays Offered to Professor Elizabeth Hill*. Cambridge, England, 1970, pp. 105–111.

———. "The Struggle for Power in North-East Russia, 1246–1249: An Investiga-

    tion of the Sources." *Oxford Slavonic Papers* 7 (1974), pp. 112–121.
————. "The Tver' Uprising of 1327: A Study of the Sources." *Jahrbücher für Geschichte Osteuropas* 15 (1967), pp. 161–179.
Fennell, John L. I. and Stokes, Anthony. *Early Russian Literature.* Berkeley, 1974.
Fisher, Alan W. "Crimean Separatism in the Ottoman Empire." In William W. Haddad and William Ochsenwald, eds., *Nationalism in a Non-National State: The Dissolution of the Ottoman Empire.* Columbus, 1977, pp. 57–76.
————. *The Crimean Tatars.* Stanford, 1978.
————. "Muscovite-Ottoman Relations in the Sixteenth and Seventeenth Centuries." *Humaniora Islamica* 1 (1973), pp. 207–213.
————. "The Ottoman Crimea in the Mid Seventeenth Century: Some Problems and Preliminary Considerations." *Harvard Ukrainian Studies* III/IV (*Eucharisterion*—Pritsak Festschrift), Part 1 (1979–1980), pp. 215–226.
————. "The Ottoman Crimea in the Sixteenth Century." *Harvard Ukrainian Studies* V:2 (June, 1981), pp. 135–170.
————. "Les Rapports entre l'Empire Ottoman et la Crimée: l'aspect financier." *Cahiers du monde russe et soviétique* XIII/3 (1972), pp. 368–381.
————. *The Russian Annexation of the Crimea.* Cambridge, England, 1970.
Foust, Clifford M. *Muscovite and Mandarin: Russia's Trade with China and Its Setting.* Chapel Hill, 1969.
Gibb, H. A. R., tr. *Ibn Batuta, Travels in Asia and Africa 1325–1354.* New York, 1929.
Golden, Peter B. "The Polovci Dikii." *Harvard Ukrainian Studies* III/IV (1979–1980) (*Eucharisterion*—Pritsak Festschrift), Part 1, pp. 296–309.
————. "The Question of the Rus' Qağanate." *Archivum Eurasiae Medii Aevi* II (1982), pp. 77–97.
Golokhvastov, D. P. and Leonid, arkhimandrit. "Blagoveshchenskii ierei Sil'vestr' i ego poslania." *Chteniia v Obshchestve istorii i drevnostei rossiiskikh pri Moskovskom universitete*, #88, 1874, kniga 1 (January–March), pp. 69–87.
Golubinskii, E. *Istoriia russkoi tserkvy,* t. II ch. 1. Moscow, 1900, rpt. The Hague, 1969.
Graham, Hugh F. "Did Institutionalized Education Exist in Pre-Petrine Russia?" In Don Karl Rowney and G. Edward Orchard, eds., *Russian and Slavic History.* Columbus, 1976, pp. 260–273.
————. "Digenis Akritas and the *Devgenievo Dejanie*—A Reappraisal." *Studies in Medieval Culture* IV/3 (1974), pp. 483–495.
————. "Digenis Akritas as a Source for Frontier History." *Actes de XIVᵉ Congrès International des Études Byzantines, Bucarest 6–12 Septembre 1971,* v. 2 (Bucarest, 1975), pp. 321–329.
————. "The Tale of Devgenij." *Byzantinoslavica* 29 (1968), pp. 51–91.
Gramoty Velikogo Novgoroda i Pskova. Ed. S. N. Valk. Moscow-Leningrad, 1949.
Grekov, B. D. *Kievan Russia.* Tr. Y. Sdobnikov. Moscow, 1959.
Grekov, B. D. and Iakubovskii, A. Iu. *Zolotaia orda i ee padenie.* Moscow-Leningrad, 1950.
Grekov, I. B. *Ocherki po istorii mezhdunarodnykh otnoshenii Vostochnoi Evropy XIV–XVI vv.* Moscow, 1963.
————. *Vostochnaia Evropa i upadok Zolotoi ordy (na rubezhe XIV–XV vv.).* Moscow, 1975.

Grigor'ev, A. P. "K rekonstruktsii tekstov zolotoordynskikh iarlykov XIII–XIV vv."
    Istoriografiia i istochnikovedenie istorii stran Azii i Afriki V (Leningrad,
    1980), pp. 15–38.
———. Mongol'skaia diplomatika XIII–XV vv. (Chingizidskie zhalovannye
    gramoty). Leningrad, 1978.
Grigor'ev, V. V. "Ob otnosheniiakh mezhdu kochevymi narodami i osedlymi
    gosudarstvami." Zhurnal Ministerstva Narodnago Prosveshcheniia ch. 17
    (1875), otdel nauk (III), pp. 1–27.
Grothusen, Klaus-Detlev. Die Historische Rechtsschule Russlands. Ein Beitrag zur
    russischen Geistesgeschichte in der zweite Hälfte das 19 Jahrhunderts.
    Giessen, 1962.
———. "Die russische Geschichtswissenschaft des 19 Jh. als Forschungsauf-
    gabe." Jahrbücher für Geschichte Osteuropas 8 (1960), pp. 32–61.
———. "S. M. Solov'ev's Stellung in der russischen Historiographie."
    Forschungen zur osteuropaischen Geschichte 4 (1956), pp. 7–103.
Grushevskii (Hrushevsky), M. Ocherki istorii Kievskoi zemli ot smerti Yaroslava
    do kontsa XIV stoletiia. Kiev, 1891.
Gudzii, N. K. Khrestomatiia po drevnei russkoi literatury. 7th ed. Moscow, 1962.
Gumilev, L. N. Khunnu. Sredinnaia Aziia v drevnie vremena. Moscow, 1960.
———. "Les Mongoles de XIIIe siècle et la Slovo o polku Igoreve." Cahiers du
    monde russe et soviétique VII:1 (January–March, 1966), pp. 37–57.
———. Poiski vymyshlennogo tsarstva (Legenda o "Gosudarstve presvitra
    Ioanna"). Moscow, 1970.
———. "Udel'no-lestvichnaia sistema u tiurok v VI–VIII vv. (K voprosu o rannykh
    formakh gosudarstvennosti)." Sovetskaia Etnografiia 1959 #3, pp. 11–25.
Halecki, Oscar. The Limits and Divisions of European History. New York, 1950.
Halperin, Charles J. "A Chingissid Saint of the Russian Orthodox Church: The 'Life
    of Peter, tsarevich of the Horde'." Canadian-American Slavic Studies 9:3
    (1975), pp. 324–335.
———. "The Concept of the ruskaia zemlia and Medieval National Conscious-
    ness from the Tenth to the Fifteenth Centuries." Nationalities Papers 8:1
    (Spring, 1980), pp. 75–86.
———. "The Concept of the Russian Land from the Ninth to the Fourteenth
    Centuries." Russian History 2:1 (1975), pp. 29–38.
———. "The Defeat and Death of Batu." Russian History 10:1 (1983), pp. 50–
    65.
———. "George Vernadsky, Eurasianism, the Mongols and Russia." Slavic Re-
    view 41:3 (Fall, 1982), pp. 477–493.
———. "The Ideology of Silence: Prejudice and Pragmatism on the Medieval
    Religious Frontier." Comparative Studies in Society and History 26:3 (July,
    1984), pp. 442–466.
———. "Know Thy Enemy: Medieval Russian Familiarity with the Mongols of the
    Golden Horde." Jahrbücher für Geschichte Osteuropas 30 (1982),
    pp. 161–175.
———. "Medieval Myopia and the Mongol Period of Russian History." Russian
    History 5:2 (1978), pp. 188–191.
———. "Now you see them, now you don't: A Note on the First Appearance of
    the Rhos (Rus) in Byzantium." Canadian-American Slavic Studies 7:4
    (Winter, 1973), pp. 494–497.
———. "Master and Man in Muscovy." In A. E. Presniakov, The Tsardom of

Muscovy. Tr. R. Price. Gulf Breeze, Fla., 1978, pp. vii–xxi.
———. "Russia and the Steppe: George Vernadsky and Eurasianism." *Forschungen zur osteuropaischen Geschichte,* in press.
———. "Russia and the 'Tatar Yoke': Concepts of Conquest, Liberation, and the Chingissid Idea." *Archivum Eurasiae Medii Aevi* II (1982), pp. 99–107.
———. "Russia in the Mongol Empire in Comparative Perspective." *Harvard Journal of Asiatic Studies* 43:1 (June, 1983), pp. 239–261.
———. "The Russian Land and the Russian Tsar: The Emergence of Muscovite Ideology, 1380–1408." *Forschungen zur osteuropaischen Geschichte* 23 (1976), pp. 7–103.
———. "The Six-Hundredth Anniversary of the Battle of Kulikovo Field, 1380–1980, in Soviet Historiography." *Canadian-American Slavic Studies,* in press.
———. "Sixteenth-Century Foreign Travel Accounts to Muscovy: A Methodological Excursus." *The Sixteenth Century Journal* 6:2 (October, 1975), pp. 89–111.
———. "Soviet Historiography on Russia and the Mongols." *Russian Review* 41:3 (July, 1982), pp. 306–322.
———. *The Tatar Yoke.* Columbus, Ohio, forthcoming.
———. "The Tatar Yoke and Tatar Oppression." *Russia Mediaevalis,* in press.
———. "*Tsarev ulus:* Russia in the Golden Horde." *Cahiers du monde russe et soviétique* 23:2 (April–June, 1982), pp. 257–263.
Hellie, Richard. *Enserfment and Military Change in Muscovy.* Chicago, 1971.
Hsiao, Ch'i-ch'ing. *The Military Establishment of the Yüan Dynasty.* Cambridge, Mass., 1978.
Hugo, Victor. *Le Rhin.* Paris, 1900.
Hung, William. "The Transmission of the Book Known as *The Secret History of the Mongols.*" *Harvard Journal of Asiatic Studies* 14 (1951), pp. 433–492.
Hurwitz, Ellen S. "Kievan Rus' and Medieval Myopia." *Russian History* 5:2 (1978), pp. 176–187.
———. *Prince Andrej Bogoljubskij: The Man and The Myth.* Studia Historica et Philologica, XII, Sectio Slavica 4. Firenze 1980.
I. R. (Prince Nikolai S. Trubetskoi). *Nasledie Chingis khana. V''zgliad na russkuiu istoriiu ne s Zapada, a s Vostoka.* Berlin 1925.
Iakubovskii, A. Iu. "Iz istorii izucheniia mongolov perioda XI–XIII vv." *Ocherki po istorii russkogo vostokovedeniia* [sb. 1] (Moscow, 1953), pp. 31–95.
———. "Iz istorii padeniia Zolotoi Ordy," *Voprosy istorii* 1947 #2, pp. 30–45.
———. "Kniga B. Ia. Vladimirtsova 'Obshchestvennyi stroi mongolov' i perspektivy dal'neishego izucheniia Zolotoi Ordy." *Istoricheskii sbornik.* Institut istorii A.N. SSSR, t. V. Moscow-Leningrad, 1936, pp. 293–313.
Ikonnikov, S. V. *Opyt russkoi istoriografii.* 2 vols. Kiev, 1891–1908.
Illeritskii, V. E. "O gosudarstvennoi shkole v russkoi istoriografii." *Voprosy istorii* 1959 #5, pp. 141–159.
Ioasafovskaia letopis'. Ed. A. A. Zimin. Moscow, 1957.
Iugov, A. "Daniil Galitskii i Aleksandr Nevskii." *Voprosy istorii* 1945 #3–4, pp. 99–107.
Kaiser, Daniel H. *The Growth of Law in Medieval Russia.* Princeton, 1980.
Karamzin, N. M. *Istoriia gosudarstva Rossiiskago.* 12 vols. St. Petersburg, 1892.
Kargalov, V. V. "Baskaki." *Voprosy istorii* 1972 #5, pp. 212–216.
———. "Mongolo-tatarskie vtorzheniia i peremeshchenie naseleniia severo-

vostochnoi Rusi vo vtoroi polovine XIII v." *Nauchnye doklady Vysshei Shkoly. Istoricheskie nauki.* 1961 #4, pp. 134–147.

———. "Polovetskie nabegi na Rusi." *Voprosy istorii* 1965 #9, pp. 68–73.

———. "Posledstviia mongolo-tatarskogo nashestviia XIII v. dlia sel'skikh mestnostei Severo-Vostochnoi Rusi." *Voprosy istorii* 1965 #3, pp. 53–58.

———. "Sushchestvovali li na Rusi 'voenno-politicheskaia baskacheskaia organizatsiia' mongol'skikh feodalov?" *Istoriia SSSR* 1962 #1, pp. 161–165.

———. *Vneshnepoliticheskie faktory razvitiia feodal'noi Rusi. Feodal'naia Rus' i kochevniki.* Moscow, 1967.

Karpovich, Michael. "Klyuchevskii and Recent Trends in Russian Historiography." *Slavonic and East European Review* 21:56 (1943), pp. 31–39.

———. "Pushkin as a Historian." In Samuel Hazzard Cross and Ernest J. Simmons, eds., *Centennial Essays for Pushkin.* Cambridge, Mass., 1937, and New York, 1967, pp. 181–200.

Kataev, I. M. "Tatary i poraboshchenie imi Rusi." In M. V. Dovnar-Zapol'skii, ed., *Russkaia istoriia v ocherkakh i stat'iakh.* Moscow, 1909, pp. 564–575.

Keenan, Edward L., Jr. "Coming to Grips with the *Kazanskaya istoriya:* Some Observations on Old Answers and New Questions." *Annals of the Ukrainian Academy of Arts and Sciences in the United States* v. 31–32 (1967), pp. 143–183.

———. "The *Yarlik* of Axmed-khan to Ivan III: A New Reading—A Study in Literal *Diplomatica* and Literary *Turcica.*" *International Journal of Slavic Linguistics and Poetics* 11 (1967), pp. 33–47.

Khozhenie za tri moria Afanasiia Nikitina 1466–1472 gg. Ed. B. D. Grekov and V. P. Adrianova-Peretts. Moscow, 1948, 2nd ed., 1958.

Kireeva, R. A. *V. O. Kliuchevskii kak istorik russkoi istoricheskoi nauki.* Moscow, 1966.

Kliuchevskii, V. O. *Drevnerusskiia zhitiia sviatykh kak istocheskii istochnik.* Moscow, 1871.

———. *Kurs russkoi istorii,* 5 vv. (=*Sochineniia,* 8 vv., vv. 1–5), II. Moscow, 1957.

Kloss, B. M. "O vremeni sozdanii russkogo Khronografa." *Trudy otdela drevnerusskoi literatury* 26 (1971), pp. 244–255.

Kochin, G. E. *Sel'skoe khoziaistvo na Rusi kontsa XIII–XIV v.* Leningrad, 1965.

Kollmann, Nancy Shields. "Kinship and Politics: The Origin and Evolution of the Muscovite Boyar Elite in the Fifteenth Century." Dissertation, Harvard University, 1980.

Kotwicz, W. "Formules initiales des documents mongoles au XIII-me et XIV-me siècles." *Rocznik Orientalistyczny* 10 (1934), pp. 131–157.

———. "Les Mongoles, promoteurs de l'idée de paix universelle au début du XIII siècle." In *La Pologne au VII-e Congrès International des Sciences Historiques.* Warsaw, 1933.

Krachkovskii, I. Iu. *Izbrannye sochineniia.* t. V. *Ocherki po istorii russkoi arabistiki.* Moscow-Leningrad, 1958.

Kuchkin, V. A. *Povesti o Mikhaile Tverskom. Istoriko-tekstologicheskoe issledovanie.* Moscow, 1974.

Kudriashev, K. V. *Polovestskaia step': ocherki istoricheskoi geografii.* Geograficheskoe obshchestvo SSSR. Zapiski, novaia seriia, t. 2. Moscow, 1948.

Langer, Lawrence N. "The Black Death in Russia: Its Effect Upon Urban Labor."

Russian History 2:1 (1975), pp. 53–67.
———. "The Medieval Russian Town." In Michael Hamm, ed., *The City in Russian History.* Lexington, Kentucky, 1976, pp. 11–33.
———. "Plague and the Russian Countryside: Monastic Estates in the Late Fourteenth and Fifteenth Centuries." *Canadian-American Slavic Studies* 10:3 (Fall, 1976), pp. 351–368.
———. "The Russian Medieval Town: From the Mongol Invasion to the End of the Fifteenth Century." Dissertation, University of Chicago, 1972.
Lattimore, Owen. "Chinghis Khan and the Mongol Conquests." *Scientific American* 209 (August, 1963), pp. 54–68.
———. *Inner Asian Frontiers of China.* 1940; Boston, 1962.
———. "The Social History of Mongol Nomadism." In W. G. Beasley and E. G. Pulleybank, eds., *Historical Writings on the Peoples of Asia.* v. 3: *Historians of China and Japan.* London, 1961, pp. 328–343.
———. *Studies in Frontier History. Collected Papers 1928–1958.* London, 1962.
Leitsch, Walter. "Einige Beobachtungen zum politischen Weltbild Aleksandr Nevskys." *Forschungen zur osteuropaischen Geschichte* 25 (1978), pp. 202–216.
Lenhoff, Gail Diane. Chapter VI. "Afanasij Nikitin's Journey Beyond Three Seas." In "The Making of the Medieval Russian Journey." Dissertation, University of Michigan, 1978, pp. 198–248.
———. "Beyond Three Seas: Afanasij Nikitin's Journey from Orthodoxy to Apostasy." *East European Quarterly* XIII:4 (1979), pp. 431–447.
———. "The Case Against Afanasii Nikitin." Paper, American Association for the Advancement of Slavic Studies Convention, Philadelphia, November 6, 1980.
Likhachev, D. S. *Chelovek v literature drevnei Rusi.* 1958, 2nd ed. Moscow, 1970.
———. *Kul'tura Rusi epokhi obrazovaniia russkogo natsional'nogo gosudarstva (konets XIV-nachalo XVI v.).*Leningrad, 1946.
———. *Kul'tura Rusi vremeni Andreia Rubleva i Epifaniia Premudrogo (konets XIV–nachalo XV v.).*Moscow-Leningrad, 1962.
———. *Natsional'noe samosoznanie drevnei Rusi. Ocherki iz istorii oblasti russkoi literatury XI–XVII vv.* Moscow-Leningrad, 1945.
———. *Poetika drevnerusskoi literatury.* Leningrad, 1967.
———. *Razvitie russkoi literatury X-XVII vekov. Epokhi i stili.* Leningrad, 1973.
———. *Russkie letopisi i ikh kul'turno-istoricheskoe znachenie.* Moscow-Leningrad, 1947; rpt. The Hague, 1966.
———. *Velikoe nasledie: Klassicheskie proizvedeniia literatury drevnei Rusi.* Moscow, 1975.
Limonov, Iu. A. "Iz istorii vostochnoi torgovli Vladimiro-Suzdal'skogo kniazhestva." In *Mezhdunarodnye sviazi Rossii do XVII v. Sb. st.* Moscow, 1961, pp. 55–63.
Lo, Jung-pang. "The Controversy over Grain Conveyance during the Reign of Qubilai Qaqun, 1260–1294." *Far Eastern Quarterly* 13 (1954), pp. 262–285.
Lur'e, Ia.S. "Izdanie bez tekstologa." *Russkaia literatura* 1960 #3, pp. 220–223.
———.*Obshcherusskie letopisi XIV–XV vv.* Leningrad, 1976.
———. "Podvig Afanasiia Nikitina (K 500-letiiu nachala ego puteshestviia)." *Izvestiia Vsesoiuznogo Geograficheskogo obshchestva,* t. 99, 1967, #5, pp. 435–442.

Mancall, Mark. *Russia and China: The Diplomatic Relations to 1728*. Cambridge, Mass., 1971.

Martin, Janet. "The Land of Darkness and the Golden Horde. The Fur Trade under the Mongols. XIII–XIV Centuries." *Cahiers du monde russe et soviétique* XIX: 4 (1978), pp. 401–422.

Mavrodin, V. V. "Levoberezhnaia Ukraina pod vlast'iu tataro-mongolov." *Uchenye zapiski Leningradskogo gosudarstvennogo universiteta*, #32 vyp. 2, 1939, pp. 39–65.

Mavrodina, R. M. "Rus' i kochevniki." In *Sovetskaia istoriografiia Kievskoi Rusi*. Leningrad, 1978, pp. 210–221.

Meyendorff, John. *Byzantium and the Rise of Russia. A Study of Byzantine-Russian Relations in the Fourteenth Century*. Cambridge, England, 1981.

McGrew, R. E. "Notes on the Princely Role in Karamzin's *Istoriya gosudarstva Rossisskogo*." *American Slavic and East European Review* 18 (1959), pp. 12–24.

McNally, Suzanne Janosik. "From Public Person to Private Prisoner: The Changing Place of Women in Medieval Russia." Dissertation, State University of New York at Binghamton, 1976.

McNeill, William H. *Europe's Steppe Frontiers 1500–1800*. Chicago, 1964.

Miliukov, Paul. "Eurasianism and Europeanism in Russian History." In *Festschrift Th.G. Masaryk zum 80 Geburtstage. I. Der russische Gedanke*. Bonn, 1931, pp. 225–236.

———. *Glavnye techeniia russkoi istoricheskoi mysli*. St. Petersburg, 1913.

———. "Iuridicheskaia shkola v russkoi istoriografii (Solov'ev, Kavelin, Chicherin, Sergeevich)." *Russkaia mysl'* 1886, VI, pp. 80–92.

Mills, James Cobb, Jr. "The Russian Autocracy in the Writings of A. E. Presniakov." *Laurentian University Review* 10:1 (November, 1977), pp. 47–65.

———. "Presniakov in Two Worlds: A 'Bourgeois' Historian and the Soviet Revolution." Unpublished essay.

Minorsky, V. "Pūr-i Bahā and his Poems." In Minorsky, *Iranica. Twenty Articles*. Publications of the University of Teheran, #775. Teheran, 1964 (originally 1956), pp. 292–305.

———. "Pūr-i Bahā's 'Mongol Ode'." In Minorsky, *Iranica. Twenty Articles*. Publications of the University of Teheran, #775. Teheran, 1964 (originally 1954), pp. 274–291.

Moiseeva, G. N., ed. *Kazanskaia istoriia*. Moscow-Leningrad, 1954.

Moses, Larry W. "A Theoretical Approach to the Process of Inner Asian Confederation." *Études Mongoles* 5 (1974), pp. 113–122.

———. *The Political Role of Mongol Buddhism*. Indiana University Uralic and Altaic Series, v. 133. Bloomington, 1977.

Mote, F. W. "The Growth of Chinese Despotism: A Critique of Wittfogel's Theory of Oriental Despotism as Applied to China." *Oriens Extremis* 8:1 (1961), pp. 1–41.

Müller, Lüdolf. *Das Metropoliten Ilarion, Lobrede auf Vladimir den Heiligen und Glaubensbekenntnis*. Wiesbaden, 1962.

Nasonov, A. N. *Istoriia russkogo letopisaniia XI-nachala XVIII veka. Ocherki i issledovaniia*. Moscow, 1969.

———. "Lavrent'evskaia letopis' i Vladimirskoe velikokniazheskoe letopisanie pervoi poloviny XIII v." *Problemy istochnikovedeniia* XI (1963), pp. 429–480.

————. "Letopisnye pamiatniki Tverskogo kniazhestva. Opyt rekonstruktsii tverskogo letopisaniia s XIII do kontsa XV v." *Izvestiia Akademii Nauk.* VII seriia. *otd. gumanitarnykh nauk.* 1930, #9, pp. 707–738; #10, pp. 739–773.

————. *Mongoly i Rus'. Istoriia Tatarskoi politiki na Rusi.* Moscow-Leningrad, 1940.

————. ed., *Novgorodskaia pervaia letopis' starshego i mladshego izvodov.* Moscow-Leningrad, 1950.

Neander, Irene. "Die Bedeutung der Mongolenherrschaft in Russland." *Geschichte in Wissenschaft und Unterricht* 5 (1954), pp. 257–270.

Nechkina, M. V. *Vasilii Osipovich Kliuchevskii. Istoriia zhizni i tvorchestva.* Moscow, 1974.

Nikitine, Boris. "Les contacts spirituels entre la Russie et l'Asie." *Russie et Chrétienité* no. 1 (1946), pp. 3–21.

Noonan, Thomas S. "Medieval Russia, the Mongols, and the West: Novgorod's Relations with the Baltic, 1100–1350." *Medieval Studies* 37 (1975), pp. 316–339.

————. "Russia's Eastern Trade, 1150–1350: The Archeological Evidence." *Archivum Eurasiae Medii Aevi* III (1983), pp. 201–264.

————. "Suzdalia's Eastern Trade in the Century Before the Mongol Conquest." *Cahiers du monde russe et soviétique* XIX:4 (1978), pp. 371–384.

Novosel'skii, A. A. *Bor'ba moskovskogo gosudarstva s Tatarami v pervoi polovine XVII veka.* Moscow-Leningrad, 1948.

Obolensky, Dimitri. *The Byzantine Commonwealth: Eastern Europe, 500–1453.* New York, 1971.

Oinas, Felix J. "The Problem of the Aristocratic Origin of the *Byliny.*" *Slavic Review* 30:3 (September, 1971), pp. 513–522.

Oinas, Felix J. and Soudakoff, S., eds. *The Study of Russian Folklore.* The Hague, 1975.

Olbricht, Peter. *Das Postwesen in China unter der Mongolenherrschaft im 13. und 14 Jh.* Göttinger Asiatische Forschungen, 1. Wiesbaden, 1954.

Orchard, G. Edward. "The Eurasian School of Russian Historiography." *Laurentian University Review* X:1 (November, 1977), pp. 97–106.

Pamiatniki drevne-russkago kanonicheskago prava. chast' pervaia: *Pamiatniki XI–XV v.=Russkaia istoricheskaia biblioteka,* VI. 2nd ed., St. Petersburg, 1908.

Pamiatniki prava perioda obrazovaniia russkogo tsentralizovannogo gosudarstva XIV–XV vv.=Pamiatniki russkogo prava, III. Moscow, 1955.

Paneiakh, V. M. *Kabal'noe kholopstvo v XVI v.* Leningrad, 1967.

————. *Kholopstvo v XVI–XVII vv.* Leningrad, 1975.

Parkhomenko, Vladimir. "Kievskaia Rus' i Khazariia (Rol' khazarskogo torgovogo kapitala v istorii Kievskoi derzhavy)." *Slavia* 6 (1927), pp. 380–387.

————. "Sledy polovetskogo eposa v letopisiakh." *Problemy istochnikovedeniia* 3 (1940), pp. 391–393.

Pavlov, P. N. "K voprosu o russkoi dani v Zolotoiu Ordu." *Uchenye zapiski Krasnoiarskogo Gos. Ped. Instituta,* t. XIII, vyp. II (1958), pp. 74–112.

————. "Reshaiushchaia rol' vooruzhenoi bor'by russkogo naroda v 1472–1480 gg. v okonchachatel'nom osvobozhdenii Rusi ot tatarskogo iga." *Uchenye zapiski Krasnoiarskogo Gos. Ped. Instituta,* t. IV, vyp. I, 1955, pp. 182–195.

———. "Tatarskie otriazi na russkoi sluzhbe v period zaversheniia ob"edineniia Rusi." *Uchenye zapiski Krasnoiarskogo Gos. Ped. Instituta,* t. IX, vyp. I, 1957, pp. 165–177.

Pelenski, Jaroslaw. *Russia and Kazan. Conquest and Imperial Ideology (1438–1560s).* The Hague-Paris, 1973.

———. "State and Society in Muscovite Russia and the Mongol-Turkic System in the Sixteenth Century." *Forschungen zur osteuropaischen Geschichte* 27 (1980), pp. 156–167.

Perfecky, George A., tr. *The Hypatian Codex. Part II. The Galician-Volynian Chronicle. An Annotated Translation.* Munich, 1973.

Petrushevskii, I. P. *Zemledelie i agrarnye otnosheniia v Irane XIII–XIV vv.* Moscow-Leningrad, 1960.

Petukhov, E. V. *Serapion Vladimirskii, russkii propovednik XIII v.* Zapiski istoriko-filologicheskago fakul'teta St. Peterburgskago universiteta, ch. XVII. St. Petersburg, 1888.

Philipp, Werner. *Ansätze zum geschichtlichen und politischen Denken in Kiewer Russland.* Breslau, 1940.

Picchio, Riccardo. "On Russian Humanism: The Philological Revival." *Slavia* 44:2 (1975), pp. 161–171.

Pipes, Richard. *Russia under the Old Regime.* London, 1974.

Pletneva, S. A. "Pechenegi, torki i polovtsy v iuzhnorusskikh stepiakh." *Trudy Volgo-Donskoi Arkheologicheskoi ekspeditsii. Materialy i issledovaniia po arkheologii SSSR,* #62. Moscow-Leningrad, 1958, pp. 151–226.

———. "Polovetskaia zemlia." In *Drevnerusskie kniazhestva X–XIII vv.* Moscow, 1975, pp. 260–300.

Polnoe sobranie russkikh letopisei. 35 vv. to date. Moscow-St. Petersburg-Leningrad, 1841–1980.

Poluboiarinova, M. D. *Russkie liudi v zolotoi orde.* Moscow, 1978.

Povest' vremennykh let. 2 vv., ed. V. P. Adrianova-Peretts. Moscow-Leningrad, 1950.

Povesti o Kulikovskoi bitvy. ed. M. N. Tikhomirov, V. F. Rzhiga, and L. A. Dmitriev. Moscow, 1959.

Prawer, Joshua. *The Latin Kingdom of Jerusalem. European Colonialism in the Middle Ages.* London, 1972.

Presniakov, A. E. *Lektsii po russkoi istorii.* t. II. *Zapadnaia Rus' i Litovsko-russkoe gosudarstvo.* Moscow, 1939.

———. *Obrazovanie velikorusskago gosudarstva. Ocherki po istorii XIII–XV stoletiia.* Petrograd, 1918.

Priselkov, M. D. *Istoriia russkogo letopisaniia XI–XV vv.* Leningrad, 1940.

———. *Khanskie yarliki russkim mitropolitam.* Zapiski istoriko-filologicheskago fakul'teta Imp. Petrogradskago Universiteta, #133. Petrograd, 1916.

Prokhorov, G. M. *Povest' o Mitiae (Rus' i Vizantiia v epokhu Kulikovskoi bitvy).* Leningrad, 1978.

Puchkovskii, L. S. "Mongol'skaia feodal'naia istoriografiia," *Uchenye zapiski instituta vostokovedeniia* VI (1953), pp. 131–146.

Putilov, B. N. "Kontseptsiia, s kotoroi nel'zia soglasit'sia." *Voprosy literatury* 1962 #11, pp. 98–111.

———. "Ob istorizme russkikh bylin." *Russkii fol'klor.* t. X. *Spetsifika fol'klornykh zhanrov* (1966), pp. 103–126.

Raeff, Marc. "Patterns of Russian Imperial Policy Towards the Nationalities." In

Edward Allworth, ed., *Soviet Nationality Problems.* New York, 1971, pp. 22–42.

Rasovskii, R. A. "K voprosu o proiskhozhdeniii Codex Cumanicus." *Seminarium Kondakovianum* III (1929), pp. 193–214.

———. "O roli Chernykh Klobukov v istorii drevnei Rusi." *Seminarium Kondakovianum* I (1927), pp. 93–109.

———. "Pechenegi, Torki i Berendei na Rusi i v Ugrii." *Seminarium Kondakovianum* VI (1933), pp. 1–66.

———. "Polovtsy. I. Proiskhozhdenie Polovtsev." *Seminarium Kondakovianum* VII (1935), pp. 245–262.

———. "Polovtsy. II. Razselenie Polovtsev." *Seminarium Kondakovianum* VIII (1936), pp. 161–182.

———. "Polovtsy. III. Predelia 'polia polovetskago'." *Seminarium Kondakovianum* IX (1937), pp. 71–85; X (1938), pp. 155–178.

———. "Polovtsy. IV. Voennaia istoriia polovtsev." *Seminarium Kondakovianum* XI (1939), pp. 95–128.

———. "Rol' polovtsev v voinakh Asenei s vizantiiskoi i latinskoi imperiiami v 1188–1207 gg." *Spisanie na B"lgarskata Akademiia na Naukite,* kn. 58. Sofia, 1939, pp. 203–211.

———. "Rus', Chernye Klobuky i Polovtsy v XII v." *Bulgarsko-Istorichesko Drushtvo, Izvestiia* 16/18. *Sbornik v pamet' na Prof. P. Nikov.* Sofia, 1940, pp. 369–378.

———. "Rus' i kochevniki v epokhu Vladimira Sviatago." *Vladimirskii sbornik v pamiat' 950-letiia kreshcheniia Rusi (988–1938).* Belgrade, 1938, pp. 149–154.

Riasanovsky, Nicholas V. "Asia Through Russian Eyes." In Wayne S. Vucinich, ed., *Russia and Asia.* Stanford, 1972, pp. 3–29.

———. "The Emergence of Eurasianism." *California Slavic Studies* 4 (1967), pp. 39–72.

———. *A History of Russia.* 3rd ed. New York, 1977.

———. "Prince N. S. Trubetskoy's 'Europe and Mankind'." *Jahrbücher für Geschichte Osteuropas* 13 (1964), pp. 207–220.

Riasanovsky, Valentin A. *Fundamental Principles of Mongol Law.* 1937; Bloomington, 1965.

———. "The Influence of Ancient Mongol Culture and Law on Russian Culture and Law." *Chinese Social and Political Science Review* 20:4 (January, 1937), pp. 499–530.

———. glava IV. "Vopros o mongol'skom vliianii na russkuiu kul'turu." In Riasanovsky, *Obzor russkoi kul'tury. Istoricheskii ocherk.* Eugene, Oregon, 1947, pp. 281–311.

Roublev, Michel, "The Periodicity of the Mongol Tribute as Paid by the Russian Princes during the Fourteenth and Fifteenth Centuries." *Forschungen zur osteuropaischen Geschichte* 15 (1970), pp. 7–13.

———. "The Scourge of God." Unpublished monograph.

———. "Le tribut aux Mongoles d'après les Testaments et Accords des Princes Russes." *Cahiers du monde russe et soviétique* VII (1966), pp. 487–530. Tr. as "The Mongol Tribute According to the Wills and Testaments of the Russian Princes." In Michael Cherniavsky, ed., *The Structure of Russian History.* New York, 1970, pp. 29–64.

Rüss, Harmut. "Das Reich von Kiew." In Manfred Hellmann, ed., *Handbuch der*

Geschichte Russlands. Band I, *Von der Kiewer Reichsbildung bis zum Moskauer Zartum,* Lieferung 3–6. (Stuttgart, 1979–1980), pp. 199–429.

Rybakov, B. A. *Remeslo drevnei Rusi.* Moscow-Leningrad, 1948.

———. "Rus' i Khazariia (k istoricheskoi geografii Khazarii)." In *Akademiku B. D. Grekovu ko dniu 70-letiiu. Sb. st.* Moscow, 1952, pp. 76–88.

Rubinshtein, N. L. *Russkaia istoriografiia.* Moscow, 1941.

Safargaliev, M. G. *Raspad Zolotoi Ordy.* Saransk, 1960.

Sakharov, A. M. *Goroda severo-vostochnoi Rusi XIV–XV vv.* Moscow, 1959.

———. "Les Mongoles et la civilization russe." *Contributions à l'histoire russe (Cahiers d'histoire mondiales).* Neuchâtel, 1958, pp. 77–97.

Salisbury, Harrison E. *War Between Russia and China.* New York, 1969.

Saunders, John Joseph. *The History of the Mongol Conquests.* New York, 1971.

Schurmann, Herbert Franz. *Economic Structure of the Yüan Dynasty. Translation of Chapters 93 and 94 of the Yüan shih.* Harvard-Yenching Institute Studies, XVI. Cambridge, Mass., 1956.

———. "Mongolian Tributary Practices of the Thirteenth Century." *Harvard Journal of Asiatic Studies* 19 (1956), pp. 304–389.

Seiden, Jacob. "The Mongol Impact on Russia from the Thirteenth Century to the Present: Mongol Contributions to the Political Institutions of Muscovy, Imperial Russia, and the Soviet State." Dissertation, Georgetown University, 1971.

Semenov, A. A. "K voprosu o zolotoordynskom termine 'baskak'." *Izvestiia A. N. SSSR, otd. literatury i iazyka,* 1947, t. VI, vyp. 2, pp. 137–147.

Serbina, K. N., ed. *Ustiuzhskii letopisnyi svod (Arkhangelogorodskii letopisets).* Moscow-Leningrad, 1950.

Ševčenko, Ihor. "The Decline of Byzantium Seen Through the Eyes of Its Intellectuals." *Dumbarton Oaks Papers* 15 (1961), pp. 167–186.

Shastina, N. F. "Obraz Chingiskhana v srednevekovoi literature mongolov." In S. L. Tikhvinskii, ed., *Tataro-Mongoly v Azii i Evrope.* Moscow, 1970, pp. 435–454.

Shpilevskii, S. M. *Velikii kniaz' smolenskii i iaroslavskii Fedor Rostislavich Chernyi.* Iaroslavl', 1899.

Silfen, Paul H. *The Influence of the Mongols on Russia: A Dimensional History.* Hicksville, New York, 1974.

Sinor, Denis. "The Barbarians." *Diogenes* 18 (1957), pp. 47–60.

———. "Horse and Pasture in Inner Asian History." *Oriens Extremis* 19 (1972), pp. 171–182.

"Skazanie o blazhennom Petre, tsareviche Ordynskom." *Pravoslavnyi sobesednik,* January 1859, chast' pervaia, pp. 356–376.

Skripil', M. O. "Povest' o Timofee Vladimirskom." *Trudy otdela drevnerusskoi literatury* 8 (1961), pp. 287–307.

Smirnov, I. I. *Ocherki politicheskoi istorii Russkogo gosudarstva 30-50-kh godov XVI veka.* Moscow, 1958.

Smith, John Masson. "Mongol and Nomadic Taxation." *Harvard Journal of Asiatic Studies* 30 (1970), pp. 46–85.

Smith, Robert E. F. *The Origin of Farming in Russia.* Paris, 1959.

———. *Peasant Farming in Muscovy.* Cambridge, England, 1977.

Soloviev, S. M. *Istoriia Rossii s drevneishikh vremen.* 15 vv. Moscow, 1963.

Spuler, Berthold. *Die Goldene Horde. Die Mongolen in Russland.* Leipzig, 1943; 2nd exp. ed., Weisbaden, 1965.

————. "Die Goldene Horde und Russlands Schicksal." *Saeculum* VI (1955), pp. 397–406.

————. *Die Mongolen in Iran: Politik, Verwaltung, und Kultur der Ilchanzeit, 1220–1350.* Leipzig, 1939; 2nd exp. ed., Berlin, 1955.

Sreznevskii, I. I. *Materialy dlia slovaria drevnerusskogo iazyka.* 3 vv. St. Petersburg, 1893–1912.

Stevenson, Burton, ed. *Macmillan Book of Proverbs, Maxims, and Famous Sayings.* New York, 1948.

Surruys, Henry. "Mongol Altan 'Gold' = Imperial." *Monumenta Serica* XXI (1961), pp. 357–378.

————. "A Mongol Prayer to the Spirit of Činggis-qan's Flag." In Louis Ligeti, ed., *Mongolian Studies* (Bibliotheco Orientalis Hungarica, XIV. Amsterdan, 1970), pp. 527–535.

Szamuely, Tibor. *The Russian Tradition.* New York, 1975.

Szczesniak, B. "A Note on the Character of the Tartar Impact upon the Russian State and Church." *Études Slaves et Est-Européens* 17 (1972), pp. 92–98.

Tataro-Mongoly v Azii i Evrope. sbornik statei, ed. S. L. Tikhvinskii. Moscow, 1970.

Tikhomirov, M. N. *Drevnerusskie goroda.* Moscow, 1956.

————. "Vossozdanie russkoi pis'mennoi traditsii v pervye desiatiletiia Tatarskogo iga." *Vestnik istorii mirovoi kul'tury* 1957 #3, pp. 3–13.

Troitskaia letopis'. Rekonstruktsiia teksta, ed. M. D. Priselkov. Moscow-Leningrad, 1950.

Tvorogov, O. V. "Redaktor XVII veka." In *Poetika i stilistika russkoi literatury. Pamiati akademika Viktora Vladimirovicha Vinogradova.* Leningrad, 1971. pp. 44–52.

Ushakov, D. N. *Tolkovyi slovar' russkogo iazyka.* IV. Moscow, 1940.

Usmanov, M. A. "Ofitsial'nye akty khanstv Vostochnoi Evropy XIV–XVI vv. i ikh izuchenie." *Arkheograficheskii ezhegodnik za 1974* (1975), pp. 117–135.

————. *Zhalovannye akty Dzhuchieva ulusa, XIV–XVI vekov.* Kazan', 1979.

V.P. (= V. A. Parkhomenko), "Polovtsy i Rus'." *Slavia* 16 (1939), pp. 598–601.

Vásáry, István. "The Golden Horde Term 'Daruga' and Its Survival in Russia." *Acta Orientalia Academiae Scientarium Hungariae,* XXX:2 (1976), pp. 187–197.

————. "The Origin of the Institution of the *Basqaqs.*" *Acta Orientalia Academiae Scientarium Hungariae* XXXII:2 (1978), pp. 201–206.

Vel'iaminov-Zernov, V. V. *Issledovaniia o Kasimovskikh tsariakh i tsarevichakh.* 4 vv. Trudy Vostochnago Otdeleniia Russkago Arkheologicheskago Obshchestva, tt. 9–12. St. Petersburg, 1863–1887.

Vernadsky, George. "A propos des origines du servage de 'kabala' dans le droit russe." *Revue historique du droit français et étranger,* 4 ser., 14 (1935), pp. 360–367.

————. *Ancient Russia.* Vol. 1 of George Vernadsky and Michael Karpovich, *A History of Russia.* New Haven, 1943.

————. "Dva podviga sv. Aleksandra Nevskogo." *Evraziiskii vremennik* IV (1925), pp. 318–337.

————. "Ivan Groznyi i Simeon Bekbulatovich." In *To Honor Roman Jakobson. Essays on the Occasion of His Seventieth Birthday,* Vol. III. The Hague, 1967, pp. 2133–2151.

————. *Kievan Russia.* Vol. 2 of George Vernadsky and Michael Karpovich, *A History of Russia.* New Haven, 1948.

————. *The Mongols and Russia.* Vol. 3 of George Vernadsky and Michael Karpovich, *A History of Russia.* New Haven, 1953.

————. *Nachertanie russkoi istorii.* ch. 1. Prague, 1927.

————. *O Sostave velikoi Yasy Chingis khana.* Studies in Russian and Oriental History, ed. G. Vernadsky, #1. Brussels, 1939.

————. "The Scope and Contents of Chinghis Khan's Yasa." *Harvard Journal of Asiatic Studies* 3 (1938), pp. 337–360.

————. "Zolotaia orda, Egipet i Vizantiia v ikh vzaimootnosheniiakh v tsarstvovanii Mikhaila Paleologa." *Seminarium Kondakovianum* 1 (1927), pp. 73–84.

Veselovskii, N. I. "Perezhitki nekotorykh tatarskikh obychaev u russkikh." *Zhivaia starina,* 21 (1912), pp. 27–38.

————. "Tatarskoe vliianie na posol'skii tseremonial v moskovskii period russkoi istorii." *Otchet Sv. Peterburgskogo Universiteta za 1910,* pp. 1–19, and separate publication, St. Petersburg, 1911.

Veselovskii, S. V. *Issledovaniia po istorii klassa sluzhilykh zemlevladel'tsev.* Moscow, 1969.

————. *Onomastikon. Drevnerusskie imena, prozvishcha, i familii.* Moscow, 1974.

Vladimirtsev, B. Ia. *Obshchestvennyi stroi Mongolov: Mongol'skii kochevoi feodalizm.* Leningrad, 1934.

Voegelin, E. "Mongol Orders of Submission to European Powers, 1245–1255." *Byzantion* 15 (1941), pp. 378–413.

Voinskie povesti drevnei Rusi, ed. V. P. Adrianova-Peretts. Moscow-Leningrad, 1949.

von Mohrenschildt, Dimitri S. *Russia in the Intellectual Life of Eighteenth-Century France.* New York, 1936.

Vryonis, Speros, Jr. "The Byzantine Legacy and Ottoman Forms." *Dumbarton Oaks Papers* 23–24 (1969–1970), pp. 253–308.

————. "Byzantium and Islam, Seventh–Seventeenth Centuries." *East European Quarterly* 2 (1968), pp. 205–240.

Waley, Arthur. *The Secret History of the Mongols and Other Pieces.* London, 1963.

————. *The Travels of an Alchemist. The Journey of the Taoist Ch'ang-ch'un from China to the Hindukush at the Summons of Chinghiz Khan, Recorded by his Disciple Li Chih-ch'ang.* London, 1931, rpt. Westport, Conn. 1976.

Widmer, Eric. *The Russian Ecclesiastical Mission in Peking During the Eighteenth Century.* Cambridge, Mass. and London, 1976.

Wittfogel, Karl August. *Oriental Despotism. A Comparative Study of Total Power.* New Haven, 1957.

————. "Russia and the East: A Comparison and Contrast." *Slavic Review* 22:4 (December, 1963), pp. 627–643, 656–662.

Zakirov, Salikh. *Diplomaticheskie otnosheniia Zolotoi Ordy s Egipetom (13–14 vv.).* Moscow, 1966.

Zdan, Michael. "The Dependence of Halych-Volyn' Rus' on the Golden Horde." *Slavonic and East European Review* 35:85 (June, 1957), pp. 505–522.

Zernack, Klaus. *Die burgstädtischen Volksversammlungen bei den Ost- und Westslawen. Studien zur verfassungsgeschichtlichen Bedeutung des Veče.* Osteuropastudien der Hochschulen des Landes Hessen. Reihe I. Giessiner Abhandlungen zur Agrar- und Wirtschaftsforschung der Europaischen Ostens, Band 33. Wiesbaden, 1967.

Zimin, A. A. "Formirovanie istoricheskikh vzgliadov V. O. Kliuchevskogo v 60-e gody XIX v." *Istoricheskie zapiski* 69 (1961), pp. 178–196.

———. "Narodnye dvizheniia 20-kh godov XIV veka i likvidatsiia sistemy baskachestva v Severo-Vostochnoi Rusi." *Izvestiia A. N. SSSR. seriia istorii i filosofii.* IX:1 (1952), pp. 61–65.

INDEX

Abbasids, 6
Abd-ul-latif, 110
Agafiia (Konchaka), 53
Agriculture, 75, 76, 79, 83
Akhmad, 35, 36–37, 72–73; and stand on the Ugra river, 59, 70–71
Alans, 45–46
Aleksandr, 53–54
Alexander Nevskii. *See* Nevskii, Alexander
Alexander Nevskii, *vita* of, 67, 71, 121
Andrei Bogoliubskii, 12
Andrei Konstantinovich, 41
Andrei Rublev, 123
Andrei Yaroslavovich, 49, 53
Anna (tsaritsa), 110, 153–54 n.18
Apocalypse, 64
Arabic language, 5, 123
Arabs: and Byzantine provinces, 148 n.9
Archers, 22–23, 91
Architecture, 120, 124, 125, 156 n.5
Argaman, 34, 36, 37
Aristocracy, 78–79, 94, 106–107, 111–13, 150 n.22
Armenians, 62
Artisans, 17, 76
Arts, 120–25
Astrakhan', 29, 60, 85, 100, 102
Autocracy: in Muscovy, 87, 90–103, 117
Avars, 47
Azerbaidjan, 27–28, 30, 79

Balkans, 15, 47, 70; Muslim and Christian interaction in, 1, 3, 6, 7
Baltic trade route, 80–81
Basileus, 71, 98, 152 n.42
Baskaki, 31, 33–40, 43, 48, 70, 129; replacement with danshchiki, 89; subsistence for, 77
Batu, 25, 30, 34, 47–48, 76, 78, 146 n.31; bookmen on, 66–68, 69–70, 71, 72–73; folktale portrayal of, 108–109

Belorussia, 52, 59, 85
Black Death, 83–84
Bolgar, 30
Bondage, 116–17
Bookmen, 104–106, 118, 121, 124; on Chingisid principle, 98–100, 101–102; on Mongol conquest, 8, 20, 61–74, 127, 129; on nomads, 8, 19–20; on t'my, 42–43; on Ugra river stand, 59
Boyar duma, 151 n.27
Boyarstvo, 95, 96
Buddhism: and the Mongol Empire, 24
Building construction, 78, 83, 84, 120, 122, 124–25
Bulgaria, 25
Bulgarians, 15, 122
Byliny (folk epics), 106–107, 152–53 n.9
Byzantine Empire, 97–98, 115, 121–22, 123, 148 n.9; compared with Golden Horde, 27; and Italian trade, 17; Muslim-Christian interaction in, 3, 5, 6; and Russian princes, 15
Byzantines, 27, 62
Byzantium, 62, 94, 113, 121–22, 126

Capital punishment (execution), 93–94
Caravan routes, 28–29, 80, 82, 85–86
Carpini, 33, 34, 35
Caspian steppe, 7, 25–27, 31
Catholic Church, 115, 122
Catholics, 3, 7, 49, 52
Cavalry, 91
Census, 35, 42, 50, 94
Chagataids, 29
Chagatai Turkic, 123
Cherniavsky, Michael, 71, 97–98, 100, 151 n.27, 152 n.42
Chernye Klobuky, 13–14, 18, 31
Children: in nomadic society, 22
China, 21–22, 23–24, 25–26, 29–30, 31, 48, 97; communications system in, 93;

economy of, 82; influence on Mongols, 93, 126; and Mandate of Heaven theory, 8, 83; Mongol legacy in, 100–101; tumens in, 41

Chingisid principle, 98–100, 101, 102

Chingisids, 42, 55, 98–101

Chingis Khan, 21–24, 29–30, 46, 98, 113; codification of Nomadic laws, 93

Chivalry, 109

Cholkan, 53–54

Christianity, 7, 61–62, 63, 97, 98, 104; interaction with Islam, 1–6; and Mongol customs, 93, 95, 103, 107; in Mongol Empire, 24; as obstacle to intermarriage, 111. See also Catholic Church; Russian Orthodox Church

Chronicles, 121, 122. See also chronicles by name

"Chronicle Tale" (1380), 69, 99

Church construction, 78, 83, 120, 122, 124–25

Church Slavonic, 122, 123

Cities, 76, 78, 79, 83–84; during Kievan period, 75

Civil wars, 28–29, 57–58, 89; in Kievan period, 14–15

Clans, 22–23, 25, 26

Clan-tribal system, 23, 25, 135 n.12

Clergy, 2, 4, 94

Collective responsibility (poruka), 93

Commerce. See Trade

Confucianism, 24

Conquest societies, 3–4

Conversion, religious, 4

Countryside, 76, 79, 83, 106, 114

Crafts, 120

Crimea, 25, 30, 42, 59–60, 81, 102

Crusades, 3, 7–8, 97, 115, 122

Customary law, Mongol, 93

Customs tax, 90–91

Dan'. See Tribute

Daniil of Galicia-Volhynia, 37, 49, 51, 67–68

Daniil of Moscow, 53

Danshchiki, 89

Darugi (dorogi), 39–40, 43

Depression (economic), 78

Desht-i-Kipchak (Polovtsian steppe), 30

"Digenis Akritas," 124

Divine Mandate, 23

Diwan system, 26, 92, 94

Dmitrii Donskoi (Dmitri Ivanovich), 58, 69–70, 136 n.27, 141 n.50; and Chingisid principle, 99; and throne of Vladimir, 41, 54; victory at Kulikovo Field, 27, 32, 55–56, 88

Dmitrii Mikhailovich, 53

Dmitrii Shemiaka, 58

Dnepr' river valley, 10, 51, 76, 143 n.17; trade route, 17

Donskoi, Dmitrii. See Dmitrii Donskoi

Dorogi (darugi), 39–40, 43

Eastern Europe, 3, 44–45, 47–48, 115

East Slavs, 7, 10–20, 61

Edigei, 29, 57

Egypt, 23, 27, 48

Elder: in nomadic society, 22

Embezzlement: of tribute, 78

Emperor. See Khan; Tsar'

Envoys (posoly), 77, 92, 139–40 n.37, 140 n.38; role in administration of Russia, 31–32, 33, 40, 43

Epifanii the Wise, 123

Epistle to Ivan IV, 72, 73

"Epistle to the Ugra," 71, 73

Etiquette, 107

Europe, 1–6, 44–45, 47–48, 115, 125

Evdokiia, 69

Evpatii, 108–109

Execution (capital punishment), 93–94

Fedor of Kiev, 35–36, 138 n.17

Fedorov-Davydov, G. A., 136 n.27

Fedor Rostislavovich, 110–11, 154 n.19

Feodor of Yaroslavl', 53

Feudalism: in Mongol Empire, 25, 135 n.12

Folk customs, 106, 152 n.6

Folk epics (byliny), 106–107, 152–53 n.9

Forced labor, 106

Forest zone, Russian, 7, 15, 57, 107; and baskak system, 33, 34

France, 3, 97

Fur trade, 80

Fur tribute (yasak), 100

Galicia, 52, 76

Galician-Volhynian chronicle, 66, 67–68, 105, 121, 157 n.9

Galicia-Volhynia, 35, 47, 51–52, 79, 120; in Kievan period, 10, 14

Genealogy: as evidence of Mongol ancestry, 111–13; of khans and emirs, 105

Germany, 81, 94, 115

Gleb Vasil'kovich, 111

Gog and Magog, peoples of, 64

Golden Horde (Zlataia orda), 7–9, 21, 25–32, 33–43; bookmen on, 61–74; first use of term, 72; influence on post-Mongol period, 87–94; legal system of, 93; and Russian politics, 44–60, 96. See also Mongols

Golden Kin, 24, 98, 100, 101

Gramota, 145–46 n.13

Grand Bolgar, 55
Great Horde, 29, 70, 73, 81, 93; destruction of, 59–60

Hanseatic League, 81
Heraldry, 111–12
Hesychasm, 123, 155 n.36
Horses, 47, 81
Hungary, 47, 52, 79
Huns, 47
Hypatian chronicle, 34

Ibn Batuta: description of Sarai, 26
Igor' Sviatoslavovich, 19
Ilkhanid dynasty, 27, 29, 31, 82. See also Persia
Imperial Russia, 87
Inner Asian steppe, 22–25, 123
"Instruction" (Monomakh), 16
Islam, 1–6, 7, 11, 24, 123–24; role in Golden Horde, 26, 29, 92, 93, 111. See also Muslims
Italy: and trade, 17
Ivan III (Ivan the Great), 59–60, 70–71, 72, 84, 125; name on coin, 100
Ivan IV, 100, 101
Ivan Kalita, 40, 54

Jagiello, 55
James (king), 3
Japan, 23, 48
Jerusalem, 3, 5
Jews, 5
Jihad, 3–4
Juchi, 25, 30
Judaism, 11
Juwaini, 100

Kabala bondage, 116–17
Kaffa, 81, 109, 153 n.14
Kagan, 11–12, 23, 98, 151 n.33. See also Khan
Kalka, defeat on the, 69
Kan, 98, 151 n.33. See also Kagan; Khan
Karamzin, N. M., 95, 96
Kargalov, V. V., 35
Kasimov, 29, 32, 59, 60, 102, 109–10
Kazan', 29, 58–59, 60, 100, 102, 110; and trade, 81, 85
Kazanskaia istoriia, 72–73
Kazna (treasury), 90
Khan, 23, 26, 98–99, 151 n.33, 152 n.42; as tsar, 71, 98, 146 n.31
Khans, 45, 114; genealogy of, 106. See also khans by name
Khazar empire, 11–12
Khazars, 11–12, 15

Khronograf of 1512, 41–42
Khwarizm, 25, 30
Kiev, 35–36, 46, 48–49, 51–52, 142–43 n.17; in Kievan period, 10, 13, 14; sack of, 105, 107
Kievan chronicle, 13
Kievan period, 7, 10–20, 75, 82, 91, 98; bookmen of, 8, 61–62, 63, 65, 68, 73–74; culture in, 120, 121–22, 152–53 n.9; political behavior in, 95, 97
Kipchaks. See Polovtsy
Kliuchevskii, V. O., 144 n.35
Konchaka (Agafiia), 53
Konstantin of Rostov, 53
Kormchaia kniga, 94
Kormlenie, 109
Kotoshikhin, Gregorii, 100
Kulikovo Field, Battle of, 27, 55–56, 69–70, 88, 91, 109
Kursk, 36, 42

Laurentian chronicle, 36, 121, 138 n.19
Legal system, 93–94
Libraries, 120
Literacy, 121
Literature, 18–19, 108–109, 120–24
Lithuania, 52, 54, 55–56, 57, 79, 112
Looting, 76–77

Machiavelli, 97
Magyars, 47
Mamai, 27, 29, 37, 55–56, 153 n.14; portrayal by bookmen, 69–70, 98–99, 109
Mamelukes, 23, 27, 48
Mandate of Heaven, 8, 63
Marriage, 18, 110–11
Martyrs: princes as, 114–15
Men: role in nomadic society, 22
Mengli-Girei, 42
Mengu-Timur, 110
Meta-Turkic language, 92
Middle East, 1, 3, 6, 7, 45
Mikhail Aleksandrovich of Tver', 51, 55
Mikhail of Chernigov, 49, 66–67, 142 n.5; vita of, 34–35, 42, 66–67, 121, 146 n.15
Mikhail of Tver', 53, 115, 116
Milei of Bakota, 34, 35, 37
Military alliances, 109–10
Min Bulat, 39, 58
Minting of coins, 76, 83, 90
Moldavia, 81
Mongol Empire, 20, 21–27, 46, 93, 137 n.14; Muscovite use of institutions, 94
Mongols (Tatars), 20, 64, 75–86; bookmen on, 104–106; campaigns of 1237–1240, 64–65; culture of, 123–24; influence on Muscovite autocracy, 87–103; military al-

liances with Russian principalities, 109–10; political behavior of, 96–97; role in Russian society, 104–119; Russian aristocracy descent from, 111–13; and Russian cultural life, 120–25; and Russian Orthodox Church, 112–16; warfare methods, 75. See also China; Golden Horde; Persia

Monomakh, Vladimir, 16, 19, 20

Moors, 3, 6

Moscow, 83, 88–89, 122, 144 n.35; sacked by Tatars, 99, 144 n.35, 144 n.36

Moscow-Vladimir, 41

Muscovites, 112, 152 n.8

Muscovy (principality of Moscow), 32, 53–60, 70, 77–86, 129, 136 n.27; and the Church, 115; culture in, 124–25; and Kasimov, 109–10; 16th-century autocracy in, 87, 90–103; social institutions of, 116–17; 1375 treaty with Tver', 143–44 n.31

Muslims, 1–6, 12, 23, 118–19. See also Islam

Names, 105, 111

Nasonov, A. N., 35, 137 n.14, 142 n.12

Nestorian Christianity, 24

Nevrui, 67

Nevruz, 41

Nevskii, Alexander, 48–51, 67, 142 n.10, 142 n.11, 142 n.12; vita of, 67, 71, 121

Nicene Patriarchate, 122

Nikitin, Afanasii, 118–19, 124

Nikon chronicle, 34

Nizhnii Novgorod, 41, 56–57, 83, 96, 122

Nobility, Russian (boyarstvo), 95, 96

Nogai, 28, 36

Nogai Hordes, 29, 31, 59, 60

Nomads, 22, 26, 80–82, 102; bookmen on, 62, 153 n.14; customary law, 93; during Kievan period, 7, 11–20; methods of warfare, 91

Novgorod, 34, 35, 50–51, 78–81, 83, 120, 122; during Kievan period, 10, 14, 17; and Lithuania, 54; veche in, 96

Novgorod First Chronicle, 34

Novgorodian Chronicle, 121, 122

Obolensky, D., 94

Old Church Slavonic, 122

Old Russian literature, 108–109, 121, 124

Olgerd of Lithuania, 54, 55

Orient: trade with, 81, 83, 85

Otrok, 18–19

Ottoman Empire, 3–6, 59, 102

Ottomans, 62, 70, 92

Pafnuti of Vorovsk, vita of, 36

Palestine, 3–4, 7–8, 48

Pastoralism, 28

Patents (yarliki), 66, 77, 145–46 n.13

Pauline doctrine, 67, 71

Pavlov, N. P., 148 n.6

Pax Mongolica, 82

Peasantry, 17, 81, 93, 94, 106–107; economic oppression of, 78, 85; in post-Mongol period, 117; and Russian Orthodox Church, 114

Pechenegs, 12–13, 62

Peoples of the Book, 4

Persia, 6, 8, 21–22, 25, 27, 29–31, 48; diwan system, 92; economy of, 82; Mongol legacy in, 100–101; Russian trade with, 85; theories on empires, 63; tumens in, 41

Peter, 114; vita of, 99–100

Photius, 58

Poland, 52, 79

Poland-Lithuania, 59

Polotsk, 79, 85

Polovtsian language, 18

Polovtsian steppe (Desht-i-Kipchak), 30

Polovtsy (Kipchaks), 13, 14–19, 31, 45–46, 62, 64

Pontic steppe, 7, 12–13, 15, 25–27, 31, 46

Population: effects of Mongol presence on, 76, 79–80, 83–84

Poruka (collective responsibility), 93

Posoly. See Envoys

Postal system (yam), 93

Povest' o razorenii Riazani Batyem ("Tale of the Destruction of Riazan by Batu"), 65, 108, 121

Povoz, 150 n.15

Presniakov, A. E., 138 n.18

Prester John, legend of, 64

Prikazy, 92, 94

Princes, Russian, 48–49, 52–53, 88, 101–102, 115, 128; and economic effects of Mongol presence, 77, 78–79, 83, 85; knowledge of Mongol customs, 107; and marriage to Mongols, 111; as martyrs, 114–15; military alliances with Mongols, 76, 78–79, 109–10; and Mongol khans, 45, 54–55; portrayal by bookmen, 62, 66; role in Mongol administration, 30, 32, 36–38, 40, 41, 89; in 16th-century Muscovy, 87, 89; and the veche, 95

Proselytization: and Christian-Muslim relations, 4

Punishment, 93–94

Puppet-khan, 55, 99

Pushkin, 122, 157 n.6

Rashid ad Din, 82

Rasovskii, D. A., 14
Religion, 24, 95, 104, 124. See also Christi-
    anity; Islam
Renaissance: and Russian culture, 122–23
Riazan', 54, 55–56, 65, 79, 112; sack of,
    108–109
Riurikid clan, 18, 48, 50, 97, 112
Rogozh chronicle, 41
Roman Empire, 121, 122; compared with
    Golden Horde, 27
Rostov, 79, 80, 96, 120, 121
Roublev, Michel, 78, 147 n.6
Russia, 30, 75–86, 104–119, 136 n.27. See
    also Golden Horde; Kievan period
Russia, Imperial, 87
Russian chronicles, 40, 45, 54, 105, 108
Russian Orthodox Church, 34, 101, 106,
    113–16, 118; and Batu, 66–67; growth
    under Mongols, 7, 129; during Kievan pe-
    riod, 10, 18; taxation of, 26, 77, 150 n.22
Russian Primary Chronicle, 11, 12
Russians: as a people, 107, 153 n.11

Said-Girei, 42
Salisbury, Harrison, 96–97, 161 n.30
Sarai, 26, 29–31, 33, 38, 55, 77; bishopric
    at, 113; Muslim culture in, 123; trade
    routes to, 80–81
Scandinavians, 15
Secret History of the Mongols, 21–22, 100–
    101, 123
Separatism: within Golden Horde, 29; in
    Kievan period, 10
Serapion of Vladimir: sermons of, 68, 106,
    114, 121
Serbs, 122
Serfdom, 117, 156 n.43
Sergius, St., 115
Serpukhov, 109
Shamanism, 7, 31, 66, 113
Shar'iat, 93
Shikhna, 39
Siberia, 25, 29
Siege warfare, 23, 75, 91
Sigismund I, 42, 59
Silver, 83, 84
Simeon chronicle, 39, 138 n.19
Skazanie o Mamevom poboishche, 56, 69–
    70
Slavery, 76, 85, 106
Slobody, 36
Slovo o pogibeli russkoi zemli, 121
Slovo o polku Igoreve, 16, 19
Smolensk, 79, 85
South Slavs, 70, 122
Soviet historians, 87, 135 n.12, 147 n.1,
    148 n.12

Soviet Union: Salisbury on, 96–97, 151
    n.30
Spain, 1, 3–7
Spanish language, 5
Sreznevskii, I. I., 65
Stand on the Ugra river, 59, 70–72, 73, 100
Steppe, 41, 76, 78, 82; during Kievan
    period, 7, 10–20, 22–23
Suzdalia, 79–80, 81. See also Vladimir-
    Suzdalia
Sviatoslav, 11
Swedes: defeat by Nevskii, 49
Symeon Bekbulatovich, 101

Tacitus, 22
Taginia, 58
Taidula, 37, 116
"Tale of Peter, tsarevich of the Horde," 114
"Tale of the Destruction of Riazan' by Batu"
    (Povest' o razorenii Riazani Batyem), 65,
    108, 121
"Tale of the Host of Igor, The," 12
Tamerlane, 26–27, 29–30, 32, 57, 99, 144
    n.36
Tamga (customs tax), 90–91
Tamozhnia, 39
Taoism: in Mongol Empire, 24
Tarkhan, 150 n.22
Tatar language, 105
Tatars. See Mongols
Tatar Yoke. See Golden Horde
Taxation, 26, 77, 78, 106, 116, 120; exemp-
    tions, 81, 113, 115, 150 n.22; in Mus-
    covy, 89, 90–91, 92; for yam, 93. See also
    Tribute
Tax farmers, 33, 38, 96, 137 n.14
Telebuga, 36, 37
Temir, 39
Tengri, 23, 24
Terem, 116, 155 n.37
Teutonic Knights: defeat by Nevskii, 49, 142
    n.11
Time of Trouble, 117
Tm'a (tumen), 41–43, 141 n.50
T'my, 48
Tokhtamysh, 27, 41, 56–57, 96, 99; defeat
    of Mamai, 29, 69
Trade (commerce), 28, 76, 80–83, 84–86;
    between Christians and Muslims, 2; dur-
    ing Kievan period, 12, 17, 75
Trade routes, 28, 80–81, 83, 85–86
Treasury, 90
Tribute (dan'; vykhod), 35, 70, 77–78, 84,
    85; calculation of amount of, 77, 147
    n.15, 147–48 n.6; collection of, 35, 38,
    89
Trinity chronicle, 138 n.19

Tsar': use as title, 71, 87, 98–99, 100, 146 n.31
Tumen (tm'a), 41–43, 141 n.50
Turco-Tatar language, 92
Türk Empire, 23–24
Turkestan, 48
Turkic language, 18, 31, 40, 92
Turkic peoples, 7, 12, 18, 23, 31
Turko-Tatars, 7
Tver', 53–57, 79–80, 83, 88, 112, 122; 1327 uprising in, 38, 96; treaty with Moscow, 143–44 n.31

Ugedei, 47
Ugra River, Stand on the, 59, 70–72, 73, 100
Uighur script, 92
Ukraine, 52, 59, 76
Ukrainians, 142 n.7, 143 n.17, 152 n.8
Ulozhenie, 117
Ulu-Mehmed, 58, 77
Ulus, 30, 136 n.27
Umayyad Arab Empire, 3, 5, 6
Uralo-Altaic people, 23
Urals, 80
Ustiug, 80–81
Uzbek, 29, 38, 53
Uzbeks, 31

Valencia, 3–7, 115
Varangians, 11
Vasilii (archbishop), 35–36
Vasilii (brother of Nevskii), 51
Vasilii II, 58–59, 77, 107
Vasilii III, 110
Vasilii Dmitrievich, 57, 58
Vasil'ko Konstantinovich, 66
Vassals, 54
Vassian, 71, 73, 116
Veche (town meeting), 95–96, 151 n.25, 151 n.27
Vel'iaminov, 144 n.31
Vernadsky, George, 147 n.5, 148 n.12, 156 n.43

Viatka, 80
Villages, 77, 79, 81, 83–84
Vitebsk, 79, 85
Vitovt, 41, 57, 58, 132 n.10
Vladimir, St.: wife of, 153–54 n.18
Vladimir, 51, 52–54, 66, 79–80, 90, 121; throne of, 41, 57
Vladimir Monomakh, 16, 19, 20
Vladimir-Suzdalia, 35, 65, 76, 80, 85, 89–90; during Kievan period, 10, 12–14, 17; politics of, 48–49, 52–53, 57, 96
Vladimir-Suzdalian chronicle, 121, 157 n.9
Voevoda, 34
Volgar Bolgar, 12, 17, 25, 31, 81
Volga river trade routes, 17, 59, 80, 83, 85–86
Volhynia, 52, 76
"Voyage Beyond Three Seas" (Nikitin), 118
Vsevolod (Big Nest), 133 n.25
Vykhod. See Tribute

Warfare, 1–3, 22, 75, 76, 91–92; during Kievan period, 11, 13–16; literary accounts of, 62, 108–109
Warlords, 22–23
Women, 22, 116

Yam (postal service), 93, 150 n.15
Yarliki (patents), 66, 77, 145–46 n.13
Yaroslav, 37, 48, 67
Yaroslavl', 80, 85, 110–11
Yaroslav Yaroslavovich, 51
Yasa, 24, 93
Yasak (fur tribute), 100
Yüan dynasty, 25, 29, 82, 126. See also China
Yurii, 58
Yurii Daniilovich, 53, 111

Zadonshchina, 69, 109
Zlataia orda. See Golden Horde